SPACEWARPS

SPACEWARPS

John Gribbin

DELTA/ELEANOR FRIEDE

A DELTA/ELEANOR FRIEDE BOOK
Published by
Dell Publishing Co., Inc.
1 Dag Hammarskjold Plaza
New York, New York 10017

Original drawings by Neil Hyslop

Delta ® TM 755118, Dell Publishing Co., Inc.

ISBN: 0-385-29366-6

Reprinted by arrangement with Delacorte Press/
Eleanor Friede
Printed in the United States of America

First Delta printing — November 1984

CONTENTS

to the far future, billions of years from now, the Universe can be pictured as an inside-out black hole.

4

Within the expanding Universe, we find islands of light in a sea of darkness. Galaxies like our Milky Way contain thousands of millions of stars—islands in space. But some galaxies seem to be involved in violent explosions, and there may be more matter around than meets the eye.

5

The most exotic objects, quasars, can be explained as black holes with masses of hundreds of millions of Suns lurking at the hearts of galaxies. Does our own Milky Way Galaxy harbor such a black hole?

6

Studies of our own star, the Sun, have surprisingly turned out to provide new insights into the fate of the Universe. Exotic particles called neutrinos flood through the Universe, and are also produced inside the Sun. It may be that most of the mass of the Universe is locked up in these invisible, almost undetectable, ghostlike particles.

7

Whatever the truth about solar neutrinos, the Sun itself no longer looks so steady and reliable as we used to think. It shakes and shrinks, on a time scale of decades and centuries, and these changes could explain climatic cycles on Earth.

8

Since space and time are two sides of the same coin, the existence of spacewarps implies the existence of timewarps as well. Einstein's theory says that time travel is possible; one theorist has described mathematically how to build a time machine. But it may not be as useful as you hoped.

9

We live in a Universe governed by the rules Einstein discovered. Life like us can only exist in a Universe like the one we see around us. Does that mean the Universe is tailor-made for humankind? Or does it imply that life is common in the Universe? Can other kinds of universe exist? Parallel worlds.

10

Einstein's theory is not the last word. Should it be scrapped in favor of a better description of the Universe? Or can a new theory be constructed that incorporates Einstein's ideas within it? Does gravity change as the Universe ages? "Supergravity" and the grand unification of physics.

SPACEWARPS

Introduction

Einstein taught us that space and time should not be regarded as distinct entities but as two sides of the same coin, different facets of the greater whole, which he called spacetime. A few years ago, I wrote a book called *Timewarps*, in which I looked at the implications of Einstein's ideas and those of quantum mechanics for our understanding of time, asking the question, "Is time travel possible?" and coming up with the answer, "Yes, but it depends what you mean by time travel." At the time I wrote that book I was aware of the artificiality of dealing with time in isolation from space, discussing timewarps without really going into any detail about the existence and implications of spacewarps. Since then, many people have made the same point to me, and my excuse, that I had already written a book which covered some of this ground (*White Holes*), was beginning to wear thin as each year brought new, intriguing developments in our understanding of spacetime and the nature of the Universe.* So here, in response to many requests, is the real counterpart to my book *Timewarps*, a look at bent spacetime with the emphasis on spacewarps.

---

*It is an astronomical convention to use the capitalized term—Universe, Moon, and so on—when talking about the "real world," the Universe we live in or the Moon that orbits the Earth. Just as other moons—those of Mars or Jupiter, for example—are not graced in this way, so the word "universe," without the capital letter, is used by the cosmologists when they are talking about an imaginary state of affairs, what the world might be like if the laws of physics were a little different—an imaginary "model" of reality. I shall follow this convention.

1

Of course, time cannot be left out of the present book, any more than spacewarps were totally ignored in my earlier book. As well as the impossibility of disentangling the two in any satisfactory manner, there have been new developments since 1978 well worth reporting—not least the explanation, from a respected mathematical physicist, of how time travel is indeed allowed within the framework of the theory of general relativity (see Chapter Eight). But *Spacewarps* deals with the tangible, observable features of the Universe, where *Timewarps* dealt more with the abstract and the philosophical. Quasars, the most energetic objects known in the observable Universe, could hardly be more tangible, and they owe their existence, it is now clear, to the extreme warping of space-time associated with a condensed supermass, a black hole; the Universe itself is thought to have exploded out of a similar superdense state, the Big Bang of creation, like a black hole in reverse, a white hole; observations of galaxies and quasars across the Universe give us clues not only to its origin but also to its ultimate fate; and new puzzles concerning the possibility that neutrinos have mass and speculations that gravity may decrease as the Universe ages provide further insight into the nature of the Universe and hint at a still better description of reality lying beyond the theory of general relativity.

It is even possible that within a few years mathematicians will be well on the road to achieving a unification of all the laws of physics within one grand theory—the unified theory that has been the Holy Grail of physicists for decades, and which Einstein himself failed to discover. Meanwhile, against this background of exciting progress in the study of spacewarps over the past few years, there runs another thread, the mystery of life. Sir Fred Hoyle and his colleague Chandra Wickramasinghe have argued loudly that life is such an unlikely thing to have occurred that the Universe must be much older than anyone else thinks, and all established theories wrong, in order for life to have had time to develop at all. Other cosmologists argue that although it seems that the Universe is tailor-made for life, in fact life as we know it is an inevitable consequence of the Universe we live in, Big Bang, quasars, black holes and all.

The violent Universe is an interesting place to live; but we are only here to witness it because it is a violent Universe.

John Gribbin
September 1982

1

Spacetime and Spacewarps

How special is our place in the Universe? Einstein's insights into gravity, space, and time tell us that there is no special place, and that the way things behave here and now depends on the structure of the whole of the Universe and its entire history.

The story of spacewarps is the story of gravity; and the story of gravity is the story of Einstein's theory of relativity. Three centuries ago, Isaac Newton's realization that gravity dominated the behavior of the observable Universe opened the way for the study of the Universe to become a branch of science, rather than philosophy or religion. But it was only in the twentieth century, with Einstein's work, that scientists were armed with an understanding of gravity powerful enough to give a true insight into the nature of the Universe at large.

Newton's great discovery was that gravity could be treated as a force, and that the gravitational force acting between any two ob-

3

jects in the Universe could be calculated simply as the product of their two masses $(M \times m)$, multiplied by a constant (usually denoted by G), and divided by the square of the distance between the two objects. This force, Newton realized, could explain the fall of an apple from a tree, the trajectory of a projectile fired from a cannon, the orbit of the Moon around the Earth, and the motion of the Earth and other planets around the Sun. For two centuries, from the late 1600s up to the end of the nineteenth century, this view of the Universe reigned supreme. At the beginning of the twentieth century, however, a revolution inspired not by the study of gravity but by the study of electromagnetism made it necessary to completely rethink gravitational theory. The laws of electromagnetism—one unified description of the behavior of both charged particles and magnetic fields—had been formulated by James Clerk Maxwell in the 1860s, and in the following decades study of electromagnetic phenomena raised new puzzles for the theorists.

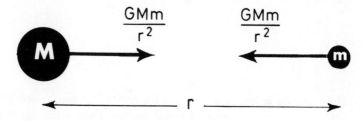

Figure 1.1 Two objects with masses M and m separated by a distance, r, attract each other with the same force, GMm/r^2, where G is the "constant of gravity." The force felt by the larger object is exactly the same as the one felt by the smaller; what matters in both cases is the product of their masses. In my case, the Earth pulls on me with a force of about 180 pounds, which I feel as my weight—but I am also pulling on the Earth with an equal and opposite force of 180 pounds.

The most famous of these puzzles is, perhaps, the failure of experiments designed to measure the difference in the speed of light caused by the motion of the Earth through what we would call space, but which Victorian scientists referred to as "the aether." It is far from certain whether Einstein himself either knew of, or was especially concerned about, these particular experiments when he was musing on the nature of electromagnetism and the behavior of light—an electromagnetic wave—in the early years of the present century. But he saw clearly that the new understanding of electromagnetic phenomena could not be reconciled with the accepted laws of dynamics based on Newton's equations of motion, and he was bold enough to accept the more modern theory—electromagnetism—and seek a new dynamical theory, rather than to stick by the older, longer established view of the Universe.

No Special Place

Einstein developed a new view of the workings of the Universe, starting from the assumption that there must be no special place in the Universe—that the laws of physics, the equations of motion and of electromagnetism and all the rest, should be the same for all observers wherever they might be in the Universe. There was no such thing as "absolute" motion, said Einstein, and no such thing as an "aether" or "fixed space" against which motion could be measured in an absolute sense. Motion was always relative, and could be described meaningfully only in relation to a specified observer in what is known as an inertial frame. All such observers move at steady speeds relative to one another, although the actual speeds measured depend on which inertial frame you are in when you make the measurements. This is why the theory is known as "special relativity." "Relativity" because it says all motion is relative, and there is no absolute "frame of reference" in which the laws of physics are uniquely true; "special" because it deals only with constant velocities—steady speed in a straight line—and doesn't attempt to tackle the problem of accelerated motion, such as the motion of an apple, or a planet, under the influence of gravity.

Such limitations might seem restrictive, and they are. But even with these restrictions special relativity produced some surprises. Einstein found that whatever frame of reference we choose as our standard from which to make measurements, moving rulers shrink, moving clocks run slow, and moving objects increase in mass as their velocity increases. All of these effects become noticeable only when the speed (measured in our chosen frame of reference) of the moving clock, ruler, or other object reaches a significant fraction of the speed of light—and the speed of light itself (usually denoted by c) is an absolute constant, 30 billion centimeters per second in all inertial frames. We have lost fixed space as an absolute standard against which measurements can be made, but gained the constancy of the speed of light as an absolute standard, the fixed referent in a Universe of relativity. With space and time losing their fixity, and becoming two facets of a greater, and flexible, space-time, special relativity also explains that matter (m) and energy (E) are interchangeable, linked by the now familiar equation $E = mc^2$.

All of these dramatic revelations have now been confirmed by direct experiments. The energy equation explains why the Sun and stars shine, and provided the basis for the development of nuclear weapons and nuclear power stations. The stretching of time (time dilation) and squeezing of space at velocities close to the speed of light have been directly measured using as probes atomic particles accelerated in giant "atom smasher" machines. The energy needed to accelerate the particles confirms their increase in mass as they speed up, while no particle has ever been found breaking the universal "speed limit" of the speed of light.

Even in the 1980s it is important to stress that special relativity is not some wild theory produced out of the hat by a long-haired scientist and having little to do with the real world, but rather a thoroughly established and experimentally proven view of the world. It is used routinely in scientific work and, if you are reading this in Europe or North America, probably contributes directly to the electricity production which is keeping your reading lamp bright. But this is not a book about special relativity, or the seemingly bizarre implications of such phenomena as time dilation. I have already covered that ground in *Timewarps*. This is a book about gravity, and as Einstein appreciated from the outset, special relativity is not a theory of gravity at all. In the ten years following the publication, in 1905, of the special theory, Einstein pondered on attempting to go beyond this theory to a more general theory, one which would include a description of gravity, and which could describe the behavior of accelerated systems. He faced two immediate problems. First, although the inverse square law provides a very good working basis to calculate the fall of an apple, the motion of a projectile, or the orbit of a planet, why should it be an inverse square law, rather than something else? And, crucially, how could gravity apparently transcend the universal speed limit?

The Puzzle of Gravity

This was the heart of the problem. With special relativity, Einstein had established that nothing could travel faster than light. But the gravitational force appeared to be transmitted instantaneously across space between any pair of objects, whether it be the apple falling from a tree and the Earth, or the Earth and the Sun. More subtly, but no less importantly, since the special theory had shown that concepts such as distance and mass depended on the frame of reference of the observer, how could it be meaningful to describe the gravitational force between two objects in terms of their masses and the distance between them? Even worse, how could inertial observers, those key members of the world described by special relativity, exist at all in a universe dominated by gravity? For gravity is an all-pervasive force, which affects every material object in the Universe, and accelerates it accordingly. The force may be vanishingly small, but in terms of Newtonian physics it is always present, and no body, or observer, can ever be regarded as unaccelerated. But this seemingly intractable problem provided the key to a new understanding of gravity, and to a general theory of relativity. Gravity is everywhere—that is the problem—so Einstein realized that it made no sense to regard gravity as something separate from space (or, more accurately, spacetime). He argued that gravity must, in fact, describe some fundamental property of spacetime, and he found that he could develop a satisfactory theory of gravity if that property is the geometry of spacetime.

The concept sounds difficult, but fortunately in this age of jet travel and pictures of the Earth from space, it is easily understood by anyone who knows that the Earth is round. The kind of geometry we learn at school is the geometry of a flat plane—a piece of paper—in which the angles of a triangle always add up to 180 degrees, a straight line is the shortest distance between two points, and two such lines which are both perpendicular to a third straight line are parallel to one another and never meet. This is Euclidean geometry, described by Euclid around 300 B.C., and used in the everyday world when we construct a bookshelf, a building, or a bridge. But Euclidean geometry is quite inappropriate for a navigator working out the most efficient route for a transatlantic flight, because the surface of the Earth, although it is flat enough not to bother us when designing a bridge or a bookshelf, is actually curved. On the surface of a sphere, the angles of a triangle always add up to more than 180 degrees (how much more depends on how big the triangle is), the shortest distance between two points is a decidedly curved line, and two such lines drawn perpendicular to the equator, for example, meet at the poles, and cannot be regarded

as parallel in the way Euclid defined the term. The geometry of a
sphere is the geometry of a two-dimensional flat surface, but one
wrapped around in a third dimension. It is possible to distort the
two-dimensional surface in other ways, producing a whole family
of non-Euclidean geometries. And Einstein's great insight was the
realization that it is possible to distort three-dimensional space (or
even four-dimensional spacetime) in similar ways, producing curved
spacetime in which the correct geometrical description of the Universe must be non-Euclidean.

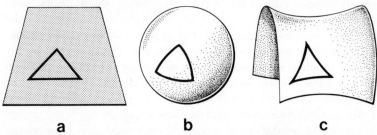

a   **b**   **c**

Figure 1.2 The three main types of geometrical surface are represented
in these three diagrams: a) Flat space, with Euclidean geometry—the kind
we learned about in school, where the angles of a triangle always add up
to 180 degrees. "Parallel lines" in flat space never meet or diverge. b)
Spherically curved space, analogous to the surface of a sphere, in which
the angles of a triangle always add up to more than 180 degrees, and
parallel lines eventually meet one another, like the lines of longitude that
all cross the equator at right angles, but all meet at the poles. c) Hyper-
bolic space, analogous to a saddle surface, in which parallel lines gradually
diverge from one another and the angles of a triangle always add up to
less than 180 degrees.

In some sense, that implies the existence of higher dimensions
around which our four-dimensional spacetime is wrapped, or otherwise distorted, but that need not worry us too much. More important, just as the angles of a triangle on a curved surface do
not add up to 180 degrees, so the physical properties of geometric
shapes are different in curved spacetime from those we know from
everyday experience. Imagine a race of intelligent beings that lived
on a permanently clouded world and had never developed space
travel, but knew something of geometry. They might decide on a
grand scientific project to investigate the curvature of their planet,
and by drawing larger and larger triangles on the surface of the
planet, and measuring the angles with scrupulous precision, they
would be able to work out that they were living on the surface of

a sphere, and determine the size of the sphere. The kind of curvature where the angles of a triangle add up to more than 180 degrees is called positive curvature; the most striking alternative, which we can picture as a saddle surface, is called negative curvature, and on such a surface the angles of a triangle always add up to less than 180 degrees. In our three-dimensional Universe, an equivalent way to measure curvature would be to measure the volume of successively larger spheres. All of us who remember geometry from school know that the volume of a sphere is given by the formula $V = (4/3)\pi r^3$, where r is its radius, but this is only true if space is flat, in the Euclidean sense. In curved space, the volume may be bigger or less than this, depending on whether the curvature is positive or negative. In principle, we could measure this—but to do so we would need to investigate the properties of spheres which occupy a significant volume of the entire Universe, and that just isn't a practical proposition. For most geometrical purposes, it makes as much sense to assume spacetime is flat as it does for a carpenter to assume the world is flat when designing a table.

Or does it? For Einstein's insight, that gravity is a property of the curvature of spacetime, brings the study of that curvature firmly into the everyday life of science, if not quite into all our daily lives. The insight is best understood by looking at the motions of projectiles and planets under the influence of gravity, and seeing how the description of curved spacetime improves on Newton's interpretation of events. To Newton, it seemed that every object in the Universe continued to move in a straight line, or to sit at rest, unless acted upon by some outside force. Without the Sun to hold them in their orbits, the planets would plough through space in straight lines; without the Earth's gravity to tug it back down, a projectile fired from a gun would continue in a straight line indefinitely (or until it came under the influence of some other body). But Einstein argued that rather than a force traveling across space instantaneously to keep a grip on all these objects, gravity acted to curve spacetime, and moving objects always followed the line of least resistance through curved spacetime.

Bending Space and Time

Far away from any material objects, the curvature of spacetime is very small, on this picture, and objects do travel in Newtonian straight lines. Near to a concentration of matter—like a planet or

a star—spacetime is distorted by the presence of matter. The projectile fired from a gun, or the planet moving in its orbit, is not
influenced by any external force, but moves in the equivalent of a
straight line at constant speed through curved spacetime. Such a
path is called a geodesic; the great circle routes used by airline
navigators to find the most efficient path from one continent to
another across the curved surface of the Earth are also geodesics,
in the context of the curvature of the Earth's surface rather than
the curvature of spacetime.

The example is a little tricky to get a mental grip on, not least
because it is hard to visualize where the time part of spacetime
comes into the picture. Most of us have trouble enough visualizing
motion in three dimensions, let alone four, but if you imagine the
orbit of a planet around the Sun as a two-dimensional ellipse, the

Figure 1.3 If we represent all the dimensions of space on a two-dimensional plane, and use the third dimension to represent time, the path of a
planet in orbit around the Sun becomes a "world line" coiling through
spacetime. The almost elliptical orbit of the planet in space alone can be
thought of as the projection, or shadow, of this world line on the space
plane. (After J. V. Narlikar, *Violent Phenomena in the Universe,* Oxford
University Press, 1982.)

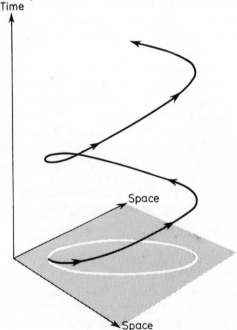

time dimension can be envisaged as stretching this into a three-dimensional helix, like the coil of a bedspring. The orbit in space is the projection of the spacetime path onto the space dimensions, like a shadow cast upon a sheet of paper by a three-dimensional object. By compressing the four dimensions of spacetime in this way, mathematicians and astronomers obtain a useful tool for describing the motion of objects in the Universe, a spacetime diagram. In the simplest of these diagrams, a plot like a conventional graph indicates the flow of time up the page, and all motion in space across the page, with the scale of the graph chosen so that motion at the speed of light is equivalent to a straight line drawn outward at 45 degrees from the point where the axes cross; on such a spacetime diagram, the region on the space axis side of such a light line is permanently inaccessible, since it could only be reached by a trip involving travel faster than the speed of light, and only the region of spacetime in a cone around the time axis bounded by the light lines can be reached by travel at less than the speed of light. We will meet spacetime diagrams again later. For now, what matters is not the details of the geometry but the difference between Newton's and Einstein's view of the Universe. In Newtonian physics, projectiles move through *flat* spacetime under the influence of a gravitational force, which propagates instantaneously throughout the Universe; in Einsteinian physics, projectiles move through *curved* spacetime without being influenced by an external force of gravity, and they follow geodesics, the paths of least resistance, the "straight lines" of curved spacetime. Special relativity, like Newtonian physics, is a description of flat spacetime. General relativity is therefore a more profound advance over special relativity than special relativity itself is over Newtonian physics.

Because of the difficulty of visualizing four-dimensional spacetime it is convenient for many purposes to separate these two facets of reality and think of the implications of spacetime curvature for space and time separately. Just as space is distorted in the presence of matter, so too is time, and the form the distortion takes is that clocks run slower—time is dilated—where gravity is stronger, that is close to large masses. For now, I will say no more about this, having made the point that both space and time are distorted by gravity, as indeed they must be if they really do form two sides to the same coin, spacetime. How can we visualize the distortions of space alone produced by gravity? Apart from the spacetime diagrams, which are a useful tool but don't actually look like anything recognizable in the physical world, relativists have another trick of

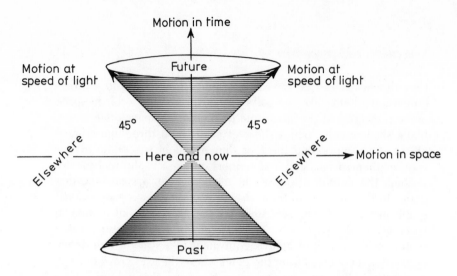

Figure 1.4 By choosing the speed of light to be one unit, by definition, the path of a light ray in a standard spacetime diagram like the one of Figure 1.3 is a straight line at 45 degrees to the time axis. Because nothing can travel faster than light, starting out from here and now we can never move outside the future light cone, or receive information about anything outside the past light cone. More than half of spacetime is inaccessible, according to relativity theory, and is called "elsewhere."

representation up their sleeves. Just as we can take a slice through an orange, or an imaginary slice through the Earth, or some other three-dimensional object, so we can imagine slices cut through the four-dimensional structure of spacetime. An imaginary slice through the Earth can be portrayed as a diagram to convey in easily assimilated form a great deal of information about what lies beneath our feet. In the same way, an imaginary slice through spacetime can be used, in diagrammatic form, to convey easily assimilated information about how space is distorted by gravity. Such a slice, a two-dimensional sheet of space, is technically known as a space-like hypersurface. You could take a different kind of slice, a timelike hypersurface, to get information about time distortion, but that is another story.

In flat spacetime—far from any gravitating masses—the hypersurface is flat, like a smooth sheet of paper. Where spacetime is distorted, the hypersurface is distorted, like a stretched sheet of rubber. Imagine a large sheet of rubber stretched tightly over a frame. Now imagine the effect of a moderately heavy object, such as a bowling ball, placed on the rubber sheet. Assuming the sheet is strong enough to support the weight, it will bend symmetrically to accommodate the heavy ball, producing a round dip in the fabric of the rubber. This is very similar to the shape of a spacelike hypersurface in the vicinity of an object like our Sun, and the curved rubber sheet can be thought of as representing the curvature of the fabric of space in the gravitational field of a star. A smaller, less massive object (a pool ball, say) distorts the "fabric of spacetime" less; a heavier object distorts it more. But the same amount of matter spread over a bigger volume causes less distortion. What matters, as far as the bending of the rubber sheet or of real spacetime is concerned, is the concentration of matter in a small volume, that is, the density. The greater the density of matter, the greater the distortion of spacetime.

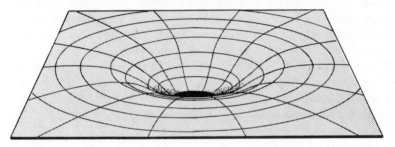

Figure 1.5 In a suitable diagram the curvature of space caused by the presence of a massive object can be represented as a pit, or well, resembling the depression in a stretched rubber sheet produced by a massive object such as a bowling ball. All of three-dimensional space is represented here by the curved two-dimensional "sheet," and time is assumed to be constant—we are taking a slice through spacetime corresponding to some instant of time.

This picture of how space is bent near a massive—or more accurately, near a dense—object immediately produces a prediction from general relativity that makes it possible to test the theory, in comparison with Newtonian physics. Imagine now our distorted rubber sheet shape, but with the bowling ball taken away to leave an empty depression. This is the two-dimensional representation of the gravitational "well" of an object like the Sun. Remember that there is no such thing as gravitational force, and that particles move along lines of least resistance—geodesics—through bent spacetime. Such a path can be traced, in our model, by rolling a marble across the distorted rubber sheet. The marble follows what we would call, in everyday terms, a curved track into the depression and out again—an orbit, if you like, past the central star. The track of the marble depends on the curvature of the sheet, and is only a straight line if the sheet is flat. Real objects in the real universe behave in a similar way as they move through spacetime. In most cases, the differences between the tracks through spacetime calculated in accordance with general relativity, and the orbits under the influence of a gravitational force calculated in accordance with Newton's equations, are indistinguishable. But light is an exception.

Light always travels in straight lines, and light can be described in terms of massless particles, called photons. If a photon has no mass, then according to Newton it cannot be influenced by gravity, since any real number multiplied by zero is itself zero, and the force of gravity acting on a zero mass particle is therefore zero, no matter how big the mass trying to tug at it may be. So, according to Newton, unlike other particles (planets or marbles), photons should travel in straight lines even as they pass close by the Sun. Einstein, however, came to a different conclusion. He said that there is no such thing as a gravitational force anyway, and that all particles, whatever their mass (or absence of mass) travel along geodesics through spacetime. Photons, therefore, should follow "bent" tracks through the distorted spacetime near the Sun, just

Figure 1.6 "Straight lines," or geodesics, in the curved space of Figure 1.5 can best be thought of as lines of least resistance. A light ray from a distant star, following such a geodesic near our Sun, will be deflected so that the position of the star in the sky shifts compared with the position where it would be seen if spacetime were flat. This deflection was first observed and measured in 1919 and was a crucial test of general relativity.

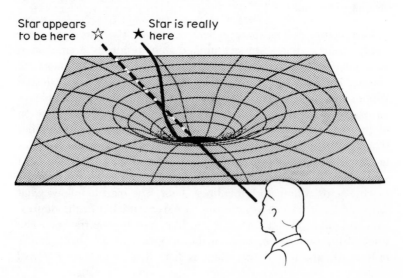

Star appears to be here ☆   ★ Star is really here

like other particles. Because of the very high speed of photons, the deviation produced by the distortion of spacetime near our Sun would be small—there would be a trade-off between the space and time parts of spacetime, so that slow-moving objects would be more strongly affected, in terms of our spacelike hypersurface, than fast-moving objects. Nevertheless, Einstein calculated that the effect of bent spacetime on light from a distant star could just be detected if the light passed very close by the Sun, deep in its gravitational well.

The effect, to an observer on Earth, would be as if the star shifted sideways slightly in the sky, compared with its usual position. Of course, the star does not move; the light rays are bent so that it *appears* to move. But how can you measure the position of a star alongside the blazing light of the Sun? The only hope is to make the measurements during a total eclipse, when the Sun's light is blacked out by the Moon, and stars can be seen during the day.

Passing the Tests

Einstein's detailed calculations of the basis of general relativity were published in 1916, and even though Europe was torn by war at the time, the English astronomer Arthur Eddington learned of this work through a colleague in neutral Holland. The next eclipse of the Sun was due in May 1919, and with war still raging, the Astronomer Royal organized two British eclipse expeditions, one to Brazil and one to Principe, an island off the coast of West Africa, where the total eclipse could be observed. Photographs of selected stars taken under normal conditions and during the eclipse showed exactly the minute shift in apparent position that Einstein had forecast, and the world seized upon the discovery with a mixture of wonder (who really understood the concept of bent spacetime?) and delight that a German theory had been confirmed by British observers while the two nations were still technically at war, the peace treaty not being signed until later in 1919.

This is not the only successful test of general relativity, although in many ways it is the simplest and most conclusive, as well as being the one that caught the popular attention six decades ago. Astronomers and mathematicians were—and are—equally interested in other ways in which general relativity produces a different picture of the world from Newtonian physics. One of the key points for astronomers was that Einstein's theory explains—indeed, predicts—a slight variation in the orbit of Mercury around the Sun, a variation which cannot easily be explained by Newtonian theory. Going back to the motion of a planet through four-dimensional spacetime, remember that the motion through space can be envisaged as the projection, or shadow, on the space part of the continuum of the actual geodesic (which is also sometimes called a "world line," for obvious reasons). A typical world line for a planet spirals up as time passes, and its projection on space traces an almost perfect ellipse. The key word there, though, is "almost." According to Einstein's description of the Universe in terms of general relativity, the ellipse traced by a planet in orbit around a star itself slowly rotates as time passes, an effect called the advance—or the precession—of the perihelion. For most planets the effect is too small to be measured, and the difference between general relativity and Newtonian physics is unobservable. But for the planet Mercury, close to the Sun and deep in its gravitational well, general relativity predicts an advance of the perihelion, at an angular rate of 43 seconds of arc per century, which is not predicted by Newtonian theory. Just such an advance of the perihelion of Mercury had been observed by astronomers in the nineteenth century.

Altogether, the measured advance in the perihelion of Mercury is 575 seconds of arc per century, but almost all of this can be explained by Newtonian mechanics in terms of the gravitational influence of the other planets in the Solar System. In the middle of the nineteenth century astronomers puzzled over the small remaining component of the perihelion advance. Just 43 seconds of arc per century remained unexplained in Newtonian theory, and they tried various ways to explain it, including the suggestion that another planet might remain undiscovered in an orbit even closer to the Sun than Mercury's. But this hypothetical planet was never found, and the astronomers were duly impressed when Einstein's theory turned out to imply exactly the extra amount of perihelion advance needed to explain the behavior of Mercury's orbit.

Since then, theorists have found other ways to produce the same effect, including the possibility that the Sun has a rapidly rotating core, so the observation of the advance of the perihelion of Mercury cannot be said to prove general relativity correct on its own. But those alternative theories seem just as contrived as the idea that an undiscovered planet lurks between Mercury and the Sun, and with the weight of other evidence—such as the bending of light—taken into account there is no doubt that general relativity is indeed a very good description of the Universe in which we live.

That does not mean that Einstein's theory is the last word. New-tonian physics is a very good view of the world as far as it goes, and the improvements provided by general relativity only become important where we are dealing with speeds close to the velocity of light, or strong gravitational fields. Perhaps under even more extreme conditions there are processes which can only be ex-plained by a theory which goes beyond Einstein's theory. The im-portant point, however, is that the success of Einstein's theory in explaining the observed behavior of the Universe means that any new theory must include general relativity within itself, just as general relativity includes both special relativity and Newtonian physics within itself. Where gravity is not involved, the equations of general relativity become the equations of special relativity; where neither gravity nor speeds close to that of light are involved, the equations reduce to Newton's equations. Relativity does not "replace" Newton for everyday purposes, and any better theory will not "replace" relativity as a description of the bending of spacetime in the region near an object like the Sun. Just where relativity might be replaced we will see later. The strength of Ein-stein's theory, however, was reaffirmed in 1960, five years after he died, when scientists developed techniques for measuring time (atomic clocks) accurate enough to measure the slowing of time on the ground floor of a building on Earth, compared with the passage of time recorded by identical clocks on the top floor, where the gravitational field of the Earth, and the bending of spacetime, is a tiny bit less than on the ground floor. Let no one tell you relativity is "just a theory" dreamed up by a crazy scientist!

What of accelerations, though? After all, the "general" in gen-eral relativity is supposed to denote an extension to deal with more complicated motion than constant speeds in straight lines, and all this talk of curved spacetime and planetary world lines may seem a far cry from that. But it is not. If an object in orbit around a star or other body is really moving in the curved-space equivalent of a straight line, and no forces are acting upon it, then it ought to behave in accordance with the equations of special relativity or, if the speeds involved are small, Newtonian mechanics. Today, we all know that this is so—we have all seen TV pictures from Skylab and other spacecraft showing that in "free fall," as it is called, ob-jects given a push really do travel in straight lines until they are given another push or collide with another object. When the spacecraft accelerates, however, everything in it is pushed to the back, just as if a gravitational field had been switched on. Einstein argued that acceleration is indeed "just like" gravity, and formulated a principle of equivalence which says that if you were inside a closed box armed with all the tools of the physicists' trade but with no window to look through, you would be unable to tell whether the box was sitting still on the surface of the Earth, with gravity holding everything in place, or accelerating through empty space at just the rate required to mimic the tug of gravity at the surface of the Earth. Acceleration is equivalent to gravity; so general relativity, a theory of gravity, also must be a theory of acceleration.

The language I have used here may be a little confusing, if you are just getting used to the idea that there is no such thing as a force of gravity tugging on anything. But the fact is, we are so used to the concept of gravitational force, and things tugging at one another, that it would be pedantic to try scrupulously to avoid such everyday terminology. The *effect* of bent spacetime on our everyday world is to produce what we think of as the force of gravity, and as long as we appreciate the underlying cause of the fall of an apple or the trajectory of a projectile, it does no harm to talk in terms of gravitational force, or to calculate using Newton's equations. The rule-of-thumb guide is that the differences between Newtonian theory and general relativity only become important where the term $GM/(Rc^2)$ is bigger than a few percent. Since G, the gravitational constant, is very small (6.7×10^{-7}, in the same system of units that the speed of light, c, is 3×10^{10}) and the speed of light very big, this magic number (usually denoted by the Greek letter alpha, α, to save writing it out in full) is very small under everyday conditions, and the predictions of general relativity are only significantly different from Newtonian predictions close to (distance R) a very massive object (mass M). Even at the surface of the Sun, α is only 2×10^{-6}, two-millionths, confirming that Newtonian gravity is a good basis to use in calculating, say, the orbit of a spacecraft to Saturn or to Mercury. Most of this book, then, will be concerned with what happens in regions of spacetime where the critical parameter, α, reaches a decent size, which means more than one percent (0.01, or 10^{-2}), and anything up to 1. By definition, that means that most of this book will be dealing with regions of curved spacetime very different from anything we encounter in our everyday lives, or which could be encountered in our Solar System. But first, a word more about the equivalence principle, and a brief mention of one of the major puzzles of the Universe.

Canceling Gravity

In spite of the success of general relativity, the equivalence principle formulated by Einstein does not hold precisely in the situation I have just described. In a closed laboratory at rest on the surface of the Earth, gravity is weaker at the top of the room than at the floor, and this difference could, in principle, be measured. Indeed, it *has* been measured, by those tests involving atomic clocks recording the passage of time on different floors in a tall building. In an identical lab (or tall building) hurtling through space propelled by powerful rocket motors, the measured force acting on a test particle—its weight—would be the same everywhere and the passage of time recorded on atomic clocks would be the same everywhere in the lab. The same sort of effect can be seen by imagining the opposite situation for our hypothetical lab.

Suppose the lab were floating freely in orbit in space. Now, everything inside would be weightless, and would obey with scrupulous accuracy the Newtonian laws of mechanics. According to the equivalence principle, it ought to be impossible to tell whether the lab is actually floating free in space far from any gravitational influence, or whether it is falling, at an ever-accelerating rate, straight down toward a planet or a star. If gravity and acceleration are equivalent, then just as acceleration can mimic the force of gravity, so a freely falling lab (like an elevator plunging to its doom after a cable has snapped) ought to see gravity "canceled out" by the acceleration. This is true up to a point—we are familiar with the momentary loss of weight we do, indeed, feel in high speed elevators, and NASA pilots are versed in the trick of flying an aircraft in a looping trajectory to produce a few seconds of weightlessness inside, giving trainee astronauts a taste of the real thing before they venture into orbit. But it is not absolutely true that the weightlessness of deep space and the weightlessness of free fall near a large mass are equivalent, as far as real observers are concerned.

Imagine our hypothetical lab falling freely down a huge shaft to the center of the Earth. The occupant of the lab, provided only with two oranges, can soon discover his predicament. If the lab were far out in space, two oranges placed at rest on either side of our tame observer would stay just where they were put. But in the lab falling down the mine shaft, each orange (and every particle of the lab and of the observer) is actually being pulled toward the exact center of the Earth, along a radius line. As the lab gets

closer to the center of gravity of the Earth, the radius lines con-
verge, and the oranges move together, meeting one another when
the lab reaches the Earth's center. Just by watching the oranges
drift together under the influence of some mysterious unseen force
the observer would know where his lab was headed, and why.

That mysterious force is a familiar one, though seen in an unfamiliar context. It is the tidal force, and tidal forces act on all real
objects, anything bigger than a mathematical point. Think again of
a simple round ball in orbit around the Earth—something like
Sputnik 1. Only the center of the object—the center of gravity, or
the center of mass—actually follows a free fall trajectory, a geodesic. Each atom of the ball except for the one at the precise center of mass would "like" to follow a slightly different geodesic, but
can't, because all the atoms are stuck together in a ball. So tidal
forces are constantly trying, unsuccessfully, to squeeze the ball one
way and stretch it another. Liquids and gases *can* be stretched and
squeezed easily, which is why tidal forces are familiar to us through
their effect on the oceans. And if gravity is strong enough—where
α starts to get big enough—tidal forces can do nasty things even
to solid objects. So the principle of equivalence seems to break
down in our hypothetical lab because the lab is bigger than a mathematical point. In fact, gravitational and accelerational forces are
indistinguishable if we are dealing with vanishingly small regions
of spacetime, and vanishingly small regions are what the equations
of physics do actually apply to. So all is well with relativity theory,
but inhabitants of the real world have to watch out for those tidal
forces.

What of those deeper mysteries? So far, we have looked only at
a very small region of spacetime, our Solar System over the span
of no more than a century or so. Gravity is weak here, yet even
within this small portion of the Universe it has proved possible to
establish a picture of how the Universe works that is so complete
and well designed that, as we shall see, it can take us back 15
billion years to describe the birth of the Universe itself, and across
millions of light-years of space to explain the enormous energy
produced by objects containing the mass of a billion Suns. This is
an astonishing achievement, but it is only possible because the
Universe seems to be a simple, well-behaved place where the laws
of physics we deduce here on Earth, and from the study of the
Solar System, apply everywhere. Why should this be so? In particular, why should the behavior of gravity and the interaction of bent
spacetime with matter be the same here as everywhere else in the
Universe?

A Universal Contribution

Another view of the differences between Newtonian gravity and general relativity may help to provide a partial answer. According to Newton's equations, the gravitational force acting on an object at any point in space is simply given by adding up the forces due to each and every mass around it—in principle, due to every mass in the Universe. So the motion of the Earth is found by adding up the force due to the Sun, the Moon, and the other planets—fortunately, the rest of the Universe is far enough away for us to ignore the weak contribution of the stars and galaxies. But, just as the curve of a stretched rubber sheet carrying a load of several different massive balls is not the same as the curve you would get by adding up the effects of each ball separately, so the curvature of spacetime in any region is not found simply by adding the influence of all nearby masses. Remember the advance of the perihelion of Mercury—general relativity makes different predictions from Newtonian physics, and, wherever tested, general relativity proves the more accurate. The curvature of spacetime in our own Solar System really does depend on the combination of all the masses in the Universe, and perhaps we cannot ignore those distant stars and galaxies after all.

Imagine a completely empty universe. Spacetime is absolutely flat, and there is no curvature of spacetime and therefore no gravitational "force." Now imagine a single object placed in that empty universe. With nothing to compare that object against, there would be no way to tell whether the object was "moving," either at constant speed or with acceleration, and motion can therefore have no meaning. If motion has no meaning, then resistance to motion has no meaning, and the Newtonian reluctance of an object to change its state of rest or of uniform motion in a straight line—its inertia—also has no meaning. If the object rotates, it experiences no centrifugal force; and so on. But now imagine adding a few more specks of material to our almost empty universe. With reference points against which it can be measured, motion immediately becomes "real," and the original object now has inertia and experiences centrifugal force and all the rest. But can two tiny specks of dust, in an empty universe, restore fully the amount of inertia that the object would have in a universe as well provided with matter as our own? Some philosophers argue that this cannot be so, and that in an almost empty universe the few objects that were present would only have a very little inertia.

Inertia, the argument runs, is a property material objects have as a result of the presence in the Universe of all the other material objects. This idea is often known as Mach's principle, after an Austrian physicist, Ernst Mach, who propounded it in detail in the nineteenth century. Although Mach was not the first person to ponder along these lines, he had a direct influence on Einstein and his thinking about the relation of the whole Universe to the local properties of matter. Clearly, the idea of curved spacetime, and the combined influence on the local curvature of spacetime of all the matter in the Universe, provides some sort of a handle on how Mach's principle might "work" in the real world—but nobody has yet been able to come up with a satisfactory way of incorporating the principle fully into general relativity. As cosmologist Edward Harrison of the University of Massachusetts put it recently, "Although its geometry is influenced by matter, and motion is controlled by geometry, the nature and existence of spacetime are not dependent on the existence of matter." *

Some physicists go further, and argue that matter only exists at all because of the way spacetime is curved—because of its geometry. Spacetime is real, but there may be nothing in the world except empty curved space, with all of the properties of matter and the laws of physics that we are familiar with in fact no more, and no less, than different manifestations of the curvature of spacetime.**

This mind-boggling possibility is more than enough to be going on with, although those deeper mysteries will surface again in due course. For now, it is enough to know that spacetime does curve. Armed with this knowledge, and treating matter as "real" in the everyday sense of the word, we are ready to take a trip into the most extreme state of warped spacetime that Einstein's theory can describe—into the black hole.

*Cosmology, p. 178; for full references to works cited, see Bibliography.
**See, for example, C. W. Misner, K. S. Thorne, and J. A. Wheeler, Gravitation. W. H. Freeman, San Francisco, 1973.

2

Black Holes and Bent Spacetime

The existence of black holes is predicted by Einstein's equations, but few people took the idea seriously until the discovery of other exotic objects in the Universe—pulsars and X-ray stars—showed that Einstein's equations really do accurately predict the behavior of matter at superdensities. Now, even more exotic ideas have their supporters.

Black holes are so much a feature of modern developments from Einstein's theory that it comes as a surprise to learn that their existence was predicted by eighteenth-century astronomers, on the basis of Newtonian ideas about gravity. Of course, those early ideas owed nothing to the concept of bent spacetime, and they rested upon a fundamental mistake about the nature of the Universe, the assumption that particles of light—photons—could be slowed down by gravity, just like material particles. We now know that photons always travel at the same speed, the speed of light. But credit where credit is due—two hundred years ago scientists were just as intelligent as modern scientists, simply a little less well informed than their spiritual heirs. And they certainly knew how to take a theory to its logical conclusions.

To the informed reader today, the fact that our forebears developed a theory to describe what we would call black holes may not seem all that surprising. After all, many books and articles, both popular and academic, have now told the story of how the great French mathematical astronomer Pierre Laplace mentioned in his book *Exposition du Système du Monde,* first published in 1796, that an object with a diameter 250 times as great as that of our Sun, and with the same density throughout as the average density of the Earth, would be invisible to outside observers because light could not escape from its gravitational pull. But this is not the end—or rather, the beginning—of the story, for it is far less well known today that although Laplace reached this conclusion independently, he had in fact been preceded by thirteen years by the work of the much less well-known English physicist John Michell. As far as we know, it is Michell who should be credited with the first published calculations describing black holes; Gary Gibbons, of the University of Cambridge, has gone so far as to describe Michell as "the man who invented black holes."

Michell's calculations were presented to the Royal Society at a meeting on November 27, 1783, and duly published in the *Philosophical Transactions of the Royal Society,* volume 74, page 35, in 1784. As part of a much larger mathematical study of how the distances to stars might be determined by measuring the brightness (or faintness) of them as seen from Earth, Michell explained in terms that still cannot be bettered the nature of a black hole within the context of Newtonian theory. "If the semi-diameter of a sphere of the same density with the Sun were to exceed that of the Sun in the proportion of 500 to 1," he said, "a body falling from an infinite height towards it, would have acquired at its surface greater velocity than that of light, and consequently supposing light to be attracted by the same force in proportion to its *vis inertiae,* with other bodies, all light emitted from such a body would be made to return to it by its own proper gravity."

The point is that the velocity an object needs in order to escape from any gravitational field—such as the Earth's—is exactly the same as the velocity an object would acquire falling into the field from infinity. Michell's calculations were impeccable; his assumption that light is affected by gravity in the same way as other bod-

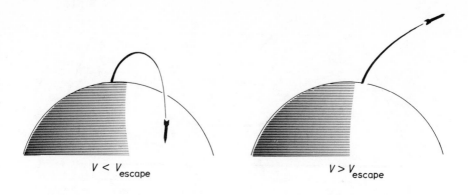

Figure 2.1 A rocket that leaves the Earth with less than escape velocity will fall back; a rocket that leaves the Earth with more than escape velocity continues outward into space even though its fuel is exhausted.

ies was wrong. But in everyday terminology, we can still grasp the concept of a black hole by describing it as an object possessing a gravitational field so strong that the escape velocity from it exceeds the speed of light. We are all used to the idea that if you throw an object up in the air it falls down, but that the faster it is thrown initially the higher it will go before falling back. Einstein has shown that nothing can be "thrown" faster than the speed of light. And a black hole is simply a place where you would have to throw things faster than light, which is impossible, for them to escape.

In terms of bent spacetime, things are a little different. The speed of light is still an all-important factor, because it is one of the fundamental constants of relativity theory. The amount by which gravity curves spacetime depends on the speed of light. Going back to the "model" of spacetime as a stretched rubber sheet with a weight on it, as the weight gets heavier the sheet is distorted more and more, making a deeper "well" with more sharply curved "spacetime" around its edges. At some point, we can imagine the fabric of the rubber sheet giving up the unequal struggle; the sides of the well pinch together, closing off the region containing our massive weight from the outside world. We are left with two separate regions—the large area of the flat sheet, equivalent to the flat spacetime of the Universe at large, and a closed off region of highly curved spacetime, equivalent to a black hole. The question is, how much does spacetime have to be bent—how much matter must we squeeze within a particular diameter of sphere—to make a black hole? And the answer provided by general relativity is exactly the same as the answer provided by Michell's Newtonian calculations, just 200 years ago.

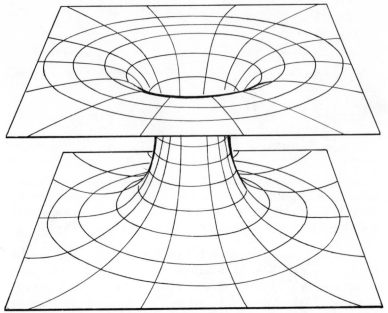

Figure 2.2 The embedding diagram of a black hole is a bottomless pit in spacetime. We have no way of telling what, if anything, lies on the other side, but it may be that the hole in spacetime joins on again to another region of flat spacetime—another universe, perhaps, or a different region of our own Universe.

Making a Black Hole

Because the important factor is the density of the matter, with a greater density leading to a greater curvature of spacetime, the radius of a particular black hole depends on its mass, and the mass you need to make a black hole depends on the radius within which you are going to pack the matter. Only two other factors enter the equation—the constant of gravity, G, and the speed of light, c, the two fundamental constants of relativity theory. The result can be conveniently expressed in terms of the radius R, so that $R = 2GM/c^2$ is the radius within which a mass M must be squeezed to make a black hole. As Michell or Laplace would have put it, an object of mass M with this radius R would have an escape velocity greater than the speed of light, c. Now G is very small, and c is very large, so unless M is big enough to make up for the tiny size of the factor G/c^2, R must itself be very, very small. To turn the Earth into a black hole, you would have to squeeze it down into a sphere of radius 1 cm, which is not a very practicable proposition. On the other hand, as Michell pointed out, a sphere 500 times bigger in diameter than the Sun, but with the same density as the Sun, would be a black hole. Our entire Milky Way Galaxy contains an amount of matter equivalent to 100 billion Suns, and that would only have to be compressed to within a radius of 0.03 light-years to become a black hole. To put that in perspective, the density of matter in the resulting black hole would be about the same as the density of water in your bathtub. Black holes don't require only superdensities, but they do require either superdensities or super-large masses, or both.

We'll come back to supermassive objects later. But first we should look at the possibility that stirred so much excitement in the 1970s—the likelihood that black holes containing a few solar masses of material had been discovered in our own cosmic neighborhood, within the Milky Way Galaxy.

Gravity is always trying to pull things together, and squeeze things down into smaller lumps, and the only reason we see such solidity and stability in the world about us is that other forces act to oppose this insistent inward tug of gravity. Our planet Earth is solid and stable because it is made of atoms and molecules, whose behavior is dominated by electrical forces. The electrical forces which maintain the arrangement of atoms in my body, or your chair, or the Earth itself, are strong enough to resist the tendency of the gravitational force produced by the mass of the Earth to crush everything into a formless blob. But if we added more and more matter to the surface of our planet, things would change. At the level of atoms and molecules, electrical forces are strong, compared with gravity. But the strength of my table doesn't increase if we stand another table on top of it, while the gravitational force gets bigger every time we add more matter to the bulk. Eventually, the gravitational force would be strong enough to crush the delicate structure of what we think of as everyday material, leaving an amorphous mass of atomic particles, nuclei and electrons. The amount of matter needed to do the job is roughly the amount of matter there is in the Sun—which is why the Sun is a star and the Earth is a planet. But when a star forms in the cold of interstellar space, it has a further means of holding gravity at bay, at least for a time, and the story of how black holes have probably formed in our Galaxy is very much intertwined with the story of how stars form and evolve.

A star forms when a cloud of gas and dust in interstellar space gets squeezed down, for some reason,* to the point where its own

---

*The reason might be the blast of a shock wave from a nearby exploding star, or the squeeze produced by the passage of a shock wave spiraling around the whole galaxy, or it may be that we have not yet discovered the trigger for star formation. Details can be found in my book *The Death of the Sun*.

gravity is strong enough to pull all the material together into a compact ball.

In practice, astronomers believe, the clouds of gas that collapse in this way are large enough to spawn several stars each, and along the way to its collapse into a ball of gas each embryonic star may throw off as a by-product rings of dusty material that themselves aggregate to form planets. But what matters for the story of black holes is that a ball of gas, being squeezed down by gravity, is produced somewhere along the line. The gas is mainly hydrogen, laced with helium and just traces of the other elements, since hydrogen is by far the dominant material of the Universe, as well as being the simplest atom—just one positively charged proton in its nucleus, orbited by one negatively charged electron.

As the protostar is squeezed by gravity it gets hot. Gravitational potential energy is converted into heat by the collapse, heat which takes the form of increased random motions among the atoms which make up the ball of gas. As the gas gets hotter, so the individual electrons are stripped off from their atoms, leaving a plasma, a hot, gaslike fluid in which protons, nuclei of helium atoms, and electrons are all mixed, hurtling frantically past one another and frequently colliding with one another. Those collisions are all-important, for as the young star gets smaller and hotter still, eventually there comes a point when the protons, instead of just colliding and bouncing off one another, sometimes stick together and fuse into new nuclei. The process, nuclear fusion, switches on in the case of a star like our Sun when the temperature at the center is about 15 million degrees.*

This is the way new elements are made. The fusion of hydrogen nuclei—protons—in a process involving several steps, produces nuclei of helium—two protons and two electrically neutral particles, called neutrons, fused together. But as well as building up new atoms, the nuclear fusion process releases energy. The mass of each helium nucleus is slightly less than the total mass of the separate particles which have been used in its construction, and the lost mass has become energy in line with the equation $E = mc^2$. This is the energy of the hydrogen bomb; it is also the energy that keeps the Sun hot. And with a source of energy at its center—a hydrogen bomb on an astronomical scale—a star can resist the in-

*The degrees are "absolute" or Kelvin, denoted by K. To convert to centigrade, just subtract 273—but for practical purposes, 15 million K and 15 million C are the same thing.

ward pull of gravity. As long as this fusion process, nuclear burning, keeps the star hot in the middle, then it is supplied with an outward pressure which can hold it up against gravity. The kinetic energy that the particles inside the star gain from the heat liberated in nuclear fusion enables them to halt the collapse of the star.

All good things must come to an end, though, and like any fuel the hydrogen at the heart of a star will eventually be used up. In the case of our Sun, hydrogen burning has been going on for about 5 billion years, and astronomers are confident that it will be a further 5 billion years or so before any drastic changes take place. More massive stars burn their fuel quicker, because more energy—more heat—is needed to resist the correspondingly greater inward push of their gravity. Less massive stars burn their fuel more slowly. But eventually all their reserves are used up, and gravity again begins its inexorable squeeze. What happens then depends very much on the mass of the star. If the temperature at the center gets hot enough because of the renewed gravitational squeeze, a new phase of nuclear fusion, involving helium, can switch on and restore stability for a time. When all the helium is used up, other fusion processes, involving nuclei of carbon, oxygen, and silicon, can each come into play at the appropriate successively higher temperatures. This is the way elements are made inside stars. But eventually all the fuel must be exhausted, and the star comes to the end of its life as a brightly shining object, supported by its own heat.

When this happens, the most massive stars may collapse suddenly in the center, releasing so much gravitational potential energy as heat that the outer layers are blasted off into space in a great explosion, a supernova. The smallest stars fade away much more quietly, cooling off so that the free nuclei and electrons of the plasma recombine into atoms; further contraction, though, soon crushes the atoms out of existence, packing the atomic nuclei tightly together in a sea of electrons. Provided the mass of the star is less than 1.5 times the mass of our Sun, this is the end of the story. The star has become a white dwarf, a type which is very common. Each white dwarf star identified in the sky represents the corpse of a star like our Sun. With the mass of a Sun packed into the volume of the Earth, contraction is halted not by electrical forces but by another form of resistance, a physical law which makes it impossible to pack electrons more closely together than a certain limit. The laws of quantum mechanics, not electrodynamics, now provide the pressure which stabilizes the stellar corpse against further collapse.

This will be the fate of our own Sun, and of many of the stars we see in the sky. But what of the bigger stars? Astronomers know of stars with ten or more times the mass of our Sun; what happens to them when nuclear fusion can no longer stop their collapse due to gravity?

Until the 1960s, astronomers could not be certain of the fate of massive stars, since they knew of no stellar remnants with masses bigger than 1.5 solar masses, the critical limit for white dwarfs to be stable. It seemed possible that all massive stars exploded with such violence that any fragment left behind had a mass less than the white dwarf limit, while most of the star's material, including the heavy elements made by nuclear fusion, went to enrich the interstellar medium and provide the raw material from which a new generation of stars would be born. But even without any observations of stellar fragments more massive than the white dwarf limit, theorists knew what they ought to be like if they did exist.

A cold star more than one and a half times as massive as our Sun can no longer be held up against its own gravity even by the quantum processes which stabilize white dwarfs. The electrons cannot be squeezed any closer together, but in effect they can be squeezed "into" the protons of the atomic nuclei they surround. One positively charged proton and one negatively charged electron combine to make one electrically neutral neutron. The whole star is converted into neutrons, and it contracts still further as a result, becoming a neutron star. The whole mass of the star has been converted, in effect, into one atomic nucleus, about the size of the island of Manhattan. A neutron star may have a radius of just 10 km, one seven-hundredth of the radius of a white dwarf, and this really is the end point of material existence, as far as we know from the present understanding of physics. Now, the same quantum effects that operate on electrons to hold white dwarf stars up against gravitational collapse operate on neutrons to hold neutron stars up against gravitational collapse—and there is no particle more compact than the neutron for these particles to dissolve into if and when gravity is strong enough to overwhelm these quantum forces.

The Puzzle of Pulsars

The concept of neutron stars was derived by Fritz Zwicky in 1934, but for three decades many astronomers doubted that such bizarre objects could really exist in the Universe. Meanwhile, the theorists pressed on to even more exotic extremes. In 1939, Robert Oppenheimer and his colleague Hartland Snyder, working at the University of California, Berkeley, described in mathematical terms the ultimate fate of a dead star too massive to be held up even by neutron pressure. There is still some doubt about just how massive a stellar remnant would have to be to overcome the neutron pressure; the best estimate today is about 2.5 times the mass of the Sun, although estimates have been adjusted slightly over the past forty-odd years, as the theories have been refined. Whatever the exact value of the critical mass, though, once neutron pressure has been overcome there is nothing left to resist the collapse of the dead star into a mathematical point, a singularity. And on the way to that ultimate fate, of course, the collapsing mass must disappear into a black hole, as it shrinks within its own critical radius.

If astronomers thought neutron stars were a little esoteric, they scarcely took black holes seriously at all. It hardly seemed likely that real, material objects could actually disappear into black holes and singularities, and the study of such outlandish possibilities remained a province of a few mathematicians, who toyed with the equations more for their intrinsic interest than through any firm belief that they described any real objects that actually existed in our Universe. All that changed in the late 1960s, however, when radio astronomers discovered a new class of astronomical objects, the initially mysterious pulsars.

I well remember the excitement of that discovery, for it was made by a team at the Mullard Radio Astronomy Observatory in Cambridge, and I had just joined Cambridge University's Institute of Theoretical Astronomy, as it then was, as a research student. What the radio astronomers down the road from my new workplace found was first one, then a handful, then many radio sources in the sky that flicked on and off with great regularity, like the ticking of a clock or the beat of a metronome. The discovery was so remarkable that when only a handful of the objects were known they were at first numbered "LGM 1," "LGM 2," and so on; when asked what the letters stood for, my radio astronomy friends replied, only half in jest, that they meant "Little Green Man," since such regular pulses could surely only be the result of intelligence at work. It didn't take long for that joke to be quietly buried, as more of these pulsars—a contraction of "pulsating radio sources"— were discovered and it became clear that they were a natural phenomenon. But exactly what natural phenomenon nobody knew for sure, and like every theorist in the world of astronomy at the time I had a stab at finding the answer.

The problem wasn't just that pulsars produced blips of radio noise with great regularity, but that the blips were very closely spaced, following each other at precise intervals of around a second. The fastest pulsar now known blips thirty times a second;* the slowest once every four seconds. And to do this with precision means that the objects have to be small.

Remember that light travels at a finite speed, and that radio waves travel at the same speed. Nothing can travel faster than light, but the radio pulses from pulsars are kept very precisely in step by some mechanism. If the pulses came from a very big star, even one the size of our Sun, they would be blurred because the "message" to set the pulse off would take a measurable time to spread over the star, and each active region would be pulsing slightly out of step with its neighbor. In round terms, an object that produces precise pulses of radio waves, or light, can be no bigger than the distance that light could travel in the interval between pulses, since otherwise different regions of pulsing activity could not be kept in step with one another. That made it very easy to set a limit on the size of the pulsars, and the limit came out as about the size of the Earth. Assuming the pulses were not, in fact, generated by intelligent beings, they had to come from an energetic natural object about as big as a planet. There was an obvious candidate—the well-known white dwarf stars.

There are two ways to produce a regularly repeating rhythm from a spherical object like a star. It might be rotating, so that the pulse is actually a beam of energy flicking past regularly, like a lighthouse beam; or it might be pulsating, breathing in and out and producing a burst of energy in all directions every time it squeezed in. In 1967, at the time pulsars were discovered, astronomers thought they knew that white dwarf stars could only vibrate in this way with periods down to about eight seconds. So most of the attention of the real experts was turned to the idea of rotation. You had to be an idiot, or a research student who knew no better, to try to find a way in which white dwarfs might vibrate rapidly enough to explain pulsars. I was a research student who not only

*In November 1982, radio astronomers discovered an even faster pulsar, which blips 642 times every second. It has been dubbed "the millisecond pulsar"—a slight, but excusable, exaggeration.

knew no better but had been set the task of writing a computer program to study how stars pulsate in just this way by my supervisor John Faulkner. Rushing in where wise men didn't bother to tread, I found, as much to my surprise as that of all my colleagues, that the standard calculations of white dwarf pulsations contained an error, and that they could actually vibrate more rapidly, with periods down to about one second. For a few heady weeks it looked as if I had solved a fundamental problem, and the first scientific paper I ever published was rushed into print in *Nature* within a week of being delivered to their office, and became the subject of several newspaper reports. But very soon more pulsars were discovered with periods much less than one second, and the vibrating white dwarf model began to look inadequate. Tom Gold, a British-born astronomer resident in the United States, pointed out that the even smaller neutron stars could comfortably explain these more rapid radio pulses, and before long the theorists agreed that pulsars must indeed be rotating neutron stars, sweeping their energetic radio beams around the sky like celestial lighthouses.*

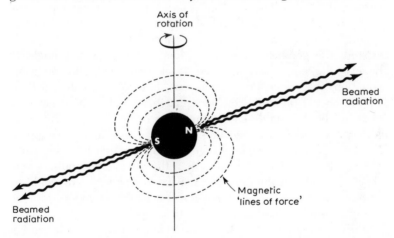

Figure 2.3 One model of a pulsar. Radiation beams out from the magnetic poles of a neutron star, which are offset from the "geographic" poles. As the neutron star spins, the resulting beam of radiation flicks past us at regular intervals, like the beam of light from a lighthouse.

---

*A flavor of the excitement of these discoveries can be obtained from the *Nature* book *Pulsating Stars* (London: Macmillan, 1968), if you are lucky enough to find a copy in your library. Graham Smith's *Pulsars* (Cambridge University Press, 1977) provides a less breathless overview of the first ten years of pulsar studies.

In some ways, this was a letdown for me in personal terms. But I had the satisfaction of knowing that I had helped to set the limits on what white dwarf stars could do, and that thereby I had helped to prove beyond doubt that pulsars must be objects even smaller and more compact than white dwarfs. Looking back over fifteen years to those days in Cambridge, that seems with hindsight like a rather more important contribution than I realized at the time, and I now appreciate that perhaps my examiners were right after all to award me a Ph.D. As Sherlock Holmes would have it, once you eliminate the impossible, whatever remains, no matter how improbable, must be the truth. It was by eliminating white dwarfs as impossible that astronomers, including myself, proved that pulsars must be neutron stars, and thereby established that neutron stars do exist.

Observing Black Holes

This was a more dramatic revelation to an older generation, accustomed to regarding neutron stars as a way-out figment of the astrophysical equations, than it was for a brash young student disappointed by the failure of his pet theory. If neutron stars really existed, the graybeards realized, then just maybe they ought to believe the equations that said black holes existed—the same equations that predicted neutron stars, but taken one step further. By the end of the 1960s the idea that black holes might not only exist but be detectable had taken a grip on the imagination of astronomers, and just at the time when they were being equipped, for the first time, to make an observational search for such exotic objects. If black holes did exist, then the discovery of pulsars very clearly hinted that the most likely place to look for them would be at the site of a former massive star, an exploded supernova. Locating an isolated black hole is clearly a hopeless task—how do you identify something that is less than 10 km across, invisible, and as far away as the stars? But astronomers soon realized that black holes need not be isolated, since very many stars—the majority—do not live in splendid isolation like our Sun, but have one or more companion stars. A black hole in a binary system wouldn't just orbit quietly around its companion star; its strong gravitational pull would tug at the companion, and if it was close enough it could easily strip off material from the companion's outer layers and swallow it. But a black hole a few kilometers across and containing a few solar masses of material is a messy eater. Gas captured from a companion doesn't just funnel neatly into the hole. It swirls

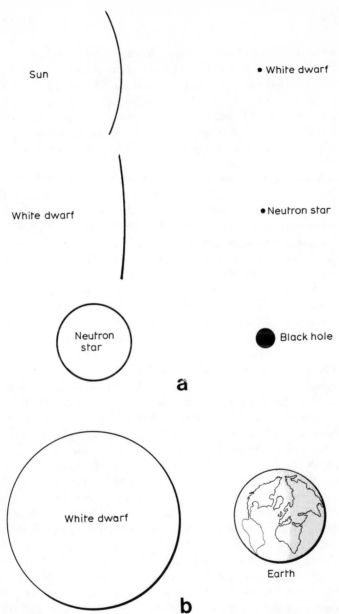

Figure 2.4 The scale of things. a) A neutron star with the same mass as our Sun is smaller than a white dwarf in about the same ratio in which a white dwarf is smaller than the Sun. But it only takes a little more compression to turn a neutron star into a black hole. So the identification of pulsars as neutron stars encouraged theorists to believe the calculations that also predicted the existence of black holes. b) The Earth is a little smaller than a white dwarf star, and a neutron star would be about as big as the island of Manhattan.

around, like bathwater going down a drain, and the colliding, swirling atoms and nuclei in the stream get hot as they fall down the gravitational well. Hot material radiates energy, and the sort of heat associated with matter falling into a black hole ought to produce a lot of radiant energy—enough to make the object detectable at X-ray frequencies. So the place to find a stellar mass black hole is as an X-ray source orbiting an ordinary star within our Milky Way Galaxy.

X rays from space are screened out by the Earth's atmosphere and can't be detected from the ground (which is just as well, since being bathed in cosmic X rays wouldn't do us any good). So X-ray astronomy only took off, literally, when rockets and balloons first carried instruments high above the ground. And it was only in the early 1970s that X-ray astronomy observatories were first put into orbit around the Earth to monitor the sky continuously at X-ray frequencies. These unmanned satellites transformed our view of the Universe and showed it to be a much more violently energetic place than anyone had suspected. They also produced at least one very good candidate in the search for black holes.

Before we look at that candidate, a slight recap seems desirable. The equations of gravitational collapse tell us that any object more massive than about three Suns, but not held up by nuclear fusion, must collapse forever under the pull of its own gravity. Once it collapses within the critical radius $R = 2GM/c^2$, however, it has become a black hole and nothing can escape to the outside world. That radius is called the Schwarzschild radius, and when I talk about the "radius of a black hole" that is the radius I am referring to. We can never see what goes on inside the Schwarzschild radius, but only events going on in the highly distorted region of spacetime just outside. In that region of bent spacetime, matter being swallowed by the black hole will gain enormous amounts of energy and radiate across the electromagnetic spectrum, including strong X-radiation. So although we can never see a black hole, we might very well detect its spoor. The math says that within the black hole matter is crushed out of existence into a singularity, a mathematical point. Where does it go? Anywhere and nowhere; your guess is as good as mine. Some guesses that have been tried include the speculation that "what goes in must come out," that each black hole has its counterpart "white hole" somewhere, or somewhen, else; that matter squeezed out of our spacetime Universe may emerge in another space, another time—another universe, or another region of our own Universe. We'll hear more of these speculations later, and they form the subject of my book *White Holes*, but first let's get back to the story of the best black hole candidate yet identified, a source known as Cygnus X-1.

Once astronomers had identified the first X-ray sources in binary systems they were well on the way to finding a black hole. Only white dwarfs, neutron stars, or black holes, among the objects with masses a little more than that of our Sun, have strong enough gravitational fields to produce X-radiation when matter falls on, or in, to them, so the search for black holes began with a search for white dwarf and neutron star explanations of binary X-ray sources. Eliminate those and what remains is the black hole. Several of the first X-ray sources identified could be eliminated because they showed periodic fluctuations, rather like X-ray pulsars, and black holes are not expected to behave in such an orderly fashion. Their X rays come from regions of chaotic interactions, not a regularly pulsed beam. Others could be happily explained as white dwarf stars, because studies of the orbital variations of the binary systems in which they were housed showed their masses to be less than the critical limit for white dwarf stability, 1.5 solar masses. Throughout the search for the first good black hole candidate, theorists endeavored to play devil's advocate. Every time a new candidate was offered, they sought any possible means to explain it away without invoking a black hole, since only by these endeavors could they eliminate the impossible in the approved Holmesian fashion. Four reasonable prospects emerged from this searching investigation in the early 1970s. All were X-ray sources in binary systems, small, energetic, and compact objects orbiting around normal stars. All showed the chaotic, noisy radiation pattern expected of matter falling into a black hole, rather than the orderly flicking of a rotating neutron star or pulsar. One had a mass 2.5 times that of the Sun, and might be a neutron star; one had a mass three times that of the Sun, still just possible for a neutron star, perhaps; the third had a mass only twice that of the Sun, not enough to eliminate the neutron star possibility; but the fourth had a mass eight to ten times that of the Sun, and now the devil's advocates were in trouble. They tried their best. Could the unseen companion actually be not one object with a mass of eight Suns, but a faint star of, say, six solar masses held up by nuclear fusion, with a third star, a two-solar-mass neutron star, orbiting around it? But as the explanations became more tortuous it became clear that here at last was a source for which the simplest explanation involved a black hole. This is still not proof; but most astronomers are now agreed that the object known as Cygnus X-1 is best explained, in the light of all the available evidence, as a black hole of at least eight solar masses in orbit around a large ordinary star.

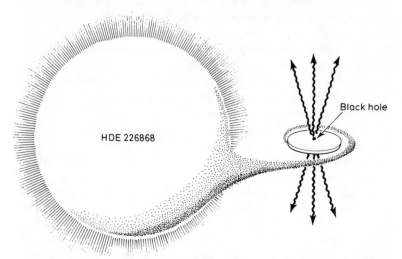

Figure 2.5 The standard model of the archetypal black hole candidate. HDE 226868 is losing matter, which streams across to a black hole in orbit around the larger star. As the gases fall into the black hole, gravitational energy is released, producing the intense X-radiation that we see as the source Cygnus X-1.

The ordinary star is not exactly like our Sun, though, and looks ordinary only in comparison with a black hole or neutron star. It is a hot, blue star catalogued as HDE 226868, with a mass about twenty times that of the Sun. The blue star and the X-ray source orbit around each other at a distance of about 30 million km, only one-fifth of the distance from the Earth to the Sun, taking just over 5½ days to complete one orbit. The diameter of the black hole is about 300 km, and it must be surrounded by a disk of gases swirling and spiraling into the hole, with atoms and nuclei rubbing shoulders in the disk until friction raises their temperature to 2 million degrees and they radiate energy at X-ray frequencies.

Cygnus X-1 is the archetypal black hole candidate, but there are others. The devil's advocates will tell you that Cygnus X-1 is still by far the best candidate, and the only well-established one, but this rather misses the point that one is all you need. If one black hole exists, then many can exist. And objects like Circinnus X-1 and GX 339-4 are also known to show the erratic flickering activity seen in the radiation from Cygnus X-1, even though they have not yet been proved to be members of binary systems, and therefore not had their masses measured. It would be nice to have stronger evidence that there are many black holes in our Galaxy, but the evidence is already strong enough to be persuasive. The objects theorists predicted almost half a century ago really do exist in our cosmic neighborhood. Just as the discovery of pulsars gave confidence in the equations that predicted the existence of neutron stars and black holes, so the discovery of even one very strong black hole candidate in our Galaxy gives confidence in the equations which say that such stellar mass black holes are merely one type, in a family which ranges from the very small—black holes smaller than atoms—to the very large—black holes containing the mass of a whole galaxy of stars. This is the real importance of the intensive study to which Cygnus X-1 has been subjected. It provides a springboard from which we can jump off into areas of science which are fully respectable, but where the direct evidence that black holes are involved is more tenuous than the evidence that Cygnus X-1 harbors a black hole. In many cases, regions of violent activity in the Universe can be most simply explained in terms of black holes, but other explanations are possible. Without strong evidence that black holes exist, the devil's advocates still have room to maneuver. With the evidence of Cygnus X-1 before them, their room for maneuver is strictly limited, and there seems little reason not to accept the simplest explanation, that black holes power many of the violent objects seen in the cosmos.

A Black Hole Miscellany

This is, perhaps, a good place to stand back again from the detail of Cygnus X-1 and astronomical observations of real black hole candidates, and look again at the implications of those equations. Although I have been careful to talk about bent spacetime, rather than just distorted space, what does the distortion of time in the region of a compact black hole really mean? In terms of a probe dropped into a black hole, assuming it could avoid getting crushed by tidal forces, time would appear to "flow" normally. But to an observer safely distanced from the Schwarzschild radius on the outside of the hole, an observer monitoring the progress of the probe through radio links, perhaps, a very curious thing would happen. Instead of the probe plummeting ever faster into the gravitational well, beyond some critical point it would seem to slow down, and eventually it would appear to be hovering on the edge of the black hole. Compared with time in the world outside, time for the space probe would be seen to the observers outside first to run slow and then come to a standstill as the probe moved deeper into the highly distorted region of spacetime around the hole. The limiting region where time comes to a halt is called the event horizon. Observers in flat spacetime can never see anything cross the event horizon—the spherical surface which has a radius equal to the Schwarzschild radius. This is the point of no return. To escape from it, you need to travel at the speed of light. To escape from within the event horizon is impossible.

But a falling space probe, or an intrepid astronaut, would notice nothing odd about the event horizon on the way in; only in an attempt to get out would the probe, or astronaut, discover that it was impossible to cross this invisible boundary. More practically, from our viewpoint as outside observers, the stretching out of time near the event horizon has a dramatic effect on light, stretching out the wavelength of each photon struggling out of the region of distorted spacetime, and shifting it toward the red end of the spectrum. This is the gravitational red shift; a similar effect, called the Doppler red shift, is produced in the light from an object receding from us with high velocity. I'll speculate more about the time distortions produced by black holes—especially rotating black holes—in Chapter Eight. Meanwhile, there are plenty of other ideas to chew over before we look again at observations of the real world.

Could energy be extracted from a black hole? Astrophysicists are always looking for sources of energy to explain the powerhouses of phenomena they observe in space; more exotically, theorists like to dabble in weird ideas, and one of the weirdest concerns the way an intelligent, spacefaring civilization could in principle extract energy from a rotating black hole. The proviso is important—static, or nonrotating black holes are much more boring objects, but since all stars rotate, and black holes presumably form from the collapse of stars, all real black holes are likely to rotate. The rotation does terrible things to our picture of a nice, spherical object with an event horizon at the Schwarzschild radius. A rotating black hole not only bends spacetime, it drags bent spacetime around as it rotates, and it has two event horizons, one inside the other, both places where time appears, to an outside observer, to stand still. The difference is that, under the right circumstances, you can still escape from within the outer event horizon. And things are also very different at the heart of the black hole.

Whereas the singularity at the heart of a static black hole is a mathematical point, the singularity at the heart of a rotating black hole is a ring, a doughnut-shaped torus. Like a lion jumping through its trainer's hoop, a probe or astronaut might dive through the ring singularity without ever being torn apart by infinitely curved spacetime (but it could never get out of the black hole, remember, since the event horizon is a one-way street). Such a journey takes us into Alice's Wonderland. Diving through the ring singularity takes you, if the equations can be accepted at face value, into a region of spacetime called negative space, where gravity pushes things up, rather than holding things down. This is way-out speculation, but just maybe it corresponds to the "other end" of a black hole, which might better be seen as a tunnel through spacetime from our Universe to something else. But let's get back to the outside of the rotating black hole, and its two event horizons. If we imagine an object dropped into the black hole from outside, it is possible to make use of the rotation in such a way that once inside the outer horizon the falling object splits into two, with half falling inward irrevocably below the inner horizon, and half gaining energy and escaping from the black hole. This is not, perhaps, a very practical way for a civilization to obtain its energy, but the idea of a particle splitting in two near the event horizon, with half going into the hole and half escaping out to flat spacetime, does lead rather neatly to the most dramatic theoretical discovery concerning black holes made in the past decade.

The most fundamental feature of a black hole is that it stays a black hole. A black hole is a black hole is a black hole, as Gertrude Stein might have said. In the 1970s, theorists elaborated on this concept. Obviously, each black hole has its own characteristic mass, determined by the amount of matter it has swallowed, and this is its fundamental characteristic. A black hole can also rotate—indeed, most real black holes are expected to be rotating—and in principle it can carry an electric charge, if it has swallowed more electrons than protons, or the other way around. It is difficult to see how a charged black hole could stay charged in the real Universe, since it should, surely, very efficiently grab hold of the amount of opposite charge needed to balance its excess; opposite charges attract and there should be plenty of charged particles in the matter falling into a black hole for it to choose from. But could any other properties be retained by a gravitationally collapsed object, a black hole? Most theorists believed that mass, charge, and rotation (spin) were the only properties a black hole could have, but at first they had no proof. Kip Thorne and John Wheeler coined the term "hair" to refer to all the other hypothetical properties a black hole might have, using the analogy that two black holes with identical mass, spin, and charge might be distinguished by some other property in the same way that two otherwise identical people might be distinguished by their hairstyle or hair color. By 1975, however, theorists had proved that mass, spin, and charge were indeed the only properties a black hole could possess within the framework of general relativity, and coined the expression "black holes have no hair" as a succinct statement of this fact. But while orderly progress was being made toward this logical development of black hole theory, the whole study of black holes had been turned on its head in 1974, when the brilliant British theorist Stephen Hawking—one of the people who developed the "no hair" theorems—published evidence that black holes do not sit quietly in space forever, but may emit particles, bubbling away until eventually they explode outward into the Universe.

"Black hole explosions?" "Black holes are hot," and "Black holes aren't black" were the headlines in the scientific journals which greeted this astonishing claim. The science behind the claim was difficult to put across to a lay audience, but the popular reports made up for that by dwelling on Hawking's genius—the nearest thing we've got to another Einstein—and the story of how, crippled by a disease which makes it impossible for him to write and difficult for him to speak, he carries all the mathematical calculations for his theorizing in his head, a skill which theorist Werner Israel has suggested is equivalent to a modern Mozart composing an entire symphony in his head. The story of exploding black holes made headlines. But it was just the latest development of a logical path of progression which had begun in Hawking's student days, in the mid-1960s. Hawking established himself as something out of the ordinary run of theorists with his work, in collaboration with Roger Penrose, which proved not only that singularities *could* exist, but that they *must* exist if general relativity is an accurate description of the behavior of spacetime. He went on to develop new theorems, proving among other things that the area of the "surface" of a black hole (the surface of the event horizon) could never decrease. The more massive a black hole is, the greater is the surface area of the event horizon, and since black holes do not lose mass, the event horizon never diminishes.

Into New Territory

This realization, simple though it seems, took black hole theorizing into new territory, since it suggests an analogy with the fundamental concept of the branch of science known as thermodynamics, the concept of entropy. Entropy is a measure of the amount of information a system contains. A highly ordered system is low in entropy, and a system dominated by random processes is high in entropy. Our Universe seems to be in a low-entropy state, with bright stars shining in a dark sky. And living things—ourselves— are a feature of high-information, low-entropy states. So entropy is something very fundamental to our understanding of how the Universe works. And entropy, like the area of a black hole, must always increase. By forging a link, however tenuous, between black holes and thermodynamics, Hawking began to unite areas of physics that had seemed unrelated. His revelation that black holes aren't black caused a great stir in the astronomical trade not so much because it flew in the face of the "black hole is a black hole is a black hole" philosophy, but because it forged a link between the two greatest theoretical achievements of twentieth-century science, relativity and quantum mechanics.

Quantum mechanics is the modern description of the behavior of the very small, the world of particles and atoms. General relativity describes the very large, the world of stars, galaxies, and the whole Universe. A link between the two would unify physics on the grand scale, and the search for such a link is the Holy Grail of modern theorists. This is not a book about quantum mechanics, and I have no space here to discuss the theory in detail. But the ideas needed to forge the link with black hole physics are quite simple, although far from "logical" in terms of our everyday lives.

Matter and energy are interchangeable. That is the meaning of Einstein's famous equation $E = mc^2$. Energy can be turned into matter, and matter can be turned into energy. But because of the factor c in the equation (c, the speed of light, is a cool 30 billion centimeters a second), you need a lot of energy to make a small amount of matter. A light shines because energy is being converted into particles, although since the particles in this case are photons and have no mass, the trick is rather easy and not too astonishing. But if you could heat something to a high enough temperature—about a million million (trillion) degrees—it would emit not just light but particles of "real" matter, electrons and positrons. This is not a practical proposition here and now, but in the world of the very small, slightly different rules apply. Where quantum mechanics is the best description of the physical behavior of particles, things are less clear-cut than in our world, and uncertainty becomes a key feature of life.

One of the key principles of quantum mechanics holds that there can be no absolute certainty about the position and motion of a particle, or its energy. For a brief interval, particles might pop into existence and disappear again before the Universe at large notices, borrowing the energy for their brief existence from the uncertainty inherent in the equations. This is a bizarre concept, but one firmly rooted in the equations of modern physics. It produces a strange picture of a universe filled with these "virtual" particles, or more strictly, particle-antiparticle pairs, that are continuously materializing and very quickly coming together and being annihilated. Such particles cannot be detected directly—by the same laws of physics which allow them to exist at all, they do not "live" long enough to be detected. But their presence does affect the behavior of "real" particles, and produces a measurable effect on the spectrum of light from hydrogen atoms, the so-called Lamb shift. What Hawking discovered, and published in 1974, was that these virtual quantum particles have a profound influence on the life of a black hole.

Hawking found that black holes emit particles at a steady rate, and that each black hole has its characteristic temperature, which it must have if the analogy between its area and entropy is to hold up. The two discoveries go hand in hand, because an object that only absorbed radiation could not have a measurable temperature —something has to get out in order to be measured. With hindsight, the twin discoveries are seen as one of the greatest breakthroughs in the history of science; indeed, in 1978 Hawking was given the Albert Einstein Award, the highest award in theoretical physics and ranking well above the Nobel prize in the eyes of the scientific community. He was just thirty-five when he received this recognition of his genius, and in spite of his disabilities his work continues. But in 1974, he couldn't believe his own calculations. As he described later in the pages of *Scientific American*: "To my great surprise I found that the black hole seemed to emit particles at a steady rate. Like everyone else at that time, I accepted the dictum that a black hole could not emit anything. I therefore put quite a lot of effort into trying to get rid of this embarrassing effect. It refused to go away, so that in the end I had to accept it."

Exploding Black Holes

Like Sherlock Holmes, Hawking eliminated the impossible and was left with the improbable, but true, evidence that black holes evaporate. The virtual particles of quantum mechanics come into the story because they explain the process. Normally, each particle-antiparticle pair annihilates itself within a tiny interval of time after its formation. But suppose the pair of particles forms near but just outside the event horizon of a black hole. Now, one member of the pair may fall into the black hole, while the other does not. Left without a partner, the spare particle can escape to the region of flat spacetime, where it seems to be a particle radiated from the surface of the black hole. The effectiveness of the process depends on the area of the event horizon, since the particle pairs can only be separated if they form just above this surface. So the temperature of a black hole—the amount of radiation it radiates—is intimately tied to the surface area, and the link with the thermodynamic concept of entropy is firmly established. But this isn't the end of the story.

Figure 2.6 In empty, flat spacetime, pairs of particles, such as electron/positron pairs, can appear out of the vacuum and then annihilate one another and disappear. If such a vacuum fluctuation occurs near the horizon of a black hole, however, one of the particles may fall into the hole before the pair annihilates, while the other escapes. The effect is as if the black hole were manufacturing particles. (After J. V. Narlikar, *Violent Phenomena in the Universe,* op. cit.)

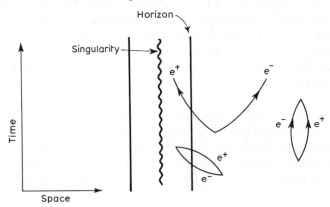

Quantum mechanics, in effect, allows a particle to escape from a black hole. The result is an effective temperature for the hole—for a black hole with the mass of the Sun, about one ten-millionth of a degree K, but for a black hole with a mass of a billion tons and the size of a proton, a temperature of 120 billion K, or 10 million electron volts. Clearly, the effect is of negligible significance for the kind of stellar mass black hole we have been talking about so far. But for a proton-sized black hole, the energy available is enough to make electron-positron pairs, as well as photons. A tiny black hole like this would radiate 6,000 megawatts of energy. Losing energy all the time, its mass would decrease in proportion. And there would come a time when the mass left in the black hole was no longer enough to close spacetime around it. The black hole would cease to be a black hole, and the remaining pent-up matter inside the now-vanished event horizon would explode outward into the Universe.

For a large black hole, the process takes a very long time. A black hole with the mass of the Sun would take 10^{66} years to evaporate in this way, and the Universe is only 10^{10} years old. Such a black hole, indeed, would gain matter faster by swallowing even odd atoms from interstellar space than it would lose mass-energy by radiation at its characteristic temperature. But if tiny black holes formed very early in the life of the Universe, they could be exploding now, releasing their pent-up mass-energy in the form of gamma rays with energy of about 100 million electron volts. It is very difficult to conceive of a way proton-sized black holes might be made in the Universe today, but astronomers believe the Universe began as a vast explosion, a Big Bang, from a state of almost infinite density. Maybe primordial black holes could have been formed then, and remain in the Universe to evaporate and explode today. The theorists are still investigating the ramifications of Hawking's discovery of a decade ago, and the observers are using their satellite-mounted instruments to check the skies for gamma ray bursts which might mark the death of black holes. But the implications of Hawking's work extend across all of our understanding of spacetime.

First, it is worth mentioning another interpretation of the production of virtual particle-antiparticle pairs. In terms of the mathematics, an antiparticle can be regarded as a particle traveling backward in time. If a positron-electron pair, say, popped into existence for a brief time and then annihilated itself, we could de-

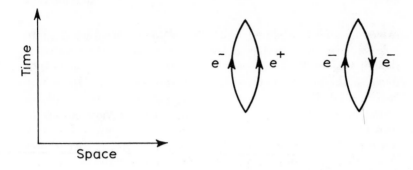

Figure 2.7 The equations of modern physics make no distinction between an antiparticle traveling forward in time (in this case a positron, e$^+$) and a conventional particle traveling backward in time (e$^-$). A vacuum fluctuation involving an electron/positron pair can also be thought of as a time loop involving one electron chasing its own tail. (After J. V. Narlikar, op. cit.)

scribe the event equally well by saying that an electron popped into existence, traveled forward a short distance in time, turned around and went back to its beginning, then turned around to travel forward as an electron, then turned around again to travel back as a positron, then . . . but you get the picture. Rather than two particles existing for a brief time, we have one particle caught in a time eddy, chasing its own tail around and around. Now look again at the pair creation process on the edge of a black hole. Instead of a particle-antiparticle pair being created and one of the pair falling into the black hole, we can say that a particle traveling backward in time emerges from the black hole, then turns around and travels forward in time and off into space once it has got outside the event horizon. In many ways, this is a more satisfactory picture, if you can live with the idea of particles traveling backward in time. Hold on to it while we go back from the world of the very small to the world of the very large, the Universe itself.

White Holes

Before the idea of black hole explosions was presented to an astonished astronomical community by Stephen Hawking, a few intrepid theorists had speculated on the possibility that a time-reversed counterpart of the black hole could exist. The equations of physics don't care which way time flows, and all of the descriptions of black hole collapse can be turned around to describe a family of exploding objects, dubbed white holes. Nobody has seen a white hole for sure (come to that, nobody has seen a black hole for sure, though Cygnus X-1 is a strong candidate), and when you look in detail at the equations there are real problems. Since time does have a fixed direction in our Universe, when you try to make a white hole mathematically you find that it tends very quickly to turn into a black hole, collapsing under its own gravity before it can expand out into flat spacetime. Still, the theorists speculate— that is their job. Suppose general relativity is not the best theory of matter and spacetime under extreme conditions, but that at some point before the ultimate singularity is reached gravity reverses, shooting the matter out again. This is not such a crazy idea. The fundamental forces of particle physics often behave like this. Two protons, for example, each with their positive charge, repel each other, and they repel more strongly the tighter they are pushed together—up to a point. At some critical distance, however, the repulsive electrical force is overwhelmed by more powerful, but short range, forces, the forces which hold the protons of an atomic nucleus together in spite of the fact that they have the same electric charge. Maybe gravity is overwhelmed by an outward urge when conditions are extreme enough. More of this, too, later.

I said that nobody has seen a white hole, but that is not strictly true. We do have a wealth of observations of one system that is exploding outward from a state of very great density—it's just that we aren't used to thinking of this particular system as it would appear to an outside observer. I refer, of course, to the whole Universe, everything we can see in space. Whole clusters of galaxies are seen to be rushing away from each other, with every galaxy cluster receding from every other, in a way which is most simply interpreted in terms of an outward expansion of spacetime, an expansion which began from a state of almost infinite density some 15 billion years ago. This is exactly what those intrepid theorists mean by a white hole, and the equations which describe the expansion of the Universe from a Big Bang origin are exactly the same equations which describe the collapse of black holes into singularities, but with the arrow of time reversed. The equations are Einstein's equations, the equations of general relativity.

The Big Bang also, as Hawking has pointed out, resembles a black hole explosion on a vastly larger scale, with particles of all kinds being formed from a sea of energy under conditions more extreme than most people can imagine. The developing understanding of how black holes radiate particles has, in the past few years, led to new insights about how the particles which make up the material Universe of stars, planets, and galaxies were created in the first split seconds after the Big Bang itself. Exploding black hole or expanding white hole, take your pick. But either way we are ready for the drama of recent theoretical developments which enable us to push our picture of the origin of the Universe back to within the first 10^{-35} of a second (a decimal point, followed by 35 zeros and a figure 1) of the Big Bang outburst from a primordial singularity, 15 billion years ago.

3

The White Hole Universe

Einstein's theories work equally well when applied to the Universe at large. From the first split second of an exploding fireball to the far future, billions of years from now, the Universe can be pictured as an inside-out black hole.

Einstein's equations—the equations of general relativity—describe the behavior of spacetime in the presence of mass-energy. The Universe we live in is a region of spacetime containing mass-energy, and it is no surprise to learn that Einstein's equations can be used to describe the behavior of the Universe. Strictly speaking, though, Einstein's equations can *only* be used to describe the behavior of a complete universe. When we use them to describe the behavior of light passing near the Sun, or the orbit of Mercury, we are actually using an approximation, because general relativity is a complete theory dealing with complete regions of spacetime, which means whole universes. The equations can happily be applied to black holes, which are universes in miniature, regions of spacetime bent around and cut off from the almost flat spacetime that stretches across the visible Universe; and they can equally happily be applied to the puzzle of how our Universe came into existence, and how it evolved into the state we see today.

That is the puzzle that Einstein set out to solve with his theory of gravity and spacetime. But his first attempts to solve the puzzle produced answers as baffling as the original puzzle. The equations that had proved so dramatically successful in solving problems like the bending of light near the Sun, or the detailed nature of the orbit of Mercury, seemed to be less successful when they were applied to the whole Universe, a complete region of spacetime which they had been designed to deal with. The paradox stemmed from a misunderstanding about the nature of the Universe which Einstein shared with every astronomer in the early part of the twentieth century.

When we look up at the night sky, we see a picture of stability. Seasons come and go, with changing patterns of stars, but apart from this regular rhythm the stars seem unchanging and constant on any human time scale. So astronomers assumed that unchanging constancy was a key feature of the Universe at large. At the beginning of the twentieth century, stars were all that astronomers knew of the Universe, and what we now think of as our Milky Way Galaxy, an island of thousands of millions of stars like our Sun, set in an almost empty sea of spacetime dotted with other island galaxies and clusters of galaxies, was all the Universe to them. So Einstein's first attempts to describe the structure of the Universe using the equations of general relativity were aimed at producing a picture of stability, a universe of flat spacetime which stayed the same, on average, forever. The equations he had set up, however, stubbornly refused to play ball. Analyze them as he might, Einstein found that in their original form they could not be made to describe such a static universe. He could get mathematical models, as we would now call them, that described regions of spacetime collapsing upon themselves under the influence of gravity (black holes), and he could get mathematical models of universes bursting outward from a singularity, like a black hole in reverse (remember the equations are time symmetric). But he couldn't get mathematical models which produced a universe balanced on the knife edge between expansion and collapse.

Of course, there were variations on the theme. Some of the expanding model universes slow down and reverse their expansion, collapsing back in upon themselves. And it is possible to build a mathematical description of a universe, consistent with Einstein's equations, which starts at infinite size, collapses down to a finite state (but not a singularity), then turns around and expands back out to infinity. Einstein even managed to find a way to fiddle a stable universe out of the equations, but only by adding an extra constant, a new parameter which had no roots in the study of gravity which had given Einstein the basis for his cosmological calculations. In later years, Einstein described this fiddle as the biggest mistake he ever made, and although theorists still dabble with models involving cosmic constants we, like Einstein in later life, can ignore such ideas. For, by the end of the 1920s, it had become clear that our Milky Way does not represent all of spacetime, and that our Universe is not delicately balanced between the alternatives offered by general relativity in its simplest form, expansion or collapse. Thanks to the pioneering work of Edwin Hubble, astronomers knew by then that the Universe contained many galaxies more or less like our Milky Way system (we now know there are thousands of millions of such islands in space), and that by and large they appeared to be rushing apart from one another. In other words, the Universe we live in is expanding, as Einstein's equations had tried to predict, and as Einstein himself refused to believe until the observational evidence came in.

The Expanding Universe

This is something that cannot be stressed too highly. Ask any cosmologist today, and he will tell you that the single most fundamental fact we know about the Universe is that it expands. Hubble's discovery of the expanding Universe came as a surprise to everybody in the 1920s. Yet Einstein's equations had predicted the discovery, whether Einstein liked it or not. The single most important thing we know about the Universe we live in was predicted by general relativity—powerful evidence indeed that general relativity provides a good description of the Universe.

How do we know the Universe is expanding? Without going into the details of Hubble's epochal discovery,* the essential point is that distant galaxies show a red shift in the light we receive from them. The light from any object, such as a star or a galaxy (which is a collection of stars) can be split into its component colors, the spectrum of the rainbow, and such a spectrum is marked by dark

*Which can be found in my books *White Holes* and *Genesis*.

or bright lines which are as characteristic as fingerprints and show which elements—which atoms—are present in the hot object which is radiating the light. The optical spectrum, the band of light visible to our eyes, runs from red to blue, with red light having longer wavelengths and blue light shorter. The light from stars in our own Galaxy shows many spectral fingerprints of different elements, and the light from distant galaxies shows the same fingerprint patterns, but shifted toward the red and away from the blue end of the spectrum. In other words, the wavelength of the light from distant galaxies has been increased, stretched somehow compared with light from objects in our own Galaxy. The simplest explanation of this is that the distant galaxies are moving away from us, and from each other. This has the effect of stretching the wavelength of light from those galaxies, in the same way that the note of a passing police car siren is deepened as the car speeds away from us.

A battery of astronomical tests shows that for the galaxies near enough for their distances to be estimated by other means, the red shift in their light is proportional to their distance from us. This is exactly consistent with the simplest models of general relativity, and very few astronomers now doubt that all galaxies obey the same red shift/distance relation, dubbed Hubble's law in honor of its discoverer. The more distant a galaxy is from us the faster it is rushing away, and the distance to any galaxy can be determined by measuring its red shift. This is the inheritance Hubble gave to astronomy, and it provides the observational evidence which backs up the reality of the simplest cosmological models of general relativity.

Einstein's equations describe, in their simplest form, a universe in which everything is receding from everything else, just as Hubble's observations show. We are not at the center of the Universe with everything receding from us—spacetime itself is expanding, carrying along the islands of mass-energy (galaxies) with it, so that everywhere in the Universe we would get the same picture of galaxies receding from us in line with Hubble's law. Imagine an infinitely large plum pudding, with no center, expanding in the same way that the Universe expands. From the viewpoint of every plum in the pudding, every other plum would be receding; but none of the plums is moving through the pudding, just as, apart from minor local motions, none of the clusters of galaxies in the Universe is moving through the fabric of spacetime. It is spacetime that expands, carrying us along for the ride.

Still, few of us are really comfortable with the idea of "empty space" being elastic, and able to stretch, squeeze, or bend. It is more comfortable to think of the galaxies, or clusters of galaxies, rushing apart like the fragments of an explosion. Up to a point, the analogy is useful. But remember, it is only an analogy, as we use it to wind our picture of the Universe back to the beginning, the Big Bang.

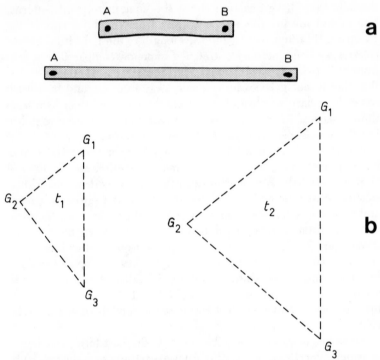

Figure 3.1 a) The red shift in the light from distant galaxies is not a result of galaxies moving through space. Rather, spacetime expands and pushes the galaxies farther apart, like two ink blobs on a stretching elastic band. The ink blobs do not migrate through the material of the elastic band any more than the galaxies migrate through space as a result of the expansion of the Universe. b) So as the Universe expands a cosmic triangle connecting three galaxies expands with it. In this case, between time t_1 and time t_2 the length of each side of the triangle doubles. Light that was emitted from galaxy 1 at time t_1 and received at galaxy 2 at time t_2 shows a red shift of 1. Exactly the same red shift is seen by observers in galaxy 2 looking at light from galaxy 1.

If all the galaxy clusters are rushing apart, then the Universe must have been in a more compact, denser state in the past, with galaxy clusters closer together than they are now. Push this to extremes, and we envisage a time, long ago, when all the galaxies were touching; before that, the Universe must have been a very different place, and if we keep pushing back in our imagination we come to a time when all the stars of all the galaxies were dissolved in a primeval superstar, a fireball—the Big Bang in which the Universe as we know it was born. So much we might have guessed from Hubble's observations of the expanding Universe, even without the aid of Einstein's equations. The beauty of general relativity, and the serendipity of its development at the same time as observers were building new telescopes and discovering the true nature of the Universe, is that it describes in great detail just how such a cosmic fireball expands from near a singularity, out of a region of almost infinite density and almost infinite temperature.

Although very few cosmologists, if any, would use the term to describe the Big Bang, it is exactly what I mean by a white hole—a black hole in reverse. We live in a white hole Universe, and the more people are familiar with the concept of black holes in the Universe the more helpful the image of a white hole universe is. What it really is, though, is Einstein's universe; the simplest model universe described by general relativity is indistinguishable from the Universe we see about us. We cannot use Einstein's equations, or any others, to describe what happens at singularities or infinities, which is why I say that we can picture the expansion of the Universe from a state of *almost* infinite temperature and density, close to the singularity in which, it seems, everything was created. But we can now get very close indeed to that singularity. To be precise, theorists now think they can get back to the first 10^{-35} of a second after the outburst from the singularity. And the conditions their equations describe there are not that different from the world of particle creation and exploding black holes described by Stephen Hawking in recent years.

The Cosmic Fireball

In the extreme conditions of the primeval cosmic fireball, particle creation was much less of a trick than it is even in the region of bent spacetime near a black hole. What matters when it comes to making particles is the energy density of the radiation around, and with almost infinite energy density it is possible to create particle-antiparticle pairs with very large masses. Of course, they don't "live" very long; like the virtual particles of "empty space" today, each particle soon meets up with its antiparticle counterpart and disappears in a puff of energy. But as the Universe expanded, it thinned out, which is another way of saying that the energy density and temperature decreased. Today, matter and radiation are still the two most important components of the Universe, but the thinning out process has gone so far that the density of the remaining background radiation is too low to make any real particles, and only the bubbling spacetime of virtual particle production remains as a theoretical reminder (and a practical one near black holes) of how the Universe began. The surprise, to theorists first grappling with all the implications of Einstein's equations in the thirty years after the realization that the Universe really is expanding, was that any matter is left over at all. In the fireball days, energy—radiation—dominated the mass-energy duality, and material particles were ephemeral visitors to the fabric of spacetime. If every creation event produces its particle-antiparticle pair, and every pair then meets and annihilates itself, how come there was any matter left over when the Universe thinned out—cooled down—to the point where particles could no longer be created from the background radiation?

Various ideas have been offered. Perhaps the Universe really contains equal amounts of matter and antimatter, but somehow the two got separated long ago. Maybe some of those galaxies we see flying away from us in the expanding Universe are actually made of antimatter. But in recent years an alternative suggestion has gained favor. It now seems that the laws of physics which govern the conversion of energy into material particles are not perfectly symmetrical, after all. A tiny asymmetry in the equations leaves scope for a tiny fraction more particles to be created than antiparticles. After the fireball era of the Universe, when all the antiparticles had met their particle partners and annihilated themselves, turning back into energy, a few particles were left over. These, the afterthought of creation, now form all the stars (and their planets) in all the visible galaxies. We owe our existence, it seems, to an imperfection in the laws of physics.

What happened to all the radiation? It's still there, and it still fills the whole of the Universe. But the Universe has expanded so much since the Big Bang that what was once a radiant fireball of heat energy is now a weak hiss of radio noise, with a temperature equivalent to just under 3 K. This is the black body background radiation, the discovery of which earned Arno Penzias and Robert Wilson a share of the Nobel prize, and provided yet another observational proof of the validity of the Big Bang theory. With modern radio telescopes, astronomers can eavesdrop on the echo of the Big Bang itself, and by taking the temperature of this radiation today and working backward in time, they get another handle on the temperature the Universe must have had when it was young and dense. We learn from the background radiation what the Universe was like the last time matter and radiation interacted, which occurred just before it cooled to the point where electrons and protons became bound together as atoms.

Electromagnetic radiation only interacts with charged particles, so the last "scattering" of the background radiation occurred when the last negative electrons and positive protons were being bound together in electrically neutral atoms. The temperature at which this happens is about the same as the temperature at the surface of the Sun today, some 6,000 K; the Universe reached that temperature about 100,000 years after the Big Bang—at that time, the whole Universe was like the surface of our Sun. Studies of the background radiation today show that it is very uniform, coming from all directions in space equally strongly, except for effects which can be explained in terms of the local movement of our Sun and Galaxy through spacetime. This tells us that the Universe itself was very uniform 100,000 years after it was born, with electrically charged particles spread evenly throughout it. And this in turn tells us that the simplest cosmological models of general relativity, the Big Bang models which describe uniform expansion of uniform universes, are indeed the best guide to how the Universe got from the Big Bang to the state, 100,000 years later, where matter and radiation finally decoupled and went their separate ways. For comparison, various estimates based on measurements of the rate at which galaxies recede from one another, and tests involving the radioactivity of samples from meteorites, show that the Universe has now been in existence for something between 10 and 20 billion years, with most tests favoring the lower end of this range. And our Sun and Solar System have existed for nearly 5 billion years, probably about one third of the life of the Universe to date.

Back to the Beginning

In order to keep some sort of a link with the Universe as it is today, we can continue our imaginary probe back toward the Big Bang itself from those last days of the fireball when matter and energy decoupled. Remember that the Universe grew from the Big Bang outward, but that we are looking at the time-reversed pattern, a black hole instead of a white hole. This may, however, be of more than passing relevance to the Universe itself, as we shall see.

Going back in time earlier than 100,000 years after the Big Bang, the Universe simply gets hotter and denser, with no significant change in its other properties, until we are within a few minutes of the singularity itself. At that time, the temperature was billions of degrees, and before then it was too hot for protons and neutrons to exist in stable atomic nuclei. From the first few minutes onward, the particles that came out of the earlier phase of the Big Bang were arranging themselves into atomic nuclei, 75 percent hydrogen and 25 percent helium, as we learn from studies of the composition of old stars, revealed by the fingerprint lines in their spectra. After 100,000 years, as we have seen, electrons became bound to the nuclei. The epoch since then has been the epoch of atomic matter, and the interval from a few minutes to 100,000 years was the epoch of nuclear matter. The first three or four minutes of the Big Bang, however, mark the epoch when the relevant physical laws were those now used by particle physicists to describe the behavior of the particles they conjure up in energetic interactions in their particle accelerators, smashing protons into each other, or into atomic nuclei, to see what comes out.

At this stage, simplicity is all. We see the Universe to be a very simple place, expanding uniformly and the same everywhere. The undoctored equations of general relativity describe just such an expanding Universe, hinting at underlying symmetry and simplicity. Back in the first few minutes, our theories are operating under conditions where they cannot be tested in the Universe today, and all we can do is follow the simplest path. But the simplest path leads to a clear, consistent picture which is certainly speculative, in that it can never really be tested, but seems to provide a working description of the birth of the Universe.

Pushing back into the particle epoch, we make the simple assumption that the Universe keeps getting hotter as it squeezes more densely together—as spacetime shrinks. At an age of 10^{-4}s (0.00001 seconds), individual protons and neutrons are packed together side by side, like the particles in a neutron star, and our everyday experience of the behavior of matter begins to break down. What happens when the particles are squeezed even tighter together? One suggestion is that they dissolve into a "quark soup," quarks being the hypothetical particles invoked to explain the events particle physicists see in their experiments. One of the best current theories says that ordinary particles such as protons and neutrons are themselves made of quarks.* But as we try to probe further back toward the singularity, even the concept of particles becomes a little fuzzy at the edges.

Remember the uncertainty of quantum mechanics. Each particle exists in a fuzzy state, spread over a small volume of spacetime, and there is a strong conviction among relativists that the real breaking point of general relativity comes where quantum effects dominate. Relativity is a "classical" theory in the sense that it deals with particles in the same basic way as Newton did, treating them as well-determined objects with precisely identifiable locations and velocities. General relativity cannot happily deal with fuzzy, uncertain objects, and back around 10^{-43} seconds after the Big Bang the Universe was so small that the quantum mechanical size of the individual quarks was significant—the time left between then and the singularity is so small that the particles can't be sure whether they are one side of the singularity or the other. This provides clues, perhaps, to the nature of the Big Bang itself.** At present, though, we have no description of gravity that includes quantum mechanics, and without such a theory we cannot get closer to the Big Bang than 10^{-43} seconds. That, however, is close enough to be impressive—the ultimate spacewarp, with quarks packed as closely as quantum uncertainty will allow, and a temperature around 10^{32} K.

---

*And, sure enough, some theorists suggest that quarks may lie in the hearts of neutron stars, where the neutrons themselves have been crushed out of existence.
**It also means, as many theorists have pointed out, that we cannot say what ultimately happens to matter involved in a black hole collapse. The laws of physics we know break down at the singularity. Does the collapsing matter "tunnel through" the singularity and burst out somewhere else? Does quantum gravity halt, or even reverse, the collapse? Those are the questions which remain to be answered, and provide some of the most exciting challenges for mathematical physicists today. Be sure you haven't heard the last of black holes.

Now it's time to turn around again and move forward from the quantum uncertainty of the singularity itself, and see how the kind of particles which make up the material Universe came to be formed out of the quark soup. One of the very few meaningful numbers which we can take over from the Universe as it is today to the epoch of particle creation relates the number of particles in the Universe today to the amount of radiation—the number of photons. The basic constituent of matter today is atomic nuclei, which are made of protons and neutrons, members of a family collectively called the baryons. From estimates of the density of matter in the Universe we can get a (very large!) number which tells us roughly how many baryons there are in our region of spacetime, and from studies of the cosmic background radiation we get an equivalent number for photons. The ratio of the two is 10^{-9}. That is, for every baryon in the Universe there are a billion photons, which is an indication of how very nearly all of the matter from the particle era did annihilate itself. A theory which can explain, even roughly, why this number should have the value it does is a theory to be taken seriously, and we now have just such a theory of the early phase of the Big Bang.

Particle physicists have in recent years been working toward the unification of their descriptions of the physical world into one grand theory. Instead of separate theories to describe the separate forces of electromagnetism and the strong and weak forces of particle interactions, they now have a Grand Unified Theory (actually, a choice of slightly different Grand Unified Theories, or GUTs, all variations on the same theme) which contains each of these forces as different facets of a greater whole. The hope is that one day gravity, too, will be incorporated into the ultimate unified theory, but that is still a remote prospect. Meanwhile, the GUTs provide new insights into the world of particle physics, including a trace of asymmetry which may well explain the presence of a trace of leftover matter in the Universe today.

New Developments

I am indebted for my own understanding of these new developments to David Lindley, now at the Institute of Astronomy in Cambridge, who first explained them to me when he was working at the University of Sussex in the early 1980s, and then, at my instigation, explained them to a wider audience in an article in

New Scientist. He pointed out that the GUTs predict the existence of superheavy particles, called X-particles, which can be produced by sufficiently energetic radiation and which themselves decay into less massive particles, producing a shower of "elementary" particles in which there is a slight excess of baryons over antibaryons. In other words, thanks to this two-step process, particle production from radiation does not always involve creation of precisely equal and opposite amounts of matter and antimatter.

The mass of each X-particle is 10^{15} GeV, one thousand trillion times the mass of the proton, which is just 1 GeV. Since the mass of a particle which can be produced out of a radiation field depends on the temperature of the radiation (a measure of its energy density), such exotic particles can only appear in the early phases of the Big Bang. Close to the singularity itself, temperatures of 10^{32} K allow the creation of particles with masses up to 10^{19} GeV, 10,000 times more massive than the X-particles; but once the temperature falls below 10^{28} K, at a time just 10^{-35} seconds after the singularity, no more X-particles can be made, and those left over from the earlier phase soon decay into a shower of baryons (or baryon-type quarks) and a marginally lesser number of antibaryons (or antibaryon-quarks). The asymmetry in the Universe which has left a trace of matter around today—just one baryon for every billion photons—was frozen into the expanding Universe at that point, 10^{-35} seconds after the Big Bang at a temperature of 10^{28} K.

To recap, in the first instant of creation, the tiniest split second, very heavy X-particles were created out of the enormously dense radiation field. A tiny split second later, the energy density was already too low for any more such massive particles to be created, and within a further billionth of a billionth of a billionth of a second the X-particles decayed, fragmenting into other particles and antiparticles. In the shower of particles created in this way, there were just a few more of the kind of quarks that make baryons than those that make antibaryons, and the result is that in the Universe today, although there is much more radiation than matter, there remains a trace of matter, just one baryon for every billion photons, sufficient to produce all the stars in all the galaxies, and all the atoms in our own bodies.

As yet, the theories are too imprecise to predict a definite number for the resulting ratio of baryons to photons, but the estimates range from 10^{-3} to 10^{-13}. This is a very big range; but there is some comfort to be drawn from the fact that the actual baryon/

photon ratio, 10^{-9}, does at least lie within it. Lindley also points out, though, that there is another way to make the baryons, using primordial black holes.

If very small, very dense black holes were present in the super-dense state of the Universe, they could themselves provide the original X-particles from which our present day baryons are descended, thanks to an extreme form of the Hawking process by which black holes emit particles. The most extreme versions of such models of the Universe even have a "cold" origin—a cold Big Bang—with the black holes doing all the work of particle production. The hot model is simplest, and therefore preferable until there is some good reason to discard it, but it is nice to know that there is yet another link between the theory of black holes and the theory of the origin of the Universe. Maybe the whole Universe is better described as an exploding black hole, rather than an expanding white hole. But this is as far as reasonable speculation can take us concerning the origin of the Universe, the ultimate spacewarp of the Big Bang, and the source of all the material around us, and within us. We have a rough idea—perhaps not so very rough—of how things got to be the way they are.* The obvious question that follows is where things are going—what is the ultimate fate of the Universe? And this depends very much on the way in which space-time is curved.

The Fate of the Universe

In science, the simplest questions you can ask are often the hardest to answer. Will the Universe expand forever? And how much matter does the Universe contain? These are prime examples of the complexity that lies behind simple speculations about the nature of the world we live in—and these two fundamental

---

*But we don't know why things started out in a Big Bang. Some questions are outside the domain of physics, and in correspondence with me on this point Graham Blackbourn, of the University of Strathclyde, made an analogy between the Big Bang and a study of a game of pool. Watching the balls move across the table, any competent physicist could work out which ball had been struck by the cue, how hard, and in what direction, in order to explain the various bumpings and bangings going on on the table. But "this tells us nothing of how the balls and table got there in the first place, why the table top is blue and the balls of different colors, and who(?) is holding the cue!" Physics doesn't attempt to answer these questions, but they are still there to puzzle us.

questions are very much linked together. Most astronomers are confident that the Big Bang model is a good guide to reality, explaining why the Universe is seen to be expanding today, and why there is a scattering of matter across the fabric of spacetime. That matter still interacts with spacetime, both locally and on the grand scale, and it is the large-scale interactions that are important when we come to the puzzle of the ultimate fate of the Universe.

Going back to the analogy of an object thrown upward from the surface of a planet (a ball, a shell fired from a gun, or a ballistic rocket), we know from everyday experience that things thrown harder rise higher before falling back, and that things thrown hard enough escape altogether, and keep going forever. Superficially, the outward explosion of the Big Bang can be understood in the same terms. If the bang was big enough, then the fragments flying apart today—the clusters of galaxies—are moving fast enough to exceed their own "escape velocity" from each other, and will keep going forever. If the bang was not big enough, however, the gravity of all the galaxies tugging on each other will eventually halt the expansion, and then cause all the matter in the Universe to collapse back into a fireball reminiscent of the Big Bang of creation.

The analogy helps, but it is actually a rather poor one now that we have some understanding of general relativity and the nature of spacetime. The galaxies moving apart in the expanding Universe aren't moving through "empty space" at all; rather, the fabric of spacetime is stretching, carrying them along with it. Two galaxies, far apart from one another today, can be likened to paint spots on a long rubber band. When the rubber band is stretched, the paint spots move further apart—but neither spot is moving through the fabric of the rubber, just as in the real world neither galaxy moves through the fabric of spacetime. For the whole expanding Universe, the equivalent analogy is of a very stretchy balloon, covered in paint spots and constantly being inflated bigger and bigger. Every paint spot—every galaxy cluster—moves away from every other as spacetime is stretched.

But just as our escape velocity analogy gave a hint of what happens near, or within, a black hole, so it sets us on the right path to investigate the fate of the Universe. The black hole, however, is an even better analog. A particle which cannot escape from a black hole, no matter how fast it moves (up to the limiting speed of light), is trapped because spacetime is bent back on itself. If the Universe is in a similar state, with spacetime bent back on itself to make a closed Universe, then in a very real sense the whole Universe is a black hole, and nothing in it can escape. This is the equivalent of a universe expanding at less than its own escape velocity. In a closed universe, if you keep going in the same direction long enough you get back to where you started, just as on the surface of the Earth if you keep going in the same direction long enough you get back to where you started.

The alternative is that the Universe is "open," and the expansion continues forever. And the one factor which decides whether the Universe is open (an eternally expanding white hole) or closed (the ultimate black hole on the greatest cosmic scale) is the amount of matter it contains. Matter curves spacetime, and if enough matter is present in the Universe then spacetime is curved enough to close the Universe and ensure that a big crunch must be its fate, just as a Big Bang gave it birth.

This is even more intriguing than it sounds. If I start a journey around the world from Boston, say, and head always in the same direction, I return to Boston from the other side. If I keep going, I repeat my original journey. In a closed universe, the big crunch isn't just *like* the Big Bang, it *is* the Big Bang, approached from the other side. If such a universe, in its collapsing phase, continues its "journey" through the big crunch, will it repeat the Big Bang, and proceed through another cycle like an Earthbound traveler foolish enough to follow the same great circle route forever? And if so, will the "new" cycle of the universe exactly follow the pattern followed by the previous cycle, or will the uncertainties of quantum mechanics, strongly brought into play during the fireball phase of the crunch/bang, ensure that no two cycles of the universe are ever quite the same?

The philosophy behind these ideas is intriguing, and it is easy to see why astronomers are so keen to find out if the Universe is open or closed. Was there just one Big Bang—an uncomfortable thought since it implies a unique, inexplicable creation event—or are we part of an eternal cycle of birth, death, and rebirth, which may be just as inexplicable but at least removes the puzzle of creation from consideration? The surprising thing is not that astronomers cannot yet answer these deep questions, but rather that they very nearly can answer them. So far, all they can say is that the Universe we live in sits close to the dividing line between being open and closed. It may be just closed, an eternal black hole doomed to pulse through its cycles indefinitely; or it may be just open, doomed to expand forever, with stars fading away and galaxies getting ever more remote from each other, getting colder and darker forever, to end not with a bang but a whimper. This itself is intriguing. Is there some reason why the expanding Universe should be in a state very close to this dividing line? We just don't know. But let's look at the evidence which gives us a guide to the state it's in.

There are two ways to tackle the problem. Just as with a more modest black hole, the key factor which determines whether the Universe is open or closed is not the actual mass of the Universe, but its density. If we could find a way to measure the density of a large enough volume of the Universe to be representative, then we would know (assuming that the Universe is the same everywhere, that is, homogeneous) whether it is open or closed. This is straightforward in principle, and if you can get some idea of the mass of a typical galaxy it certainly ought to be possible to get an idea of the amount of matter in a particular region of space simply by counting the number of galaxies in it. Unfortunately, although astronomers know the masses of stars quite well, and can guess the mass of a galaxy by its brightness, which indicates how many stars it contains, this doesn't seem to tell the whole story.

The Missing Mass

Just as the planets of the Solar System are bound to the Sun by gravity, and all the stars of our Milky Way Galaxy are bound together by gravity, so clusters of galaxies, presumably, maintain their identity because the gravitational interactions between all the galaxies in a cluster stop them from flying apart. We can measure the velocities of galaxies in such a cluster—their random, local velocities, with the recession velocity due to the expanding Universe subtracted out—and from these measurements (made using the ubiquitous Doppler shift technique) we can calculate how much mass each cluster needs, altogether, to be bound together by gravity as a stable system. Almost always, the numbers astronomers come up with from these calculations are bigger than the numbers they get by estimating the mass of each galaxy from its brightness and adding all the individual masses together. If clusters really are held together by gravity, there must be a great deal of dark matter around, invisible material which we can't see but which exerts its gravitational influence.

This dark matter needn't be in the form of black holes, although it just might be. It could simply be cold gas and dust between the stars, or dead stars like white dwarfs, or planet-sized objects—anything as long as it isn't hot enough to shine by the glow of its own nuclear fires burning inside. The point is that some of the mass in the Universe, for sure, cannot be seen. Astronomers used to call this the "missing mass" problem, but lately they've changed this to "missing light." After all, we know the mass is there, it's just that we cannot see it!

Even when they look at individual galaxies, astronomers find evidence of more matter than we can see. It is now possible to measure the speed with which individual galaxies rotate about their centers, and these measurements show, time and again, the dragging effect of dark matter, carrying the visible stars around with it. If you stir a cup of black coffee, and then add a little cream to it, you get a beautiful spiral pattern which is very much like the pattern of our rotating spiral Galaxy, and galaxies like it, viewed from outside. On the latest evidence, the picture is even more realistic than astronomers used to think, for just as the cream is swirled into a spiral pattern by the coffee in which it floats, so the bright stars in the spiral pattern of a galaxy like our own are carried around embedded in the gravitational field produced by surrounding dark matter.

This doesn't tell us what the dark matter is, but it does pin down where it is—or where some of it is. Only one-tenth of the matter needed to keep galaxy clusters stable is generally found in the bright galaxies, and now it seems that each bright galaxy is like the tip of an iceberg, surrounded by ten times more dark matter than we can see. Nine-tenths of the matter in the Universe is essentially invisible, undetectable to our telescopes, its presence revealed only by the influence of its gravity on the visible matter of stars and galaxies. Ninety percent of the mass in the Universe we just don't see at all, and that makes galaxy counting a poor way to estimate the matter density of our region of spacetime.

Now, it happens that these discoveries, made only in the past few years, are a great help to astronomers in some ways. The best current theories of how galaxies formed in the first place, after the fireball era, suggest that a mass of stars formed long ago, and that they ran through their life cycles and died away as neutron stars, white dwarfs, or even black holes. These formed supergalaxies, ten times as big as the visible galaxies we see today but burnt out and fading even when the Universe was young. A trickle of leftover material, gas and dust blown out from these first generation stars, plus hydrogen and helium left over from the Big Bang, would gather at the hearts of these dead galaxies, like water falling down a well, and in the swirling eddies of this gas new stars could form. These, it seems, are the bright stars of our Milky Way and other galaxies—afterthoughts of creation, leftover embers still burning amid the ashes represented by the dead corpses of the original stars. All the real activity happened within ten million years of the Big Bang itself. But without that activity we wouldn't be here to tell the tale, or puzzle over it, since without the framework provided by those dark, supergalaxy halos the galaxies we know would not have formed a few billion years ago.

So counting galaxies is a poor way to estimate the mass of the Universe, or its density. When they do try this, however, astronomers come up with a total density for the bright matter we can see which is almost one-tenth of the density needed to close the Universe. This is the density parameter, often referred to by the Greek letter omega Ω; a value of 1 for the density parameter would mean that the Universe is just closed. Clearly, since some of the matter in the Universe is dark, the value we get for omega by counting bright galaxies is a lower limit, and we can say for sure that the density parameter is actually bigger than this—but how much bigger? Using the rule of thumb that in the galaxies whose rotation has been measured, and in the clusters that seem to be made of galaxies bound together by gravity, 90 percent of the matter is dark and invisible, it looks already as if the Universe sits very close to that crucial dividing line. But this isn't the end of the story.

There is a completely independent way to test whether the Universe is open or closed, by measuring the speed with which it is expanding, and the way that expansion velocity has changed as the Universe has aged. We see objects which are far away from us across space as they were long ago, when the light we are now seeing left them. We see a galaxy that is 1,000,000 light-years away as it was 1,000,000 years ago, and the velocity of recession which we measure from its red shift indicates how rapidly the Universe was expanding that long ago. Such a short time is but an eyeblink in the life of the Universe, but many objects are now known which show red shifts so large that, if they are due solely to the expansion of spacetime following the Big Bang, we are looking back billions of years into the past. The objects with the biggest known red shifts are the quasars, great powerhouses of energy which must be immensely bright to be visible at all across such vast stretches of space and time, and which are thought to be closely related to galaxies.

Remaining Puzzles

The most distant quasars are seen as they were shortly after the Big Bang, and at that time, according to Einstein's equations as well as to common sense, the Universe was expanding more rapidly than it is today, since subsequently the outward expansion has been slowed down by the influence of gravity. This means that Hubble's famous red shift/distance relation is only an imperfect tool, since really there is a different red shift/distance relation for each epoch in the Universe's life. If we had an independent way to estimate the distances of quasars, we could see how the Hubble relation has changed as the Universe has aged, and that would tell us how quickly the expansion is slowing down. Checking this against the different cosmological models described by Einstein's equations, we could then determine whether the expansion will eventually slow so much that it turns into a collapse, or whether the Universe will indeed expand forever.

There's only one way, other than the red shift, to estimate the distance to a quasar, and that is by its brightness. Presumably, the quasars that look faintest are actually farthest away. But this is a pretty rough and ready guide. Some measurements have suggested that the actual brightness of a quasar can be estimated by measuring the proportion of its energy emitted in a particular band of the electromagnetic spectrum, the ultraviolet. This helps, because if we know the true brightness of a quasar then its apparent brightness is a good guide to distance, just as you could accurately measure the distance to a 100 watt light bulb by measuring its apparent brightness. And with a lot of quasars—and hundreds have now been identified—you can make some sort of statistical guesstimate and come up with a number, the deceleration parameter, which gives a clue to the fate of the Universe. The quasar studies, and similar estimates based on measurements of the most distant known galaxies, both indicate that the Universe is closed. The evidence is not absolutely conclusive, and there is no consensus among astronomers about which side of the dividing line between open and closed the Universe actually lies on. Some measurements, and some astronomers, still support the idea of an eternally expanding Universe. But it seems to me that the closed Universe is a better bet, not least since every time astronomers look at bigger systems they seem to find more evidence of "missing light."

Counting galaxies alone gives a density estimate about one-tenth of the amount needed to close the Universe; small groups of galaxies clearly show the influence of dark matter, and by the time we look at large clusters, such as the relatively nearby Virgo cluster, it is clear that there must be as much as four-tenths of the matter needed to reach the critical density. On bigger scales still the numbers get even closer to the critical limit. How far can this curious relationship be pushed? I asked John Huchra, an observer based at the Smithsonian Institution Observatory in Massachusetts, for his view. Huchra has been closely involved in studies aimed at determining the expansion rate of the Universe, and unraveling the details of the mass-to-light problem (M/L), as it is often called. He told me, early in 1981, that "I would have to say the question is still very much up in the air. I can't really believe that the M/L of systems keeps monotonically increasing . . . it is extremely unlikely that the mass of the Universe (or mass density) is more than twice that required for closure. My own interpretation of the existing data is that the Universe is open, but only by a factor of 3 to 5. From a philosophical point of view, an optical observer would quickly lose interest in observational cosmology if the Universe was dominated by things he couldn't see."

That last sentence is important. Even with this confessed bias, an observer such as Huchra is willing to accept that the Universe could contain twice as much matter as is needed for closure, and the fairest interpretation of all the evidence seems to be that the actual value of the density parameter omega probably lies somewhere between 0.5 and 1.5. Either way, there is a lot more gravitationally active matter in the Universe than we can see. My own prejudice is that the Universe is closed—I'm a theorist, not an observer, and a closed universe gives the theorist more room to speculate, even if it diminishes the interest of the observers. What could the extra mass be? The suggestions keep on coming. Maybe the dark matter is just gas between the galaxies; maybe it is in the form of black holes; maybe (as we shall see in Chapter Six) it could be in the form of a sea of particles, each almost undetectable but each with a tiny mass, filling the entire Universe. As a theorist, I am comforted to know that there is still so much room for speculation. But to back up that case, the best evidence that the Universe is closed comes from those studies of quasars. And that evidence in turn depends on the assumption that quasars really are closely related to galaxies, and that quasar red shifts really are produced, like galaxy red shifts, by the expansion of the Universe. Those are questions which have been the subject of debate over the past twenty years, and I have, perhaps, been a little cavalier in introducing both quasars and galaxies as features of the expanding Universe without going into a little more detail about them. The time has come to make good this omission, and look at the links between quasars and galaxies and the Universe itself. Then we will be armed to tackle the puzzle of what exactly quasars are, and where they obtain the great quantities of energy they need in order to shine so brightly.

4

Galaxies, Quasars, and the Universe

Within the expanding Universe, we find islands of light in a sea of darkness. Galaxies like our Milky Way contain thousands of millions of stars—islands in space. But some galaxies seem to be involved in violent explosions, and there may be more matter around than meets the eye.

We live in an expanding Universe. Einstein's equations of general relativity, the equations which describe the bending of spacetime, predicted that the Universe would be found to expand, even though Einstein himself at first refused to accept the prediction. Confirmation that the Universe expands came from the study of the red shifts in the light from distant galaxies, and as far as the study of the Universe is concerned galaxies are no more than insignificant "test particles," minute specks of matter carried along by the expansion of spacetime in the same way that raisins are carried apart from one another in an expanding cake as it cooks. But from our point of view one galaxy, at least, has a far greater significance. We

71

live in a galaxy of stars, the Milky Way Galaxy, and as far as life as we know it is concerned stars and galaxies are the most important components of the Universe.

Almost everything you can see in the night sky is part of our Galaxy. A few of our nearest neighbor galaxies can be seen as faint patches of light if you live in the right part of the world and view the night sky far from the city lights, but otherwise all of the heavenly bodies visible with the naked eye are part of the same galactic family. Until well into the twentieth century, most astronomers believed that this family of stars represented the entire Universe. The pioneering work of Hubble and his colleagues first established that many of the faint patches of light—nebulae—visible with the aid of telescopes are indeed other galaxies of stars in their own right, and only then that these external galaxies are receding from us in the expanding Universe. Galaxies are collections of stars, but there may be more to galaxies than the stars which are so obviously visible, as we shall see.

On a dark night, away from the bright lights, the main structure of our Galaxy shows up as a faint band of light across the sky, a band which has been referred to by many different cultures as a "road" or a "way," and which is widely known now as the Milky Way, from the Romans' Latin description of its appearance, the Via Lactae. Even a small telescope, or a pair of binoculars, reveals that this milky band of light across the sky is actually composed of many individual stars, which make up a flattened disk. We live in the disk of our Galaxy, so when we look through the plane of the disk we see many stars as a band of light; when we look in other directions, we are looking out of the disc and see far fewer stars dotted around the dark sky. This is a typical structure as far as many galaxies are concerned: A disk, in the case of our Milky Way Galaxy, about 30 kiloparsecs in diameter and only one-tenth of a kiloparsec thick, with the stars in the disk forming a spiral pattern as viewed from outside. There are other galaxies which do not show this spiral structure—ellipticals, which as their name suggests are cigar shaped, and the irregulars, which have no discernible structure. Our Galaxy contains some 100 million million (100 trillion) stars, and our Sun is an ordinary star located in the disk of the Galaxy about two-thirds of the way out from the center, which is about 10 kiloparsecs away.* All of this disk is embedded in a

---

* 1 parsec is just over 3¼ light-years; a kiloparsec is the distance light travels in rather more than 3,250 years, traveling at a speed of 30 billion centimeters a second.

more tenuous, spherical cloud of stars which is called the halo. Halo stars are old, and seem to be left over from the formation of the Galaxy; disk stars are younger, and stars are still forming in the disk today.

Galaxies, of course, are held together by gravity. Each star is in orbit around the center of the Galaxy, just as each planet in the Solar System is in orbit about the center of mass of the Solar System. The center of the Galaxy is a region where stars are closely packed together, compared with the emptiness of space out near the edge of the disk where we live; and there is almost certainly more than just stars at the centers of most, if not all, galaxies. There can be no better place to search for a massive black hole, a region where large quantities of matter have been concentrated by gravity into a region small enough for gravitational collapse to have occurred. In recent years there has been an accumulation of evidence that energetic processes go on at the hearts of galaxies, and there is a growing suspicion that black holes may be responsible. What is certain, though, is that the stellar populations of galaxies evolve and age as the stars within them are born, live, and die. First-generation stars were composed solely of hydrogen and helium, the leftover material from the Big Bang; the nuclear reactions that keep stars hot build these simple elements up into heavier elements, including the oxygen that we breathe and the carbon atoms which make up much of the structure of our bodies. As old stars die, often in violent explosions, these materials are scattered through space and can be incorporated into later generations of stars that form from collapsing clouds of gas and dust in space. So the stars of the spiral arms are enriched with heavy elements compared with the stars of the halo, and the differences between them show up in the light they emit, where each atom produces its characteristic fingerprint of lines in the visible spectrum. In the same way, the averaged light received by a telescope from a whole galaxy of stars shows spectral features which tell us whether the stars of that galaxy are young or old, and this technique reveals that elliptical galaxies contain stars more like those of our halo (old stars deficient in heavy metals) than those of the disk, like our Sun.

Our Humdrum Home

There are billions of galaxies in the Universe, and billions of stars—even trillions of stars—in most of those galaxies. Our home in space is both insignificant and typical, an average location which has no distinguishing features except that it is the place we live. Most galaxies occur in groups, called clusters, which may contain anything from a handful to hundreds of galaxies, of all types, bound together loosely by gravity. The mass that does the binding is largely invisible—if gravity really is holding these clusters together, then there must be 10 to 100 times more matter present in the clusters, in some form or another, than we can see as bright galaxies. The distance from our own Galaxy to its nearest large neighbor, the Andromeda galaxy, is typical of the distances between galaxies—about 670 kiloparsecs, roughly twenty times the size of our Galaxy itself.

Where do galaxies come from? It is unwise to be dogmatic about any theories of what happened early in the history of the Universe, just after the time of the Big Bang, some 15 billion years ago. But theorists believe that they can explain satisfactorily how a seething brew of hot particles, expanding and thinning away from the singularity of creation, developed into a dark Universe dotted with bright island galaxies. Probably the best of these current theories envisages random disturbances in the primeval sea of particles becoming large enough to hold together under the influence of their own gravity, and these initial clumps were probably more the mass of stars than of galaxies. The initial irregularities themselves grouped into larger collections of matter, galaxies, and the galaxies are grouped into clusters and clusters of clusters in a hierarchical arrangement. All of this is very much borne out by measurements of the way galaxies rotate. It takes hundreds of millions of years for a galaxy like our own to rotate once, so these measurements cannot be made directly. But the Doppler shift in light from stars on either side of a galaxy can reveal how fast one side is approaching us and how quickly the other side is retreating, once the overall red shift due to the expanding Universe has been subtracted out. Such studies show that the visible bright galaxies do not rotate as they should if the visible stars were all that they contained; instead, there is a clear dragging effect which is best explained as due to the gravitational influence of superhalos of dark material surrounding each bright galaxy. Theorists such as Professor Martin Rees, of the Institute of Astronomy in Cambridge, have suggested that as much as 80 percent of the original matter which burst forth out of the Big Bang condensed into stars early in the life of the Universe, and these formed supergalaxies which are now represented by the dark halos. Such early stars may have been very large, so that they

1. The spiral galaxy M 101. Our Milky Way Galaxy would look something like this if viewed from outside. (Lick Observatory Photograph)

consumed their nuclear fuel rapidly and are no more than burnt-out hulks—perhaps black holes—today; or they may be very small stars, too faint to be visible across the depths of intergalactic space. Either way, the visible galaxies that provided Hubble's generation of astronomers with such a startling, expanded vision of the Universe beyond the Milky Way are actually no more than the dregs of creation, a few stars forming among the embers at the heart of each original supergalaxy.

This new picture of the Universe is very much in line with the need for ten or more times as much dark matter as visible matter to explain how gravity holds clusters of galaxies together, and moves us a stage closer to the total amount of matter needed to make the Universe closed. It is a dramatic shift from the ideas of even ten years ago, which saw the visible galaxies as representing almost all of the matter in the Universe, but there is independent evidence that the idea of superhalos made of very old, dead stars is correct. Studies of the microwave background radiation have now reached such a stage of refined subtlety that observers can detect very small differences between the actual background radiation and a "perfect" black body spectrum. One such subtlety is a small bump in the spectrum, in just the right place to be explained by the emission of silicate dust very early in the history of the Universe. But the explanation only stands up if very nearly all of the matter needed to close the Universe was processed into stars, each contributing its share of silicates to the total, early in the history of the Universe. This fits very well the developing picture of galaxies in which 90 percent of all the material in the Universe is thought to be dark material, black holes or dead stars, left over from the initial burst of star formation long ago.

It is even possible that the dark matter is in the form of black holes produced still earlier in the history of the Universe, at the critical time when the quark soup was "condensing" into the sort of matter—hadrons—that we think of as the elementary particles of our world of atoms and molecules. This happened when the "age of the Universe" was about three-millionths of a second, and its temperature had cooled to the point where some quarks began to join together to make hadrons. The effect is similar to the phase transition when water vapor condenses, and just as water vapor condenses unevenly, into droplets, so the quark soup would have condensed unevenly. Matt Crawford and David Schramm, of the University of Chicago, have calculated the sort of unevenness that might result, and come up with some intriguing numbers.*

The result is a variation of density across the Universe as it enters the hadron era, with some patches more dense than others. At the time when all this was happening the Universe was still

*Nature, vol. 298 (1982), p. 538.

very dense, and it wouldn't have taken much of a density fluctuation to produce a black hole. In particular, the calculations show that any volume of space that contained about 10^{30} grams of matter at that time could be squeezed into the black hole state by such a density fluctuation. That is about a thousand times the mass of the Earth, three times the mass of Jupiter, or one-thousandth the mass of the Sun.

One important feature of these black holes is that they would have been "processed" before baryons began to dominate the Universe, and so their mass does not come into the calculations of element abundances, particularly the helium abundance, which set a relatively low density on the whole Universe, on the basis of how much hydrogen was processed into helium in the Big Bang. Even if Crawford and Schramm's calculations turn out not to be the last word, they are certainly telling us that the helium abundance calculations are themselves far from being the last word on whether the Universe is open or closed. Equally intriguing, a cluster of such black holes bound by gravity could well provide the "seed" on which a galaxy could grow, with their gravitational influence holding back matter that would otherwise be dissipated in the expanding Universe. Planetary mass black holes are ideal candidates for the dark matter of galactic halos, and for the "missing mass" astronomers need to explain why clusters of galaxies behave as if they contain much more matter than we can see as brightly visible stars.

The story is a fascinating one, at the heart of presentday research into the nature of the Universe. But it has little relevance to the story of spacewarps. Much more relevant and interesting, from our present point of view, are the conditions at the centers of galaxies, where large amounts of matter are concentrated in relatively small regions of space. Many galaxies show signs of violent activity at their hearts, and the most violent and energetic objects in the Universe, the quasars, are now known to be violently active galactic nuclei. Intermediate between quiet galaxies, like our own, and the violence of quasars is a whole range of activity, with one class shading indistinguishably into the next.

Quasars

Quasars were first discovered in the early 1960s, a historical accident which caused considerable confusion to astronomers. At the

2. A rich cluster of galaxies. Each fuzzy blob is a galaxy containing thousands of millions of stars, like our Milky Way Galaxy. (Royal Observatory, Edinburgh)

time, quasars seemed to be so different from anything else known in the Universe that serious doubts were raised about our understanding of the Universe, and even of physics. Over the next ten years, however, a whole range of violently energetic objects were studied by astronomers, ranging from X-ray stars and pulsars in our own Galaxy up through a variety of active galaxies to the quasars themselves. Some of these objects had been known before, but were thought of as rare freaks; it was the work of observers in the 1960s and 1970s that showed the Universe to be a place full of violence, on every imaginable scale. If the quasars had only just been discovered, they would be regarded as the logical culmination of a whole series of such discoveries; but because they were

discovered first, bursting upon the awareness of unprepared astronomers, they produced one of the biggest of astronomical surprises.

The surprise related to their red shifts. Quasars look like stars,
but have red shifts appropriate for distant galaxies. If the same red
shift/distance relationship that works for galaxies can also be applied to quasars, then quasars are as far from us as galaxies—indeed, many quasars are much farther from us than any known galaxy. In order to be visible across such great distances, and yet to
appear starlike on photographs, quasars must produce huge quantities of energy from very small regions of space. In round terms,
a quasar produces as much energy as a whole galaxy like our own,
but it comes from a region of space no bigger across than our Solar
System. Some astronomers argued that there must be a mistake
here. Either the red shift could not be taken as a true indicator of
the distances to quasars, so that they are actually much closer and
correspondingly fainter, or the laws of physics as we know them
must break down at the heart of a quasar, since how else could so
much energy be produced from such a small object? But over the
past two decades evidence has grown both that quasars are at the
"cosmological" distances their red shifts imply and that the laws of
physics formulated from experiments here on Earth and studies of
our Solar System really can explain where quasars get their energy. This is the second great triumph of general relativity. The
same equations of bent spacetime that forecast the discovery of the
expansion of the Universe can explain the energy production of the
most powerful objects in the Universe, in terms of spacewarps and
black holes. When Einstein developed those equations, remember, astronomers thought that our Milky Way Galaxy was the entire Universe, and that the Universe was a quiet, orderly place;
previous great theories, like those of Newton, explained known
patterns of behavior, but Einstein's theory *forecast* the discovery
of objects and phenomena that nobody had any inkling of at the
time the theory was formulated. This has to be the greatest single
achievement of science. It is only in the 1980s, sixty years after
Einstein developed the equations of general relativity, that the full
power of those equations has really become clear, through the study
of quasars, and that the reality of black holes has thereby been
acknowledged.

There are certainly plenty of quasars to puzzle over. Several
hundred have been identified, and the statistics of their distribu-

tion suggest that as many as a million might be detectable in principle using modern techniques. Many of that million have already been photographed, but since they look just like stars on photographic prints they will never be identified as quasars unless for some reason some astronomer decides to look closely at the spectrum of a particular starlike object. One of the occasions that astronomers look more closely at starlike objects is when they are found to be associated with radio noise, and that is how the first quasars were discovered. An object that looks like a star but produces intense radio emission is obviously interesting, and so many of the known quasars are also radio sources. But many are radio quiet, and it is a mistake to assume that radio noise and quasar activity inevitably go hand in hand. Still, this does provide one important link with galaxies, since many galaxies show the same sort of activity at radio wavelengths as quasars do, and it would be strange indeed if the two kinds of radio phenomena were not related. Other galaxies show violent activity of different kinds at their hearts. One type, dubbed the Seyfert, has properties which overlap those of quasars seen at low red shifts, which means relatively nearby. Another class of galaxies, called N-galaxies because they have bright nuclei, look like mini-quasars shining at the hearts of galaxies. And a class of objects named after the first of the kind discovered, BL Lacertae, look like quasars but have no measurable spectral lines and so their red shifts cannot be estimated. When BL Lac objects were shown to lie at the hearts of large galaxies, in the middle of the 1970s, few astronomers were left in any doubt that quasars must be superenergetic galactic nuclei. It was only in 1982, however, that the clinching evidence was reported.

The problem was to photograph the surrounding galaxy against the bright light of the central quasar. Ordinary stars are so faint by comparison with a quasar that it is like trying to photograph the light of a candle alongside a searchlight; any photographer knows that a film exposed long enough to pick up the candle light will be burnt out by the bright light from the searchlight. So although several quasars were found to be identified with much fainter wisps of material, it took the development of a remarkably sensitive new instrument, coupled with the 200-inch Hale telescope in California, to measure the spectrum of one such wispy nebulosity and establish that it is exactly the spectrum expected from a galaxy of stars surrounding the quasar 3C 48. What is more, the light from the surrounding galaxy shows exactly the same red shift as the light from the quasar, convincing evidence that the red shifts of quasars embedded in galactic nuclei can be taken as indicators of their cosmological distances.

By a happy coincidence, in the same week this study of 3C 48 was reported (the first week of April 1982) an Anglo-Australian team announced that it had found a quasar with the largest red shift of any yet measured. The object is identified by the number PKS 2000-330, and has a red shift of 3.78; this means that it is receding from us at 90 percent of the speed of light, and that the light by which we see it left the quasar when the Universe was only one-tenth of its present age. Astronomers still debate exactly how old the Universe is, but if the age of the Universe is 15 billion years, then we see back 13 billion years into the past when we look at photographs of PKS 2000-330; if the Universe is 20 billion years old, then we see the quasar by light that has been 18 billion years on its journey.

But this is very much a freak. A red shift of 2 corresponds to recession at 80 percent of the speed of light, and astronomers have techniques which should be able to measure red shifts as large as 4.7. But PKS 2000-330 is the first quasar with a red shift bigger than 3.5 found since 1973, in spite of several intensive searches and the natural competition among observers to "break the record." When astronomers carry out surveys of quasars, they find increasing numbers of these objects as they look out or back in time to red shifts of about 3.2, but relatively few in the interval from 3.2 to 3.5, and only PKS 2000-330 with a red shift above 3.7. Interpreting this in terms of the way quasars enable us to look back in time to earlier epochs of the Universe, because it takes light a finite time to get to us, this seems to be telling us that very many quasars suddenly "switched on" a few billion years after the Big Bang, that they were active for a while, and that then their activity died away as they settled down to become ordinary galaxies like those we see in our immediate cosmic neighborhood. This discovery fits in rather well with the idea that present-day galaxies are the remnants of much more spectacular supergalaxies that went through their phase of youthfully extravagant activity long ago. There is, though, still room for debate about the exact nature of quasars.

The evidence is that quasars switched on, lived for a certain time, and died away. But how long does a quasar live? Most of the experts, led by Maarten Schmidt of the California Institute of

Technology, argue for a short lifetime. Schmidt has described a
detailed version of this model in which quasars experienced a brief
heyday more than 10 billion years ago. But other theorists, such
as Janet Cheney and Michael Rowan-Robinson, of Queen Mary
College in London, have put forward an alternative theory which
says that the observed distribution of quasars in the Universe can
be equally well explained if each quasar has a long lifetime, about
3 billion years, roughly one-fifth of the age of the Universe. Gary
Chanan, of Columbia University, is another proponent of this idea,
and he argues that quasar activity may continue throughout the
Universe right up to the present day. This provides an important
difference from the standard theory. Theorists who follow Schmidt's
line of argument say that virtually every galaxy must have been a
quasar long ago, but briefly; the alternative is that only a very few
galaxies—one in 30,000—ever become quasars, but each one stays
active for correspondingly longer. The weight of evidence at present lies with the idea of a quick burst of activity affecting every
galaxy. But there is one important piece of evidence that the alternative theory explains better. We happen to have a very bright
quasar, 3C 273, almost on our cosmological doorstep, at a rather
modest red shift of 0.158. Indeed, largely because it is both close
and bright (and a radio source), 3C 273 was the first quasar identified. It is receding from us at only 15 percent of the speed of light,
and we see it as the Universe was only 2½ to 3 billion years ago.
If quasars are a feature of the early Universe, 10 billion or more
years ago, 3C 273 has no right to be there. On the alternative
picture, that quasars are scarcer but much longer lived, the presence of 3C 273 in our neighborhood of the Universe is much less
surprising.

Long Ago and Far Away

The puzzle of quasar lifetimes still has to be resolved, but already the quasars are providing us with detailed information about
the nature of the Universe long ago and far away, near the Big
Bang. They also provide comforting reassurance that our laws of
physics really are universal. Studies of the spectra of quasars provide a wealth of information about the conditions in spacetime close
to them. The exact positions of the lines in the spectrum, after
allowing for the red shift, depend on such factors as the ratio of
the mass of a proton to the mass of an electron, the constant of
gravity, and a factor called the fine structure constant, which we

shall meet again in Chapter Ten. All of the tests applied to quasar spectra to date show that the same physical processes are (or were) at work in them as in our region of spacetime. If this were not the case, there would be little point in trying to understand the workings of the Universe at all, so the discovery came as a major relief, if not a surprise, to astronomers. And yet there are still heretics who claim that new laws of physics are needed to explain the observed behavior of quasars. Some of these heretical claims are easily dismissed; others rest upon more solid ground. But all are worthy of discussion.

The most spectacular example of the light "bending" which provided one of the first, and best publicized, tests of general relativity inevitably comes from quasar studies. In 1979, a team of British and American scientists working with the new multiple mirror telescope in Arizona reported finding what looked like a pair of quasars alongside one another—a binary pair—but which was actually a double image of one quasar, produced by the bending of spacetime to make a gravitational lens. The gravitational lens effect is the result of a rare alignment of a massive galaxy exactly in line between us and the single quasar whose two images we see, almost exactly like the rare alignment of Earth, Sun, and Moon which produces an eclipse during which the bending of starlight can be detected. Light comes toward us from the quasar, and some is bent one way around the intervening galaxy by gravity and some bent through a different route, so that we see two images of the quasar alongside the image of the galaxy on the photographic print.

Figure 4.1 Just as light from a star is bent as it passes the Sun (see Figure 1.6), so light from a distant quasar can be bent as it passes an intervening galaxy. In this case multiple images of the quasar are sometimes seen from Earth—two or more views of the same quasar, slightly displaced from one another.

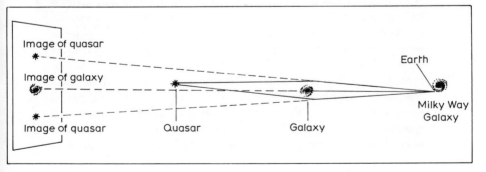

The two images have exactly the same spectral features, each indicating a red shift of 1.4, corresponding to a distance of some 5 billion light-years. When this quasar pair, 0957+561, was first discovered, the similarity of the spectral features immediately suggested that this was a gravitational lens effect, not two separate quasars in orbit around one another, and the subsequent detection of the faint galaxy that is producing the splitting of light from the quasar, lying just between the two images, confirmed this. By the spring of 1982, two more examples of this gravitational lens effect had been discovered, one producing three images of the same quasar in a triangle on the sky separated by 3 seconds of arc, roughly one six-hundredth of the diameter of the full Moon viewed from Earth. At the time of writing, some astronomers are now puzzled that they have found so few multiple images of this kind, since if nearby "lens" galaxies are randomly aligned with distant quasars then there should be many more such pairs and triplets visible. But this is a minor puzzle which may well have been resolved, by the discovery of yet more gravitational lenses, by the time you read these words. Yet again, though, the observation of these multiple images produced by the gravitational distortion of spacetime is a triumphant confirmation of the broad applicability of general relativity theory to the Universe.

Quasars Faster Than Light?

A slightly stranger confirmation of the power of general relativity has come from a discovery that seems at first sight to fly in the face of Einstein's theory—quasars that seem to be expanding faster than light. It is a basic tenet of relativity theory that the speed of light is both constant and an ultimate speed limit, and yet astronomers have found two radio source components within the quasar 3C 273 that seem to be separating from one another at ten times light speed. Other quasars show similar effects, and the discoveries produced some spectacularly misleading headlines in popular newspaper accounts along the lines of "Einstein's theory overthrown." Astronomers and physicists, however, were less disturbed when the news broke. First, they had known about such phenomena for ten years, even though the newspapers only picked up on the story with the release of the news about "superluminal components" in 3C 273 at the end of 1980. Secondly, they already knew how the appearance of superluminal velocities can arise as an optical illusion even when nothing in the distant radio source is actually moving faster than light.

The appearances, although deceptive, are impressive. Many quasars and galaxies which are also radio sources show a complex structure in which there are localized patches of strong radio emission. Very often, there is a double structure with one strong patch of radio emission on either side of the central bright quasar, or galaxy. This suggests that energetic components or particles have been shot out from the center, a suspicion that is very much strengthened by the appearance of some of these objects, including 3C 273, which have jets of material seemingly blasting outward from the central active nucleus. The jet in 3C 273 is typical— a bright streak on photographic prints, with its tip precisely at the place where intense radio emission is coming from, and a second radio source centered on the bright nucleus of the quasar itself. With modern radio techniques, astronomers can resolve details of such structure down to an angular size of 1 second of arc, which corresponds, if the red shift of 3C 273 is indeed produced by the expansion of the Universe and follows the same Hubble's law as the red shift in light from galaxies, to features 10 light-years across in this particular source. The more distant a source, the less detail we can see, which is why the nearby quasar 3C 273 is yet again in the news; it isn't that 3C 273 is unusual, just that it is relatively nearby and therefore easy to study.

When 3C 273 was mapped by these detailed radio techniques in 1977, the astronomers found a strong double radio source, with the two sources separated by about 62 light-years, assuming 3C 273 is at the distance of 3 billion light-years that its red shift implies. This was in 1977. By July of 1980, however, the same two radio sources within the quasar showed a separation of 87 light-years, apparently having moved apart by 25 light-years in the span of just three years, seeming to move at eight times the speed of light. The resolution of the puzzle depends on the alignment of the beam of particles being shot out from the quasar. These particles are chiefly electrons, negatively charged particles moving through magnetic fields and producing radio emission as a result; the moving radio source is a knot of electrons in the beam, a burst pushed out by some disturbance at the heart of the quasar and moving outward at a sizable fraction of the speed of light. The beam from 3C 273 happens to be pointing almost directly toward us, within 12 degrees of the line of sight, so that radio waves from the central source are racing along almost parallel to the beam, while the electrons which produce the secondary radio source are themselves racing in our direction at almost the same speed as the radio waves by which we detect their presence. The result is that the beam seems to be moving faster than it would if viewed at right angles—if it were moving directly across our line of sight. This is very different from how moving objects look in everyday life, when we are dealing with speeds much less than that of light, but it is purely a geometrical effect, which owes nothing to the bending of spacetime, or time dilation, or any of the other curious effects of relativity. The only strange thing about the whole business is that the nearest bright quasar should have a beam pointing in our direction, but after all the beam has to point somewhere, and it may well be that the brightness of 3C 273, which led to its early discovery, is a result of this alignment of the beam in our direction.*

But there may yet be more to the tale of quasar alignments and jets than can readily be explained by the standard theories. Some quasars do occur in groups that are genuine, not just a result of multiple imaging through a gravitational lens, and some of the jets from quasars and galaxies seem to be intimately connected with these groupings. Add in the evidence that some physically connected quasars, or members of quasar/galaxy pairs, have different red shifts from one another, and you are left with a puzzle that troubles some astronomers deeply, although the majority dismiss it lightly—too lightly, in my opinion.

It is only recently that the first definite identification of a cluster of quasars was made, in 1981, using a newly developed instrument which produces a miniature spectrum of each object in a telescope's field of view on one photographic plate. This makes it much easier to identify objects with similar spectra than the traditional technique of looking first at the photographic plates, then selecting objects of interest and taking a spectrum of each one in turn, each consuming hours of observing time on the largest telescopes in the world. The new technique showed that three quasars lying within a circle 1.8 minutes of arc across on the sky have very similar red

---

*For those interested in geometry, the relevant formula for the apparent speed of a beam moving toward us in this way is $v = v_0 \sin A \, / \, (1 - (v_0/c)\cos A)$, where c is the speed of light, v_0 the actual velocity of the beam, and A the angle of the beam to the line of sight. For a beam traveling at close to the speed of light, this becomes $v = c \sin A /(1 - \cos A)$, while at speeds much less than the speed of light it reduces to the formula applicable in everyday life, $v = v_0 \sin A$.

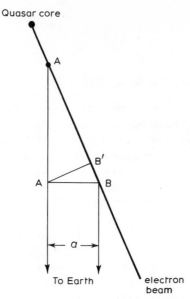

Figure 4.2 If a quasar jet is pointing toward us, simple geometry can make it seem that the jet expands faster than the speed of light. Light from blob A speeds toward us only slightly more quickly than a disturbance travels along the jet to blob B. Once blob B is disturbed the two beams of light race along parallel tracks to us, but information from the disturbance at A reaches A' and B' at the same time. It looks to us as if information travels from A' to B "faster than light" along a distance a; in fact the "extra" distance traveled by the information is from B' to B, a much smaller distance, which it covers, in the time available, at less than the speed of light.

shifts, with exact values 2.048, 2.054, and 2.040. These red shifts are different enough to establish that this is not a case of one quasar showing up as a multiple image through the gravitational lens effect, but close enough to establish that the three objects really are physically associated in space, and not at very different distances from us along the line of sight. Since galaxies have long been known to occur in clusters and clusters of clusters, and quasars are thought to be associated with galaxies, this is a very important discovery. It tells us that there is at least one quasar cluster, and that it is about 9 million light-years across, a size very much like the size of a typical cluster of galaxies, and the differences in the red shifts show that the quasars in the cluster move relative to one another at speeds of a few hundred kilometers per second, speeds which, once again, are typical of the relative motions of galaxies within clusters. There is very little room to doubt that these three quasars are the brightly shining active nuclei of three galaxies in a cluster so distant from us that neither these galaxies nor the other members of the cluster can be seen.

Are All Quasars the Same?

But there is much more room for doubt and speculation about other apparent associations of quasars. Although this cluster of three, lying in the direction of the galaxy M82 but far beyond it in space, is the first unambiguously identified as a physical association, some astronomers have been arguing for many years that other sets of quasars which seem to be aligned on the sky really are physically associated. The problem is that in these cases the various quasars in each set have different red shifts from one another, so that according to Hubble's law they must be at very different distances from us, and their apparent grouping on the sky ought to be just a chance pattern. In the same way, the Sun and Moon, although at very different distances from Earth, seem to be lined up together just before, during, and just after an eclipse of the Sun. It isn't only quasars that show this pattern of alignment of objects with discordant red shifts; there are chains of galaxies that seem to be physically connected to one another and which have different red shifts, and there are many known galaxy/quasar pairs in which the quasar sits alongside a galaxy but has a much bigger red shift. These may be chance alignments, but there are enough of them to make some astronomers, notably observer Halton Arp and theorist Geoffrey Burbidge, consider alternative explanations.

There is certainly something here that needs explaining. First, in many of these associations a quasar or compact galaxy seems to be not just alongside a larger galaxy but lying at the end of a trail of material apparently ejected from the galaxy; jets like the one seen in 3C 273 often point in the direction of companion quasars; and the compact companion objects always have bigger red shifts than the larger "parent," never smaller. It is at least arguable that some violent process in the heart of a galaxy or quasar can emit a fragment of material (where a "fragment" in this case may still have the mass of millions, or billions, of Suns), and that the emitted fragment gains some extra red shift above and beyond the red shift due to its recession from us in the expanding Universe. Hold on to that idea while we look at some of the evidence.

Most of it has been gathered by Arp, and virtually all of it is dismissed as coincidence by all but a handful of astronomers. But it is unwise to be complacent about our understanding of the Universe, and alternatives to the established view ought to be looked at. As such alternatives go, this is the major contender.

Historically, Arp's interest in these peculiar phenomena has developed from whatever observations come to hand. Like the discovery of quasars itself, the observations don't occur neatly at the right time to fit in with developing theories, but as much through luck as judgment. In telling the tale, however, it makes sense to put things in some order by looking first at galaxies and working our way outward to quasar alignments. A key step in the chain, but one only discovered in the mid-1970s, is a galaxy which can be seen in the act of emitting three narrow jets of material. The galaxy is called NGC 1097, and the jets all point directly away from the nucleus of the galaxy, its central region. Many other galaxies are seen to possess jetlike trails of material stretching away from their hearts, but in most cases these can be explained as the products of tidal interactions, trials pulled out of the galaxy by the gravitational attraction of a passing neighbor.* The NGC 1097 jets are clearly not a result of such a close encounter, and they each lie in the plane of this spiral galaxy, squirting out through the stars which make up the spiral arms. This is at least intriguing, and pushed to extremes—which may not be justified—provides evidence in support of an extreme maverick view of the way galaxies work, a theory which holds that all of the material of the spiral arms of a galaxy like our own has been shot out from the nucleus in a series of such eruptions, with the jet material subsequently being wrapped around the galaxy by rotation.

By the end of the 1970s, the weight of evidence accumulated by Arp over a period of fifteen years began to raise doubts even in the minds of some of the strongest opponents of the idea that not all quasar red shifts are produced solely by the expansion of the Universe. In one study eight quasars were identified in the region of the sky around a triple galaxy system, NGC 3379, 3384, and 3389. Six of the quasars have similar red shifts to one another, and all eight are aligned with the axis of the galaxy NGC 3384, in pairs on either side of it. The two quasars closest to the central galaxy are aligned precisely through the nucleus, which happens to be violently active, and have identical red shifts to one another; the next pair outward are similarly aligned, and also have identical red shifts to one another, although slightly greater than the red shifts of the inner pair. This is exactly the pattern that would be produced if the quasars are being shot out on opposite sides of the galaxy in a sequence of violent events. In another study, like the previous one reported in 1979, Arp and his colleagues drew atten-

---

*In the case of pairs of objects with different red shifts, of course, it makes no difference whether the jet has been ejected from one galaxy or whether it has been pulled out by the tidal influence of its neighbor. Either way, if the trail of matter links the two objects it is evidence that they are physically associated in space, evidence which all too often runs counter to the red shift evidence.

tion to a galaxy, NGC 1073, which seems to have quasars embedded in its spiral arms, suggesting a more gentle expulsion from the central regions of the galaxy. By 1980, Arp had found four examples of galaxy pairs in which a large, lower red shift "parent" is physically connected to a smaller, higher red shift companion. In terms of the indicated Doppler recession velocities, the parents are moving away from us at speeds in the range 4,600 to 10,400 km per second; the companions' indicated Doppler velocities range from 16,400 km per second up to 46,900 km per second. Yet in every case filaments of material are seen physically connecting the pair together. Some of the greatest excitement in this continuing search of the heavens came, however, later in 1980 when Arp joined forces with Cyril Hazard, of the Institute of Astronomy in Cambridge, to describe an incredibly precise triplet alignment of quasars—not one triplet, but two, in the same part of the sky.

Too Much of a Good Thing

Apart from the unusual nature of the alignment itself, this discovery was significant in terms of the acceptance of Arp's ideas by the astronomical community. By the 1980s, Arp had a reputation as a maverick, and it was scarcely news that he had found another alignment of objects with different red shifts. But it was another matter to see Hazard's name on the same scientific paper. Hazard was responsible for the accurate radio measurements which led to the identification of the first known quasar, 3C 273. He has an impeccable astronomical pedigree, and had previously gone on record as favoring the view that quasar red shifts can be explained by the cosmological effect of the expanding Universe alone. But his appearance alongside Arp in this case didn't mean that the bastions of the establishment had fallen to the "maverick." When I spoke to Hazard shortly after the discovery was announced, he said that he was still far from convinced that all of Arp's ideas were correct, but neither was he convinced that they were entirely wrong. It is quite possible that there is some component of red shift in any cosmological object that is produced by its own local, random velocity or by the gravitational red shift, and in each case this must be added to the cosmological red shift. The question, said Hazard, was how big the intrinsic red shift might be. Objects moving at speeds close to that of light can produce a red shift even if they are not moving directly away from us, because of the way time is stretched by relativistic effects, and if objects are being shot out of the nuclei of galaxies then this effect must come into play somewhere along the line.

So what is the evidence that raised at least some doubts in Hazard's mind? In their joint paper in the *Astrophysical Journal* (vol. 240, p. 726) Arp and Hazard described two groups of quasars found close together in the sky. One contains nine quasars, five of which form a close group clustered at a density thirty times greater than the average density of quasars in that part of the sky. Two of the five have identical red shifts but are too far apart (2.6 minutes of arc) to be explained as a gravitational lens double image. The others have different red shifts. But it is the second grouping of quasars that provided a big talking point in the trade late in 1980 and on through the next couple of years. Just a few degrees of arc away from the cluster of nine quasars there is a small area of sky which contains two separate triplets of quasars. Each triplet has a bright quasar in the middle, with two fainter quasars precisely aligned on either side. The red shifts of the two central objects are 0.54 and 0.51, while the flanking quasars have red shifts of 1.61 and 2.12 in the first case and 1.72 and 2.15 in the second.

Figure 4.3 a) When we see two quasars close to one another on the sky, are they really near neighbors in space or is their apparent proximity simply the result of a chance projection? b) Two triplets of quasars discovered by Halton Arp and Cyril Hazard are very precisely aligned. If the red shifts (marked) are solely due to the expansion of the Universe, this must be a chance projection. But the precision of the alignments, and the repeated pattern of high and low red shifts of similar value suggests that there may be some other explanation.

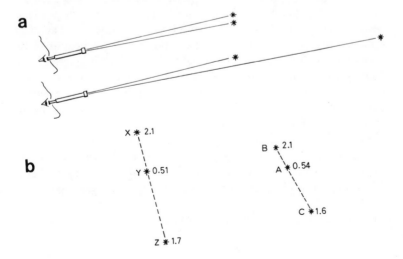

The likelihood of even one such precise alignment occurring by chance is small; the occurrence of two in the same part of the sky, coupled with the remarkable similarity between the red shifts and the pattern of red shifts (low for the central object, high for the flankers) is simply baffling in terms of any conventional explanation of quasars. The simple expanding Universe explanation says that the larger red shift objects are further away from us, yet the alignment suggests that the members of each triplet are physically associated with one another and therefore at the same distance. Of course, with hundreds of quasars now identified the patterns some of them make on the sky are bound to look a bit odd, and it could just be that this pattern is no more than a random juxtaposition on the sky of objects which really are at different distances from us. A study carried out by a team at University College, Cardiff, used a computer to produce random patterns of dots to mimic the distribution of quasars on the sky, and found that in an area equivalent to the size of the photographic survey plate on which Arp and Hazard found their patterns there were, on average, one or two such alignments. Arp and Hazard found four alignments, including those in the cluster of nine quasars. Whether this seems too great a deviation from the random pattern or not, seems to depend on whether you are prejudiced for or against the idea of intrinsic red shifts in the first place. In 1982, another calculation of the likelihood of such triplets appearing by chance out of the random quasar distribution was made by E. J. Zuiderwijk, at the Royal Greenwich Observatory. Zuiderwijk says that the chance of two such triplets lying together in the way they do on the sky is two in a thousand. Since the plates from which this pattern was picked out probably include 5,000 quasars, as long as no more are found the statistics seem to favor the established view of quasar red shifts. The argument is impeccable as far as it goes, but takes no account of the repetition of the pattern of a bright, low red shift quasar being flanked by a pair of faint, high red shift objects. So the evidence can still be interpreted whichever way you fancy. Like Geoffrey Burbidge, who has provided a great service to astronomy by reviewing all of the evidence of this kind at many astronomical gatherings and in several important review articles, I believe that the overall evidence is too strong to ignore.* Each case on its own might be dismissed as a statistical fluke; but the evidence keeps piling up, more of it, and more compelling, as the years go by.

* See, for example, his article in *Nature*, vol. 282 (1979), p. 451.

It is absolutely clear that many quasars are indeed the brightly shining nuclei of active galaxies, that their red shifts are the same as those of the galaxies in which they lie, and that these red shifts are produced by the expansion of the Universe. But it seems almost equally clear that some quasars have red shifts which are bigger than they should be on the simple cosmological explanation, and that these quasars are physically associated with other quasars, or galaxies, that themselves have "ordinary" red shifts. It is just possible that there are two different types of object which have both, mistakenly, been put in the same category by astronomers, and that this has caused the confusion. It may be that the "quasars" with discrepant red shifts have been shot out from the nuclei of active galaxies, and that the material surrounding them and carried along for the ride may settle down into a new galaxy of stars in its own right. The first question to be tackled, though, is where the extra red shift comes from.

5

Black Holes or White?

The most exotic objects, quasars, can be explained as black holes with masses of hundreds of millions of Suns lurking at the hearts of galaxies. Does our own Milky Way Galaxy harbor such a black hole?

The cosmological red shift associated with distant objects in the expanding Universe is not really a Doppler red shift. The distant galaxies are not moving away from us through empty space; empty space between ourselves and the distant galaxies is stretching, and stretching the light from distant sources in the process. So one possible explanation of the "extra" red shift which some quasars seem to possess is that this is indeed a genuine Doppler effect. These objects really might be moving away from us through space, although in that case it seems odd, at least at first sight, that there are no examples of quasars with smaller red shifts than their cosmological distances imply, which would be the result of motion toward us through space, partially canceling out the cosmological

94

red shift. Alternatively, thanks to the distortions of time produced by relativistic effects, it could be that the objects with excess red shifts are traveling across the line of sight, at speeds comparable to the speed of light. At such relativistic velocities, time is slowed down in the quasar's frame, as observed by us, and the result is that light emitted from the fast-moving object is seen as red-shifted in our frame of reference, even if the object is traveling almost directly toward us. And there is a second, completely different way to produce a large red shift, through the gravitational effect of a supermassive object.

All of these variations on the red shift theme have been invoked at one time or another to explain all or part of the observed red shift in the light from quasars. Two of Arp's general observations are crucial to this debate. First, he has pointed out that the colors of the quasars with discrepant red shifts differ systematically from the colors of most quasars, the ones which do seem to be unambiguously identified with active galactic nuclei. Secondly, the galaxies involved in the quasar/galaxy associations that he has described are loosely termed "peculiar" galaxies, and don't fit the standard image of galaxies. Both the quasars and the galaxies in the Arp associations are different from the majority of quasars and galaxies, and the kinds of differences they exhibit are consistent with Arp's suggestion that these quasars have been ejected at high velocity from the active centers of the peculiar galaxies.

According to Hoyle

Sir Fred Hoyle has taken up this theme recently, jumping off from the peculiar alignments found by Arp and Hazard. He estimates the chance of this pattern of objects in the sky occurring by accident as about 1 in 10,000, and he has provided one of the clearest accounts for a general reader of the way in which relativistic effects ensure that we see only red shifts from fast moving objects ejected from galaxies in the way required to explain these triplet alignments.*

Hoyle extends the Doppler red shift idea with a proposal that light is emitted only backward from the ejected quasars, like the exhaust emitted from the back of a fast moving rocket. That certainly ensures that we would see only red shifts, since we would only "see" quasars when we were looking up the tailpipe of the

*In *The Quasar Controversy Resolved;* see Bibliography.

rocket. The puzzle then is how we can see pairs of quasars on either side of a galaxy, when presumably if one is moving more or less away from us the other ought to be moving toward us, and so its "exhaust" should be invisible. But once again relativity comes to the rescue. The geometry of the situation is very similar to the geometry of the radio sources that seem to be expanding faster than light, but the effect now—called aberration—is that an observer can see "round the corner" of an object moving almost precisely toward him at close to the speed of light. The faster the object is moving, the more of the "back" becomes visible, and if the quasar "exhaust" is emitted backward over a fan 20 degrees of arc or so across it becomes very easy for an observer on Earth to see this red-shifted light even when the quasar is moving our way.* Again, the result is not common sense; but our idea of common sense is based on everyday life and experience with objects that move at speeds only a tiny fraction of the speed of light.

What happens if the jet is pointing precisely toward us? In such a very special case, the effect of the relativistic motion of the particles—assumed to be electrons—that are radiating the energy by which we see the jet is to produce a very bright, intense blue-white light. This bright light from the core of the quasar would completely swamp any radiation from surrounding stars or clouds of material, producing a source which looked like a bright quasar but with a featureless spectrum showing no lines, and so offering no means of measuring its red shift. It just so happens that a few years ago astronomers found just such an object, called BL Lac, and they have followed this find with the discovery of several similar "lineless quasars," dubbed "BL Lac objects." In the summer of 1982, radio astronomers working with an array of telescopes spaced across western England and east Wales (the MERLIN system, from "Multi-Element Radio-Linked Interferometer Network") found faint halos around seven BL Lac objects. These halos look just like the characteristic double-lobed structure seen in many radio galaxies and quasars, but viewed end on. BL Lac objects are, therefore, almost certainly quasars in which the jet is directed straight toward us, and we get a view down to the active power-house of the object, the black hole (if such it is) itself.

This identification of BL Lac objects holds whether or not you accept Hoyle's more general ideas of the role of relativistic aber-

* These ideas have since been refined and strengthened by J. V. Narlikar and K. Subramanian in *Astrophysical Journal*, vol. 260, p. 469.

ration in producing quasar red shifts, but it represents an extreme version of the effects he discusses. If you find the idea of relativistic aberration hard to swallow, I recommend a careful perusal of his monograph, which in any case is a highly entertaining read, being full of his anecdotal accounts of astronomical research in the 1960s, the decade of the discovery of quasars. He presents the most extreme view, that *all* quasar red shifts can be explained by the relativistic Doppler effect, and very few people—myself included—would swallow this whole. But it is only fair to discuss all the alternative theories, if only in order to show how good the better theories are in comparison with the worse.

At the end of his monograph, Hoyle says that "if the Doppler theory fails for some proper reason, the gravitational theory . . . must be reconsidered." Two astronomers who would agree with that are R. E. Wilson, of the Max-Planck Institute for Astrophysics, and S. T. Gottesman, of the University of Florida. They have turned Arp's argument on its head, arguing that the distortions we see in the peculiar galaxies which are the companions of the Arp quasars have been produced not by explosive outbursts, but by the gravitational tidal effects of close encounters with supermassive objects. The classic jet and counterjet structure seen in so many peculiar galaxies has now been shown by computer modelers to be an archetypal feature of such tidal encounters, while the characteristic blue color, very great brightness, and pointlike image of a quasar are all features that would naturally be associated with compact, very dense masses that are generating energy through accretion of material, swallowing up gas and dust from clouds in space. This is exactly the image of a massive black hole, and Wilson and Gottesman have argued* that the Arp associations may actually be ordinary galaxies that have been disrupted by the tidal influence of a massive black hole which has drifted into their vicinity. Such a black hole, perhaps long dormant as it has drifted through space, could have become activated as it moved into the region of the galaxy, and began to suck in gas. Unfortunately for this rather neat idea, it is very difficult to produce the amount of extra red shift needed to explain Arp's observations from the gravitational field of such a black hole, and there is nothing in this theory to explain why quasars with similar excess red shifts should occur in pairs on either side of a peculiar galaxy, as in the now famous triplet examples.

*Astrophysics and Space Science, vol. 70 (1980), p. 531.

If you rule out the transverse Doppler effect and the gravitational red shift, and if you accept Arp's increasing weight of evidence that some quasars do have extra red shift and are associated
with peculiar galaxies, the known laws of physics are no longer
adequate. Any other explanation of the excess red shifts would involve nonstandard physics. That hasn't stopped some people trying
to develop such explanations, as we shall see. But before moving
on to such exotica it is, perhaps, best to take stock of the status of
the vast majority of quasars, the ones which do seem to have no
more than their cosmological share of red shift, and which do lie
at the hearts of galaxies. I don't want to make the common mistake
of dismissing the Arp associations out of hand; I'm sure that these
observations are telling us something important about the Universe. But neither do I want to make the far greater mistake of
suggesting that conventional physics is inadequate to explain the
great majority of quasars and other phenomena in the Universe.
Indeed, these explanations of the most violent and energetic phenomena known in the Universe provide one of the great success
stories of scientific endeavor, and the fact that there remain a few
oddballs that we cannot yet explain is not, if you think it over,
very surprising at all.

The "Best Buy"

Martin Rees, probably the leading proponent of the idea that
quasars are powered by supermassive black holes, has described
such models as a "best buy," in the sense that they are the most
powerful and economical models that can explain these events
within the framework of conventional physics. Commenting on the
rather large number of theorists who seem eager to embrace revolutionary new ideas in a package to explain quasars and related
phenomena, he has also said that he is "a reluctant conservative. I
wish the radicals were right, but am sceptical about the arguments
they have advanced, and doubtful that the need for new physics
has yet been justified . . . progress has been slower than we hoped,
but by no means slower than could reasonably have been expected."* The point is that, as long as conventional physics can
explain these phenomena, the need for a revolution in astronomy—or in physics—is hard to see. Geoffrey Burbidge, the theorist who best expresses the opposed view, stresses that we have no

* Quote from *New Scientist* (19 October 1978), p. 191.

proof that black holes lie at the hearts of galaxies and quasars, that the evidence is at best circumstantial, and that we may be barking up the wrong tree altogether. Maybe, but using the best theory we have, general relativity, we can indeed explain all the observed properties of quasars.

Although some theorists dabbled with the idea of black hole quasars in the 1960s, the idea only really began to take off in the 1970s. The discovery of the X-ray source Cygnus X-1, whose properties can best be explained in terms of a black hole in orbit around an ordinary star in our own Galaxy, gave the whole of black hole theory a boost, and astronomers became more willing to entertain the possibility that the supermassive big brothers of Cygnus X-1 might power active galaxies, radio sources, and quasars. By 1976, Rees and his colleagues at the Institute of Astronomy in Cambridge were arguing the case for a black hole at the center of the galaxy Centaurus A, which is flanked by two lobes of powerful radio emission. In 1977, theorists Peter Young, Gregory Shields, and Craig Wheeley were reporting a detailed model of how black holes could disrupt stars at the center of a galaxy, producing energetic outbursts on the scale of Seyfert and similar galaxies. In 1978, it was the turn of the giant galaxy M87 to come in for close scrutiny. M87 has a bright jet stretching out from its central nucleus, a streamer of blue light reaching outward from a central pinpoint of intense brightness, estimated by Jerome Kristian and colleagues at the Mount Palomar Observatory as equivalent to a hundred million suns. M87 is a galaxy, but one which shares very many properties with quasars, and this discovery was seen as strong evidence in favor of the supermassive black hole idea. But how does the energy get out of the black hole and into the surrounding galaxy? Why does a quasar shine so brightly, and how does it influence vast stretches of space, millions of light-years across, to produce the characteristic double lobes of radio sources?

The extent of the influence of a quasar may reach over several million light-years, observed by its radio activity, whereas the central powerhouse, the energy machine that drives all this activity, is in a region less than one light-day across. If the central object is a black hole containing the mass of a million suns or more, it would have no difficulty converting the matter of the galaxy that surrounds it into energy. Remember Einstein's equation $E = mc^2$. Gas and dust from the surrounding galaxy, or whole stars ripped apart by tidal forces, would be sucked into the central black hole, and on the way they would form a spiraling whirlpool of material, a

3. The peculiar galaxy NGC 5128, also known as Centaurus A, is a strong source of radio "noise" and may harbor a massive black hole. (Photograph from the Hale Observatories)

disk in which atoms were colliding with one another and converting gravitational potential energy into heat. At a conversion efficiency of only 10 or 20 percent, in terms of $E = mc^2$, a supermassive black hole could produce enough energy to flare as brightly as a quasar if it swallowed a mere one or two solar masses of material per year, so that a couple of hundred million solar masses, still only a small percentage of the total amount of material in the surrounding galaxy, would keep it going for a hundred million years. All these figures fit in with the observations, including the likelihood that quasars are short-lived phenomena that die away into shadows of their former selves as time passes. On this now standard model, that happens when the central regions of the galaxy the black hole inhabits have been swept clean and there is little or no interstellar matter left to gobble up. Seyfert, N-galaxies, and the like are intermediate stages, and a relatively nearby, modestly active radio galaxy like Centaurus A, at a distance of 5 Megaparsecs, could be such a quasar on its last legs.

In the past couple of years, this vague but plausible model of quasar activity has been refined by improved calculations of the way matter falls into rotating black holes, and by the inclusion of calculations of magnetic effects. One of these recent insights is that if quasars and other active galactic nuclei really are powered by matter falling in from accretion disks then the disks must be very fat indeed. The picture painted by Marek Abramowicz and Tsvi Piran in a 1980 study is more like a tangerine with a knitting needle stuck through it than the LP record with a hole in the middle beloved of SF moviemakers. Abramowicz and Piran, working at the University of Texas, came up with this model after looking at the remarkable way the beams of material—jets and radio "trails"— ejected from such sources are "collimated," streaming into space in the same precise direction for millions of years from openings which can be measured to allow a spreading of no more than 20 degrees of arc, determined from radio observations.

The long time scale over which the collimation process operates is shown by the activity of quasars and other double-lobed sources, where regions of intense radio emission may lie many light-years outside the central active body. If the material that is producing the radio noise has come from the central regions, then even traveling at close to the speed of light it must have taken comparably many light-years to reach its presently observed position. Velocities of 70 percent of the speed of light and beams of particles millions of light-years long are invoked to explain the observations, but the beams have to be very narrow. Just as a long-barreled rifle is more accurate over a longer range than a snub-nosed revolver, such beams must emerge from deep, narrow "tunnels" reaching out from the "poles" of a rotating black hole through the cloud of surrounding material.

4. The radio source Cygnus A is one of the brightest in the sky, even though the radiation comes from a faint, distant galaxy. In this Hale Observatories photograph, the galaxy is near the center. The superimposed contour lines outline the very extended region from which the radio radiation comes. (Photograph from the Hale Observatories)

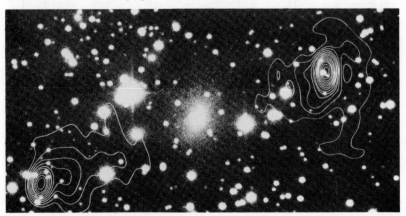

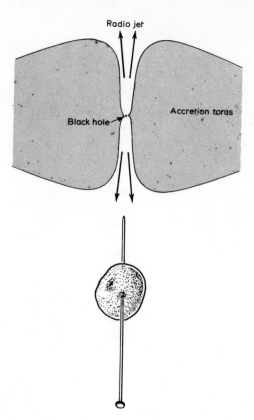

Figure 5.1 The accretion torus of matter around a massive black hole leaves only two long, narrow channels through which energy and matter can escape. Does this explain the jets in some galaxies and quasars and the characteristic double-lobed structure of radio sources? From farther away the production of two precisely collimated beams from such an object would give an appearance like a tangerine with a knitting needle stuck through it.

How, then, can a central black hole maintain its precisely aligned influence over distantly expanding radio lobes when it has eaten up most of the accretion disk—or accretion tangerine, as we should perhaps call it? This is where magnetic effects become important, as Rees and his colleagues from California pointed out late in 1981. In effect, the magnetic fields associated with a spinning quasar allow the radio source to tap the energy of the spinning black hole itself. The last dregs of the accretion tangerine are now seen as a torus of more tenuous material, surrounding the black hole like a doughnut wrapped around its center. Such a cloud of material would not be made of electrically neutral atoms, but atoms stripped of their electrons to leave positively charged nuclei behind, and electric currents flowing through this material and around the black hole itself make the black hole behave like an electrostatic generator—a Van de Graaff generator or Whimshurst machine on the cosmic scale—which accelerates charged particles to very high energies. The energy comes from the spin of the black hole; in principle, the hole spins a little more slowly as the particles are squirted out, but you don't slow down a hole with the mass of a hundred million suns very much by shooting a few electrons out of it! And the only gas you need is enough to anchor the magnetic fields in place, just a remnant of the original material that powered the source when it was a quasar.

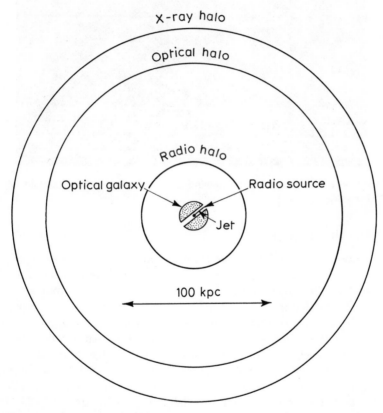

Figure 5.2 A schematic diagram of the source M87. At the heart of the source, probably a black hole, a jet of matter is being ejected from a galaxy. Both the jet and the region around the galaxy produce radio noise, and activity can be detected at optical and X-ray wavelengths over a vast region around the galaxy, an expanding halo of electromagnetic "noise." One kpc is about 3,262 light years. (After J. V. Narlikar, *Violent Phenomena in the Universe*)

5. The active galaxy M 87, showing jet. (Photograph from the Hale Observatories)

An Alternate View

The story certainly hangs together, but even within the framework of conventional physics there is an alternative to this standard model. Bill Saslaw, of Cambridge University, has championed the possibility that more than one black hole may be needed to explain each such source. Rather than one supermassive, spinning black hole at the heart of a quasar, Saslaw suggests that a collection of massive black holes might gather in such a location. Stars, after all, are born in clusters, not singly; why shouldn't black holes also be born in clusters? If they are, then the laws of orbital mechanics predict that, sooner rather than later, one or more of the objects will be ejected from the cluster of black holes, through a process called the "gravitational slingshot" (the same process, by the way, used by NASA to take advantage of Jupiter's gravity to speed a space probe on out to Saturn). Detailed calculations of the process for a system of three black holes show that one is ejected while the other two form a gravitationally bound system and recoil in the opposite direction. There is no problem here of explaining how a beam of particles is collimated, since a massive black hole plowing out from the center of a galaxy at a sizable fraction of the speed of light would take a lot of deflecting, let alone stopping. And radio galaxies like M87 are often found to produce a large amount of their radio emission from "knots," concentrations of energy, in their jets. Could such knots mark the sites of outward-moving black holes, the true powerhouses of the radio emission? One further calculation lends weight to the idea. The lifetime of an electron moving through intergalactic space and radiating energy is about twenty years, before it loses so much energy through radiation that it slows down and ceases to be detectable at a particular wavelength. In the case of M87, electrons traveling at close to the speed of light would take 5,000 years to travel from the central nucleus to the bright outer knots of the jet, and this time scale is typical. The radio emission from the knots must surely be produced locally, some theorists argue, and the knots in radio sources may be the best place to look for supermassive black holes.

Such ejected black holes might escape from their parent galaxy altogether, explaining some or all of the Arp associations, or they might move outward at less than escape velocity before falling back in. The slingshot effect provides an interesting meeting ground for conventional and unconventional ideas about quasars, and perhaps offers the best hope of linking Arp's discoveries to the mainstream. Perhaps for that reason, though, it doesn't seem to have had a very good press or to have aroused much interest in the trade. The mainstream theorists seem happy with their image of a single, central black hole, consigning Arp and Burbidge to the regions beyond the pale; and some of the nonmainstream theorists, far from being eager to bridge the gap with conventional theory, are seemingly eager to burn all their bridges behind them.

Are We Barking Up the Wrong Tree?

One totally different way of looking at cosmological red shifts has been developed by Fred Hoyle and Jayant Narlikar. The nub of their argument is that all our observations which seem to show that the Universe is expanding can be equally well understood if there is no expansion, spacetime is flat, but the masses of all particles in the Universe increase as the Universe ages. The point is that something has to vary in Einstein's equations, or their equivalent,

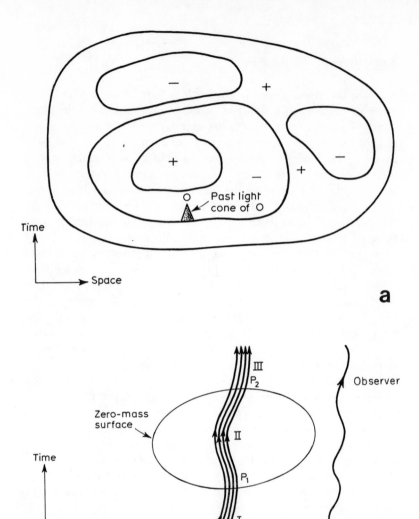

Figure 5.3 a) Perhaps all of the region of spacetime we can observe is simply a local region of something much bigger and more complex. The beautiful simplicity of the Big Bang theory may apply only to our own past light cone, and the Big Bang may in fact be the boundary between a region of positive mass and a region of negative mass in a complex steady state universe. b) In such a universe an observer whose own world line stays in one mass region may observe the effects of other particles' world lines passing through a region of opposite mass. As the bunch of world lines crosses a zero mass surface, the observed effeft may be either that a black hole forms (region I), or that a white hole becomes a black hole (region II), or that a white hole forms (region III). (After J. V. Narlikar, op. cit.)

but that the "something" can just as well be mass as distance, or what is sometimes termed the "scale factor." This is an unusual approach, and one which runs counter to common sense, although in the world of relativity theory and its derivations that in itself doesn't mean much. In this cosmology, the spacetime singularity of the Big Bang is replaced by a time—a universal epoch—when everything has zero mass, which in some ways seems closer to everyday physics, since we know particles with zero mass (light particles, photons) but nobody has ever seen a singularity. The Hoyle-Narlikar cosmology is not taken very seriously today, chiefly because mainstream cosmologists don't see any need to step outside general relativity until forced to do so. But it is at least of passing interest in the context of the anomalous red shifts shown by some quasars, because on this model the "cosmological" red shifts of galaxies are a result of the smaller mass of the particles in their atoms when the light by which we see them was being emitted. Narlikar and his colleague P. K. Das have elaborated this into a model where local irregularities cause distortions in the "zero mass hypersurface" so that in local regions of high density there are aggregates of particles with even less mass than the figure appropriate for their surrounding region of spacetime. These would show up as objects with unusually high red shifts.*

This has a counterpart in more conventional cosmology, where some theorists have suggested that local regions of spacetime may be delayed in their expansion from the Big Bang singularity, forming retarded, or lagging, cores of expansion. They would be seen bursting forth into the Universe as fountains of exploding matter, cosmic gushers which are best described as the opposite of black holes and are therefore dubbed white holes. Many of the observations of active galaxies and quasars can be explained in terms of white holes, and I championed this theory (perhaps, with hindsight, a little too enthusiastically) in an earlier book. The idea is still viable, although it has never been fashionable. Narlikar and Das have produced a more exotic variation in which quasars are concentrations of matter, initially with zero mass, fired out from the hearts of galaxies and gaining mass as they travel, so that their initially highly anomalous red shifts eventually settle down to the value appropriate for their cosmological distances. The calculations hang together, and although opponents argue that the model is somewhat contrived they cannot say that it is wrong in any absolute sense.

Astrophysical Journal, vol. 240 (1980), p. 401.

Fred Hoyle has recently developed another old idea produced originally in collaboration with Narlikar, that when enough matter is packed together in a small region of spacetime, gravity alone is no longer sufficient to explain its behavior, and we have to invoke another negative energy force called the C-field. The C-field acts like a gravitational repulsion, causing expansion or explosion out and away from what would otherwise be a singularity, and if you don't like the idea of singularities then such a cosmic repulsion has its attractions, so to speak. There are many exploding objects in the Universe, from stars up to galaxies and quasars, not to mention the Universe itself, and it is surprising, perhaps, to find most astronomers and physicists unwilling to look at such theories at all. It has to be said that this may be in no small measure because Sir Fred is the chief supporter of the idea; his Yorkshire bluntness and inability to suffer fools at all, let alone gladly, has not endeared him to all of his colleagues, and even today there is a feeling among some researchers that anything Fred proposes is worth opposing, a knee-jerk reaction that doesn't conform with the myth of the objective scientific method, but certainly shows that scientists are more human than they are sometimes given credit for.

The key feature of the C-field, in the present context, is that if the C-field is real then there are no black holes. Compact objects may indeed lie at the nuclei of galaxies, says Hoyle, but so far from collapsing into a black hole singularity such an object squirts matter explosively outward. Some of this outward bound material might show up as a quasar like those seen in the Arp associations; some might settle down as stars to make up the halo of bright stars that surrounds the spiral disk of a galaxy like our own; many more blobs of dark matter might form the superhalo which is now known to be a feature of most galaxies; and only the disk material of the spiral arms itself has formed, on this picture, by the conventional "outside in" collapse of gas down toward the center of gravitational attraction.*

Once you start tinkering with the laws of physics you can invent a theory to explain anything, and that is why most theorists prefer to stick with one well-established set of rules, general relativity, as long as this can explain our observations of the real Universe. The difference of opinion is between the bulk of astronomers, who be-

*What is a Spiral Galaxy? by Fred Hoyle, Preprint Series No. 76, Department of Applied Mathematics and Astronomy, University College, Cardiff, 1982.

lieve that although stretched to the limit general relativity can do the job, and the mavericks who believe that some observations cannot be explained by Einstein's theory, while the fact that Einstein's theory predicts the existence of singularities is seen in those quarters as hinting at some fundamental flaw in its makeup. It's worth mentioning, perhaps, that the C-field was originally invented to do away with another singularity, the Big Bang of creation. Hoyle has never been happy with the idea of a unique origin for the Universe, and has tried for decades to establish the alternative steady state theory, which in its original form acknowledged that the Universe is expanding, but proposed that new matter is eternally being created to fill the gaps as old galaxies recede from one another. In such an infinite universe (infinite in both space and time), the view would always be much as we see it now, and there need never have been a singular origin. The C-field provides one mechanism for making the necessary new matter. Slight but increasing evidence that our Universe is indeed aging—including the evidence that there were more quasars active shortly after the Big Bang—makes it harder to cling to the steady state idea, and evidence that there has been at least one singularity in spacetime, at the Big Bang itself, can be viewed as evidence both that Einstein's theory really is an accurate portrayal of reality and that singularities, whether we like it or not, are features of the real Universe.

The balance of evidence favors the Big Bang, black holes, and singularities. But let's not pretend everything is clear-cut. Doubts are still expressed from time to time about the basic techniques used to measure distances to nearby galaxies, the first stepping stone to the red shift/distance relation, and nobody can be absolutely confident that we have got the universal scale of distances and times down accurately yet; the blobs in the jet of M87, whatever they are, seem to be shot out from the center in the same direction at regular intervals of between 500 and 1,000 years; even in the classic quasar, our near companion 3C 273, welcome evidence that the fuzz surrounding it is actually a galaxy has to be weighed against measurements showing that the center of quasar activity is displaced by about 10 kiloparsecs (33,000 light-years) from the center of the galaxy. In spite of Rees's reluctant conservatism, it is hard to believe that the glib standard model of a central black hole, a funnel of distorted spacetime into which matter falls, radiating energy the while, is actually the last word on the subject.

All of our cherished laws of physics, even general relativity, have been developed on the basis of studies within our small Solar System, and most of them on the surface of one small planet. In 1982, astronomers using the European Southern Observatory's 3.6 meter telescope in Chile reported measurements of a huge cloud of gas around a quasar, MR 2251-178, measurements which enabled them to give, for the first time, a direct estimate of a quasar's mass. It checks in at around 1.3 million million times the mass of our Sun. In the enormous range from studies in our local region of space-time to such incomprehensible concentrations of matter—let alone back to the Big Bang itself—there must, surely, still be room for a few more surprises. The mainstream view of quasars as black holes at the hearts of galaxies is certainly the best buy for now, but it should never be regarded as the last word, doctrine handed down from above. And in particular I wouldn't be at all surprised to learn one day that new observations establish beyond a reasonable doubt that the quasars in the Arp associations really are massive, compact objects shot out, in some way, from the hearts of their companion galaxies—although I don't believe that any of the maverick theories proposed to explain just how they are ejected have yet got close to the truth.

At the Heart of the Milky Way

Closer to home, and perhaps closer to the truth about one galaxy at least, the growing awareness of the importance of violent events in galactic nuclei has naturally led to increased interest in the heart of our own Milky Way. Do all galaxies harbor black holes at their centers? One astronomer who thinks so is Michael Ryan, of the University of Texas at Austin, whose calculations suggest that the existence of a galaxy in the expanding Universe is evidence for a black hole at its center, since without the gravity of the black hole to hold things together the galactic material would have been dissipated by the universal expansion. It would be natural to follow up such a suggestion by looking for a black hole at the center of our Galaxy, which could be the nearest large mass black hole, and would provide a testing ground for theories about black holes at the hearts of active Seyfert galaxies, N-galaxies, and quasars. Unfortunately, because our Sun lies in the disk of our spiral Galaxy, it is hard to see the center, since we are looking through the thickest concentration of stars, dust, and other material. But radio waves, and infrared radiation, can penetrate this obscuring material, and throughout the late 1970s as more observations were made there was increasing evidence that there is a compact, powerful source of energy just where we would expect there to be a black hole if our Galaxy does harbor one. There is clearly a special object—a source less than 0.02 seconds of arc across, emitting strong radio noise—at this special place, and some studies have shown that 25 percent of the energy from the galactic center source is coming from a region no more than one-thousandth of a second of arc across, which translates into a linear measurement of less than 1 billion miles, smaller than our Solar System. The size would be appropriate for a black hole of up to 100 million solar masses, and the kind of energy emitted by the central object is the kind of radiation theorists expect to be produced by matter falling into such a black hole. By late 1981, the first high-resolution infrared survey of the galactic center region had been carried out, by a team from the Anglo-Australian Observatory in New South Wales, Australia, and the Royal Greenwich Observatory. Visible light is dimmed a million million times on its way across the 10 kiloparsecs from the galactic center to us, but a camera using near infrared light shows a tiny double "star" at the heart of the Milky Way, just at the site of the previously detected radio emission. The current conjecture among the experts is that this double system is actually a superheavy "star" of about 10 million solar masses, in orbit around a black hole rather less than a hundred times more massive still, which maintains its activity by sucking in a streamer of matter from its companion. One intriguing feature of such a system is that the disk of matter which forms around such a rotating black hole can produce outbursts in double jets, similar to those seen in some quasars and active galaxies; evidence of just such jets, bent by rotation into an elongated "S" shape, shows up in radio surveys of the galactic center made with the Very Large Array (VLA), a linked series of twenty-seven radio telescopes in New Mexico. High-energy electromagnetic radiation (X and gamma rays), energetic particles (positrons), and other pieces of evidence add weight to the growing suspicion that there really is a black hole at the center of our Galaxy, and astronomers hope that with the next generation of spaceborne instruments, including the Space Telescope planned for use with the Shuttle, they will be able to find out enough about this unique source to confirm their suspicions and test out their theories of black holes and quasars.

Studies of other galaxies are beginning to point the same way—the Seyfert NGC 1068, for example, has now been shown to have a bright center (equivalent to 5 billion Suns) less than 6 light-years across, with another bright group of objects 20 to 40 light-years away. Once again, the obvious explanation is that the galaxy harbors a black hole. So Ryan's theoretical prediction looks to be sound, and it is natural to ask whether our own Galaxy ever was, or ever could be, a quasar, and what the implications might be for life on Earth.

The first part of the question is easily answered. If there is a black hole at the center of the Milky Way, all the evidence agrees that its mass is too modest for it ever to have distorted spacetime sufficiently to provide the powerhouse of a quasar. If quasars really were uniquely features of the early Universe, that would be the end of the story. But the slightly puzzling presence of 3C 273 in our neck of the cosmological woods hints that our own Galaxy could have an active future ahead of it. Maybe the initial burst of quasar activity, long ago and far away across spacetime near the Big Bang, was indeed associated with black holes that started out big and went with a bang until they used up all the matter nearby. But Robert Brown, of the U.S. National Radio Observatory, has pointed out that the black hole at the heart of the Milky Way could yet grow quietly, absorbing matter and increasing in mass, until its gravitational reach extended out into the starfields of our galaxy—or at least, of the central regions of our Galaxy—to a size where quasar activity switched on.

Even though such an occurrence lies hundreds of millions of years—at the very least—in the future, it might seem an alarming prospect, especially to anyone who has read the science fiction novel *The Inferno*, by Fred and Geoffrey Hoyle.* In that book, the Hoyles draw on Fred's experience as an astronomer to describe the destruction of civilization on Earth when the heat and cosmic radiation from an explosion at the center of our Galaxy pulses out past the Solar System. The idea got into the respectable scientific literature by this back door, and some astronomers, not realizing the dramatic license taken by the Hoyles in developing their story, began to produce serious works commenting on the fact that the existence of life on Earth could be attributed to the relative weakness of the source at the heart of the Milky Way, compared with the powerhouse of a Seyfert or quasar. This in turn produced a response from astronomers who took the trouble to do the calcu-

*New York: Harper & Row, 1973.

lations properly, with conclusions disappointing for readers of SF but reassuring for the prospects of life in a galaxy like our own, or even in a galaxy surrounding a quasar.

A. P. Fairall, of the University of Cape Town, South Africa, was first off the mark, pointing out that at our comfortable distance of 10 kiloparsecs from the galactic center a quasar at the heart of the Milky Way would be no brighter than "a romantic full Moon"; Robert Smith, of the University of Sussex, then had the last word (so far) by pointing out that because of the obscuring effects of the dust and gas in the plane of the Galaxy, if the object at the nucleus became a quasar it wouldn't even be visible to the naked eye in daylight, and would only be noticed by regular observers. Apart from the evidence that the mass of the central black hole is too small, our own Galaxy could have been a quasar in its past, with no harmful effects on the dinosaurs or whatever creatures inhabited the Earth at the time.*

If this comes as a disappointment after the catalog of superlatives generally associated with quasars, there are still some impressive statistics left to consider. The largest radio sources known in the Universe are radio galaxies in which the central object is spanned by lobes of radio emission covering 18 million light-years (in the case of 3C 236), 16 million and 10 million light-years, respectively, for the sources 3C 380 and 3C 293, and an astonishing 78 million light-years for the radio noise around the quasar 3C 345. This last dimension is so huge that it is thirty-five times the distance from our Galaxy to its neighbor, the Andromeda galaxy, and although 3C 345 is 5 billion light-years away (according to the cosmological interpretation of its red shift) the radio source is twice as large on the night sky as the Moon.

Even our old friend 3C 273 is now known to have radio lobes extending across 13 million light-years, and in all of these objects the faint outer lobes are thought to be remnants of great bursts of activity from the central compact object, outbursts that happened about 100 million years ago. We see the central objects as bright and unusual today because they are undergoing new outbursts; this might give a clue to why 3C 273 is active now when most quasar activity occurred when the Universe was young. Recurrent activity in the hearts of galaxies and quasars is clearly of crucial importance, although very poorly understood today. Another source, 3C 111, shows two lobes extending over a more modest 800,000 light-

*A. P. Fairall, *The Observatory*, vol. 100 (1980), p. 7; Robert Smith, *The Observatory*, vol. 100 (1980), p. 123.

years, with the central, active galaxy itself a tiny double radio source with two lobes separated by a mere 3 light-years, but aligned precisely along the same axis as the outer lobes.

It's hard to know what all this means, although it does clearly show that there are many more mysteries in the Universe still to be explained. As far as the Universe at large is concerned, however, the confirmation that many, if not all, quasars are at the cosmological distances implied by their red shifts, and do lie at the centers of galaxies, makes it possible to take at face value the many studies which attempt to interpret the overall properties of the Universe from the statistics of the distribution of quasars in time and space. As long as quasar red shifts are cosmological, the bigger the red shift the further back in time we are looking when we look at the quasars, and so, by comparison with objects that are closer in both time and space, quasar statistics give us a hint of how the Universe is evolving. In particular, they tell us how the outward expansion of our local region of spacetime compares with the rate of expansion when the Universe was young, and how quickly the expansion is slowing down. This deceleration parameter is a key indicator of whether the Universe will expand forever, or whether it is destined first to halt its expansion and then collapse back into a singularity like the one in which it was born. On the basis of estimates of the amount of visible matter in the galaxies of the Universe, the expansion "ought" to continue forever. The discovery of evidence of superhalos suggests that there might be nearly enough matter to cause the Universe to recollapse—to "close" it— but most cosmologists today favor the open models. The parameter used as a guide, Ω, the deceleration parameter, has a value less than one for an open universe, and one or more if the Universe is closed; and the quasar studies are consistent with a deceleration parameter in the range from 1 to 3.5.* This is a surprising result to many cosmologists, and I should stress that it is not accepted by all of them. But it is another pointer to the existence of more mass in the Universe than we can see. What is it, and where might it be? The latest proposed answers to these questions take us far away from the study of quasars, black holes, white holes, and the like. From the largest known objects in the Universe, we have to turn our attention to the smallest; from the depths of space we have to return home to the depths of a gold mine in South Dakota. It may seem a curious detour, but it leads us to a story well worth hearing.

*Cheng Fu-hua, T. Kiang, and Fang Li-zhi, *Chinese Astronomy and Astrophysics*, vol. 6 (1982), p. 48.

6

The Mystery of Neutrino Mass

Studies of our own star, the Sun, have surprisingly turned out to provide new insights into the fate of the Universe. Exotic particles called neutrinos flood through the Universe, and are also produced inside the Sun. It may be that most of the mass of the Universe is locked up in these invisible, almost undetectable, ghostlike particles.

"Is there any other point to which you would wish to draw my attention?"
   "To the curious incident of the dog in the night-time."
    "The dog did nothing in the night-time."
"That was the curious incident," remarked Sherlock Holmes.

     "Some Snarks are Boojums."

It takes a mixture of Conan Doyle and Lewis Carroll to convey the flavor of the recent debate about the puzzle of the "missing" solar neutrinos, and the implications of a possible resolution of the puzzle for the Universe at large. The neutrino saga is at first sight

115

reminiscent of the curious incident of the dog in the night described by Conan Doyle in his tale "Silver Blaze," for the curious thing is that although nuclear physics theory predicts that copious floods of these particles should be pouring from the Sun every second, solar neutrinos, like the dog who failed to bark in the night, have yet to make the expected impression on the observer, which in this case consists of a detector the size of a swimming pool, buried in a gold mine in South Dakota.

The analogy has been only slightly marred by the fact that the detector does find a few solar neutrinos—about one-third of the expected number. The dog has failed to bark, but may just have managed a whimper. But the Carrollian aspects of the story are absolutely clear-cut. Not just the hunting of the Snark, but the absurdity of Alice in Wonderland seems to apply to the curious idea of burrowing into the ground to build a detector designed to study the interior of the Sun; even curiouser is the recent revelation that the underground detector may be telling us as much about the origin and fate of the whole Universe as it does about the Sun. And then again, it takes a mind like that of the mythical Sherlock Holmes to unravel all the twists of logical argument in the tale.

Inside the Sun

All good stories have a beginning, a middle, and an end. Here and now, writing in the summer of 1982, the story of neutrino mass has only a beginning and a middle. The end is yet to be written, and is still the subject of debate among the experts. But the story so far is intriguing enough to merit reporting.

The beginning came with the prediction by nuclear physicists that the fusion reactions which keep the Sun hot ought to be producing floods of the subatomic particles called neutrinos. To most people, even the idea of the neutrino itself seems a little crazy. These singularly elusive particles have zero mass (according to the original theories) and no electric charge, travel through space or "solid" matter at the speed of light, and are identifiable only through a property the particle physicists dub "spin," which enables them, occasionally and reluctantly, to interact with ordinary matter. They are produced in nuclear reactions, but once produced have little to do with the material world, being unaffected by any conditions much less extreme than those at the heart of a star.

Without going into details* it is worth noting that those condi-

*They can be found in my book *The Death of the Sun.*

tions are extreme indeed. Stars shine because of the nuclear reactions going on inside them, and in a star like the Sun the main process is the fusion of nuclei of hydrogen (protons) into nuclei of helium. In this way the Sun, basically a ball of hydrogen 1,392,000 km in diameter, has stayed hot for the 4.5 billion years that the Earth, judging by the geological evidence, has been basking in the sunlight. Astrophysical calculations tell us that the nuclear reactions take place in the heart of the Sun in a region where the density is 160,000 kg per cubic meter (twelve times the density of lead) and the temperature is 15 million degrees.

Trying to catch a neutrino using ordinary matter seems even crazier than the idea that neutrinos exist—far worse than the problem of locating a black cat in a coal cellar at midnight. But one man had the chutzpah to tackle the task, and set about building a neutrino detector two decades ago. The saga of Professor Ray Davis and his tank of cleaning fluid has to be skimmed over here, but it is easy to understand the motivation behind Davis's work. Just because neutrinos are so elusive, detecting them is likely to be highly rewarding. If the theories are correct, any solar neutrinos detected here on Earth have been unaffected by anything since they were born in the heart of the Sun. Measuring the flow of neutrinos would be like opening a window to the center of the Sun itself. All our knowledge of stars to date has been gained by studying the light from their surfaces, and all our theories about how stars work are based on deductions about their interiors derived from studies of their surfaces. Astrophysicists think their theories are good—but a direct view of the heart of a star would be an almost unimaginable new insight for them.

Davis's now famous detector was built, in effect, to take the temperature of the heart of the Sun. The detector had to be large by human standards, since the more atoms it contained the more chance there was that a passing neutrino would interact with one of them. And it had to be buried deep belowground so that the layers of rock above would shield it from other stray particles, the cosmic rays, and avoid recording any spurious interaction "events." The theories predict that no less than 4 billion detectable solar neutrinos should be flooding through every square centimeter of the Earth every second; even with a tank containing 100,000 gallons of fluid, however, the forecast was that Davis should detect no more than twenty-five neutrinos each month. In fact, over a run of more than ten years, the tank has found no more than eight solar neutrinos each month. The dog has failed to bark, and that is the end of the beginning of the story. A variety of more or less wild ideas have been offered up to explain why the dog has failed to bark, and these form the middle of the story. But with no one of those seemingly wild ideas yet proved correct, we have a choice of possible endings to our tale.

Solving the Puzzle

In simple terms, the puzzle is that the Davis tank detects only one-third of the expected number of solar neutrinos. Many careful tests show that the detector system works, and that this result can indeed be taken as meaning that only one-third of the expected number of detectable neutrinos is arriving from the Sun. Explanations of the puzzle come in two kinds. Most of the "answers" proposed during the 1970s were astrophysical in nature—they started out from the assumption that only one-third of the expected number of these neutrinos is being produced inside the Sun, and that they all then travel across space to the Earth, and beyond, unchanged. In everyday terms, this approach seems to look promising. Whereas standard astrophysical theory says that the temperature at the heart of the Sun is 15 million degrees, the neutrino observations could be explained if the temperature were just 10 percent less than the theorists predict. That doesn't sound like much of a difference, and if the theorists have predicted the temperature at the heart of the Sun with only a 10 percent error you might think they've done a good job.

But there are problems. Glossing over the details once again, the theorists are pretty sure they know how stars tick, and they are convinced that the Sun's temperature must be 15 million degrees, at least on average. The catch is that "on average" refers to a lifetime lasting billions of years. Maybe something could happen to make the Sun go "off the boil" temporarily—where "temporarily" could easily mean anything up to a million years.

So the astrophysical "solutions" to the solar neutrino puzzle revolve around the possibility that, for whatever reason, the Sun is at present in an unusual state, a little cooler than usual in its heart. Whatever the reasons for it being off color, there are interesting implications for life on Earth, not least the possibility of a link between the Sun's present allegedly unusual state and the recent occurrence of a wave of Ice Ages, producing stress conditions for life which led, ultimately, to the emergence of intelligent human beings on our planet. But here I want to take up the other thread of the story, the possibility that the Sun's interior really is at a temperature of 15 million degrees, that it is producing all the neutrinos predicted by theory, but that somehow only one-third of them are getting through to Ray Davis's detector.

This alternative approach to the problem implies that it is the particle physics, not the astrophysics, that needs revision. And the whole saga is reminiscent of one of the greatest debates in the history of science, when nuclear physics and astrophysics came into head-on collision half a century ago.

It was as recently as 1926 that the pioneering astrophysicist Arthur Eddington wrote that "it is reasonable to hope that in a not too distant future we shall be competent to understand so simple a thing as a star." Over the next few years, he and his colleagues made calculations similar to those astrophysicists make today, feeding into their equations the known mass and size of the Sun, and its measured surface temperature, to predict what conditions must be like in its interior. They came up with the same answers as today, including a central temperature of 15 million degrees. Just as today, theorists knew half a century ago that the only process which could keep the Sun hot over its long lifetime is nuclear fusion. But the nuclear physicists of the day said that, according to their best theories, the hydrogen fusion reaction couldn't work at a temperature of "only" 15 million degrees.

Something had to give—the astrophysicists and nuclear physicists couldn't both be right. And the story is that Eddington told his overconfident nuclear physics colleagues to "go and find a hotter place"—a polite way of telling them to go to hell. In due course, he was proved right. A better understanding of nuclear physics explained how the fusion process can occur at a temperature of 15 million degrees, and incidentally helped pave the way for the development of the hydrogen bomb. What would be the comparable implications today, if once again the astrophysical theories stand up to the test, and it is the particle theorists who have to change their ideas to resolve the solar neutrino puzzle?

But one of the ironies of the present rematch between particle theory and astrophysics is that this time around both parties seem less sure of their ground. Rather than some present-day Eddington telling the particle theorists to "go and find a hotter place," the astrophysicists were almost indecently eager, throughout the 1970s, to produce ever more exotic "nonstandard" theoretical models of the Sun to explain the absence of neutrinos. Meanwhile, the few particle physicists who bothered themselves with the problem were no more sanguine about their own theories, and happily offered an explanation of where they might be wrong and the standard astrophysical models right. As a former astrophysicist myself, I fell into this pattern of inverse chauvinism when I reported the debate in 1980, so much so that in my book *The Death of the Sun* I neglected to mention the particle theorists' resolution of the puzzle, even though I had been one of the first reporters to be given the story, by Professor Willie Fowler, of Cal Tech.

Fowler, a nuclear physicist with a strong interest in astrophysics, visited England in the fall of 1978, and on October 9 gave a talk on the solar neutrino puzzle at the University of Sussex. Outlining the observations I have described above, and noting the fact that just one-third of the expected number of neutrinos was being detected, he discussed the possible astrophysical resolutions of the puzzle, and then went on to break new ground. My own scepticism at the time can be seen clearly in the way I reported what ensued for the magazine *New Scientist* on October 19, 1978:

> With his tongue, perhaps, in his cheek, Fowler drew the attention of his audience to the growing belief in elementary particle circles that a "new" lepton, the tauon, has been discovered to rank alongside the electron and the muon in the same family. Electrons and muons each have their own associated neutrinos, and it makes sense to guess that there must also be a tauon neutrino, bringing the size of the lepton family up to six.
>
> Is it possible that, on their way to us from the Sun, electron neutrinos produced in reactions in the solar interior are involved in resonances—oscillations between the members of the family—which distribute their numbers evenly among the three kinds of neutrino now thought to exist? Since Davis's detectors can detect only electron neutrinos, this would solve the problem nicely. Too nicely, perhaps—Fowler himself says it is "too good to be true" and points out that the discovery of another lepton and its neutrino would cut the rug from under the hypothesis by providing four states for the resonance. Meanwhile, the desperation of such a proposal, even suggested only half-seriously, indicates the extent to which the solar neutrino problem is still puzzling the theorists.

As *The Death of the Sun* went to press, a year after those words were written, Fowler's half-serious proposal seemed too desperate to mention; when the book appeared in 1980, the papers were full of stories about neutrino oscillations and the implications for our understanding of the Universe, and I was the one with egg on my face. What happened in the interim was that several different groups of experimenters claimed they had found evidence for just the kind of neutrino resonance needed to explain the solar neutrino puzzle. More recent experiments have cast some doubt on the validity of those particular claims, but leave the issue still open. I'm certainly not going to ignore the idea twice, however, especially since it turns out that if neutrinos do change their coats in this way, then they must have at least some mass. The mass of each neutrino may be very small, but the Universe is full of neutrinos. It now seems possible that there is more mass in all the neutrinos put together than in all the visible matter—stars and galaxies—put together. So far from being insignificant, those crazy, almost undetectable particles may actually be, in gravitational terms, the most important feature of our expanding Universe, and their mass may be the factor which decides whether the Universe expands forever or collapses back into a cosmic fireball. And that is the possible ending to the solar neutrino story which is relevant to my present discussion of the nature of the Universe in which we live.

The Neutrino Saga

The neutrino story goes back more than fifty years. It was in 1931 that Wolfgang Pauli suggested that a new particle, previously unknown to physics, must exist in order to account for the behavior of atomic nuclei when they eject an electron—beta decay, as it is known. Observations showed that in this decay process, the energy of the emitted electron did not always match the recoil of the atom it was ejected from, apparently contradicting the law of conservation of momentum. The truth, suggested Pauli, was that an additional, invisible particle carried some of the momentum away with it, restoring balance to the equations. Soon after Pauli aired his proposal, Enrico Fermi gave the name "neutrino" to this hypothetical particle. Physicists took the idea of the neutrino seriously—they had to, if they weren't to abandon the concepts of conservation of energy and momentum—but Pauli never expected that these elusive particles would be detected, and wagered a case of champagne that they would remain elusive. In 1956, when Frederick Reines and Clyde Cowan found direct evidence of the existence of neutrinos, a delighted Pauli paid up with good grace.

Cowan and Reines found their neutrinos by looking at the particles produced in the Savannah River nuclear reactor in South Carolina. Such a nuclear reactor produces many neutrinos as a result of beta decays, so many that some of them are bound to interact with a large tank of suitable material placed nearby. The form of this reaction is the opposite of beta decay. Instead of an electrically neutral neutron emitting a negative electron and a neutrino while changing into a positively charged proton, a proton absorbs a neutrino and emits a positively charged positron, itself becoming a neutron. The detector used by Cowan and Reines actually recorded flashes of light produced by the passage of the positrons (the positively charged "antiparticle" counterparts to electrons) produced by the neutrino reaction.

This proof that Pauli's idea was right came twenty-five years after he suggested the existence of neutrinos; and it was all but twenty-five years after the first direct observations of neutrinos that Reines was involved in one of the dramatic new experiments that suggested neutrinos had mass. Working once again with the Savannah River nuclear reactor, but now with colleagues Elaine Pasierb and Henry Sobel, Reines found that only half of the number of neutrinos that theory predicted were being produced in the beta decay reaction were reaching the detector, just 11.2 meters away.

By 1980, this did not come as a complete surprise, although it was certainly an exciting result. In the intervening years since 1956, several studies had shown that neutrinos come in more than one variety. For example, the neutrino produced in the beta decay reaction is, strictly speaking, an "electron antineutrino," while there is also a mirror image particle, the electron neutrino, and neutrino/antineutrino pairs associated with each of the particles called muons and tauons; together with the electrons and the corresponding three antiparticles, these make up a family of particles called the leptons. Back in 1963, a Japanese team suggested that free neutrinos might "oscillate" between these different states, changing from electron neutrino to muon neutrino, and so on. A Russian team reached the same conclusion independently, and on purely theoretical grounds the idea that neutrinos might change their spots had become current in the world of particle physics by the 1970s, long before anyone became very concerned about the shortage of detectable solar neutrinos.

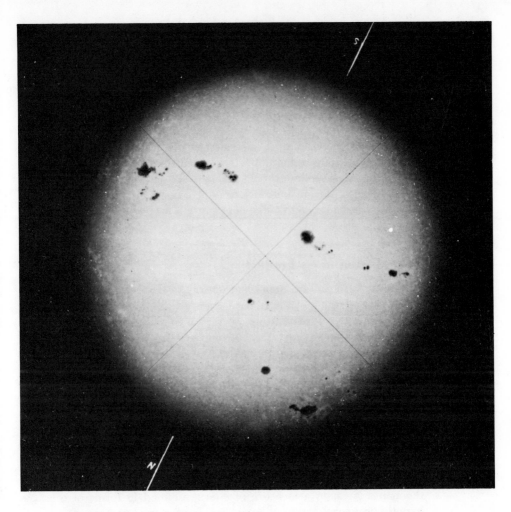

6. The Sun, photographed near the maximum of its activity cycle, on April 1, 1958. The north and south solar poles have been marked on the photograph. (Royal Greenwich Observatory, Herstmonceux)

Such spot-changing seems very odd to all of us used to the everyday world, where a table is a table and doesn't suddenly decide it is going to become a chair. But it is a familiar pattern of behavior in the world of the particle physicists, where such oscillations are allowed by the laws of physics, provided certain quantities like energy and spin are conserved, and the oscillations only involve members of the same family of particles, such as the leptons. The best way to think of it is that neutrinos may be composed of particles which are even more basic, and which Reines dubs "neutrettos"; on this picture the face a neutrino shows to the world depends on the changing pattern of the neutrettos of which it is composed, like the changing pattern in a kaleidoscope. What matters for my present discussion, however, is that the spot-changing can only occur if at least some of the neutrinos have mass. The oscillations are related to slight differences in the speeds with which the particles move, and all massless particles always travel precisely at the speed of light. It doesn't matter, yet, what the mass may be. It can be infinitesimally small, as long as it is not precisely zero. But in order for neutrinos to oscillate—to change their spots from electron to muon to tauon neutrino and back again—they must have some mass.

The Missing Mass Found?

Reines, Pasierb, and Sobel had no way of determining the possible mass of the neutrinos from their experiment at Savannah River. But they suggested that the reason they found only half the expected number of electron neutrinos was that the other half had changed into muon neutrinos in the time it took to travel the 11.2 meters from the reactor to the detector. With a detector impervious to muon neutrinos, that could certainly explain the observations. And about the same time V. Lyubimov and colleagues at the Institute of Theoretical and Experimental Physics in Moscow were reporting experiments in which they claimed to have measured the mass of the electron neutrino.

To measure such small masses, physicists use units which are convenient for them but unfamiliar to us. The electron volt, eV, is the name given to a measure of energy defined in terms of the hypothetical acceleration of an electron across an electric potential difference. The mass energy of an electron (mass and energy are interchangeable) in these units is 500,000 eV, and although the comparison is hardly meaningful we can get something of a feel for the size of electron volt units by noting that in grams the mass of an electron is denoted by a decimal point followed by 27 zeros and a number 9 (9×10^{-28} gm). The Russian experiments suggested that the mass of the electron neutrino could be anything from 14 to 46 eV, but was most probably about 34 eV, less than one ten-thousandth of the mass of the electron.

Actually measuring the mass of such a light particle, whatever the units you use, is no easy task. The Russian team used a technique which depends on measuring the energy carried away by an electron during beta decay, and comparing this with the recoil of the parent atom. The energy available is divided between the electron and neutrino (strictly, antineutrino), which is why Pauli first realized the neutrino must exist, and the exact amount of energy carried by different electrons depends in a subtle way on the mass of the neutrinos involved in the reaction. By measuring electron energies in many beta decay reactions the Russians believed that they had clear statistical evidence that the neutrinos had mass, and they were able to use those experimental statistics to make an estimate of that mass.

The interest these claims roused among the specialists related to the way the possibility of neutrino mass fitted neatly into their "Grand Unified Theories," which we met in Chapter Three. Although by the middle of 1980 experts were expressing caution about the interpretation of both the Savannah River and the Russian results, casting doubt on the statistics used by the experimenters to back up their claims, theorists were quick to point out that the results would certainly fit nicely into the currently favored theories. Writing in *Nature* (vol. 286, 21 August 1980, p. 755), A. De Rújula, of CERN in Geneva, and Sheldon Glashow, of Harvard University, pointed out that "many [of the Grand Unified Theories] demand that neutrinos have mass, but say nothing of what these masses are." And just at the time excitement was being stirred by the experimental claims for neutrino mass, a flurry of scientific papers on the implications of such mass for the Universe at large was also appearing—a flurry based not upon the experimental results, which had not been reported when the papers were being written, but on the sound theoretical reasons for suspecting neutrinos had mass.

Very simple Grand Unified Theories require that the three types of neutrino known today, all "left-handed" in terms of their spin, should form a family with at least one much more massive right-handed neutrino. The mass of such a hypothetical particle is so large—at least 10 million times the mass of the proton (which is itself a billion eV)—that it cannot be made or detected in particle machines today, but would have played a part in the interactions that took place in the early, energy-rich phase of the Big Bang. The presence of the massive right-handed neutrino at that time does not affect the standard picture of baryon production outlined in Chapter Three, but it does "explain" the presence of three almost massless, left-handed neutrinos in the Universe today.

Now, this starts to be very interesting on a far greater scale than that of the Sun and Solar System. Of course, a resonance, or oscillation, which "shares" the original solar electron neutrinos equally among three separate states, only one of which triggers Ray Davis's detector, could exactly explain the observations of just one-third of the expected number of solar neutrinos. But the implications extend far beyond, across the Universe. Each neutrino must be light, but there must be a very great number of neutrinos in the Universe, since they are produced in profusion by nuclear reactions, including those of the Big Bang itself, and are very reluctant to interact with anything after they are produced. In round terms, there ought to be as many neutrinos in the Universe as there are photons of light, about a billion times as many neutrinos as there are protons and neutrons together (remember the baryon/photon ratio?). Most of the mass of stars and planets, most of the mass of the visible galaxies and clusters of galaxies, is in the form of baryons bound together as atomic nuclei. But if the mass of each neutrino is as great as 10 eV, then most of the mass of the Universe is in the form of these invisible, almost undetectable particles. On this evidence, every astronomical observation ever made, except for Davis's solar neutrino study, and every theory constructed from those observations, has been dealing with only a minority of the material in the Universe, the small fraction which makes up the visible stars and galaxies. If the mass of the electron neutrino is as great as the Russian experimenters claim, then there is enough to curve spacetime so much that the Universe is closed, and its present expansion phase will inevitably be halted and followed by collapse back into the cosmic fireball. Even with a smaller mass than the Russian studies indicate, the neutrinos could still dominate the Universe. Equality between the total mass of neutrinos and baryons in the Universe only occurs if the neutrino mass is a mere 1.4 eV, and the baryons dominate only if the neutrino mass is even less than that.

These are startling possibilities, which many astronomers find abhorrent. One cosmologist I spoke to while researching this book said that he was sure these conclusions must be wrong, and that if he found that most of the mass of the Universe really was in the form of neutrinos then he would feel that his entire career, based upon studies of the Universe derived from observations of the bright, visible matter, had been a futile waste of time. So science faces a dilemma—the experimental evidence for neutrino mass is far from clear-cut, but the particle theorists now expect neutrinos to have mass, and will be disappointed if it turns out they don't.

Many cosmologists, on the other hand, firmly believe that the Universe is open, and would be unhappy to find neutrinos with masses of tens of electron volts. Somewhere in the middle of the debate, but of less cosmic importance, is the prospect that the presence of any neutrino mass, no matter how small, could resolve the solar neutrino puzzle. And even those cosmologists reluctant to consider the possibility that neutrinos may actually dominate the curvature of spacetime on the grandest scale and the evolution of the whole Universe admit that a small neutrino mass could solve one of their other outstanding problems.

Cosmological Implications

This problem is the so-called "missing mass" of clusters of galaxies. By measuring the Doppler red shifts of galaxies in clusters, astronomers are able to estimate the velocities of the galaxies relative to one another. Like a rocket launched from the ground, a galaxy will "escape" from the cluster if its speed exceeds a certain value, the escape velocity. Estimating the mass of a typical galaxy from its brightness, which presumably is related to the number of stars it contains, and counting the number of galaxies in a cluster, astronomers can calculate the speed a galaxy would need to escape. All too often, calculations based on these estimates of the mass of galaxies imply that clusters are not stable—the overall gravitational pull of the cluster members is insufficient to stop them flying apart from one another, dispersing the cluster into the depths of space. "Extra" mass is required in order to explain why clusters exist at all—and a sea of trillions of neutrinos, each contributing 10 eV or so of mass energy to the cluster, could do the job very well.

What the observations really tell us, assuming that clusters are stable, is that there must be dark, unseen matter present. For this reason, some astronomers prefer to talk about the "missing light" problem—why don't we see this material?—rather than the "missing mass" problem. With yet another twist to the saga of neutrino mass, however, it now seems that some of the "missing light" may have been seen.

In 1980, A. De Rújula, of CERN in Geneva, and Nobel prizewinner Sheldon Glashow, whom we have already met, proposed on theoretical grounds that massive neutrinos ("massive" simply meaning "having mass," however small) left over from the Big Bang ought to "decay" into lighter neutrinos, and that when they did so

they should emit photons. Every known massive particle except
the electron and proton decays in this way, and theorists believe
that protons would decay if they had time, but that the Universe
is far too young for this incipient instability to have shown up yet.
The massive neutrinos would be concentrated around galaxies and
clusters of galaxies—indeed, on this picture it is the concentration
of neutrinos that really matters, with galaxies embedded in the
neutrino sea like raisins in a cake. And the photons emitted during
the decay, said De Rújula and Glashow, ought to be in the energy
range equivalent to ultraviolet light. Scarcely was the ink dry on
the paper making this prediction (in *Physical Review Letters*, vol.
45, 1980, p. 942) when Floyd Stecker, of the Goddard Space Flight
Center in Greenbelt, Maryland, published a claim that the ultraviolet light produced by the decay of massive neutrinos had already been found.

Stecker based his claim, also published in *Physical Review Letters*
(vol. 45, 1980, p. 1460), on a reanalysis of existing studies of the
sky at ultraviolet frequencies, which had been made years before
with instruments carried above the atmosphere on rockets. He
found a blip in the spectrum which could be interpreted as the
ultraviolet radiation produced by decaying neutrinos in a superhalo
surrounding our Galaxy, and deduced that the observations were
consistent with the existence of neutrinos with a mass of about
14 eV, which decay so reluctantly that only one neutrino in 10
million has decayed since the Big Bang. The proposed mass would
certainly solve the puzzle of what holds clusters of galaxies together, just about "agrees" with the Russian estimate of neutrino
mass, and would imply that neutrinos do dominate the Universe,
making up about 90 percent of its total matter.

But these claims remain suggestive rather than authoritative.
University of Chicago astrophysicist David Schramm said that there
could be "half a dozen other explanations" for the ultraviolet observations, and Stecker himself described his interpretation as only
a "conjecture." "Conjecture," "half-truth," and "speculation" seem
to be the key words in any discussion of neutrino mass in the early
1980s. But this is the way science progresses, and amid all the
confusion there is a clear scent of something exciting in the air. It
now looks as if the original claims that the neutrino's mass had
been measured were premature, but if the unified theories of
physics are to work in their description of neutrinos in the simplest
way, then neutrino oscillations should happen, and the neutrino

should have some mass, however small. There is an obvious analogy with the way general relativity predicts that gravity waves must exist, and experimenters made premature claims that these waves had been discovered in the early 1970s. Those claims proved false, but most theorists still believe that gravity waves are real, just that they haven't been found yet. Few physicists now believe that the neutrino mass has yet been measured, but many believe that the neutrino must have mass.

Perhaps, after all, the best evidence we have for neutrino mass is that Davis's detector finds only one-third of the expected number of solar neutrinos. If the neutrino does have some mass, the cosmologists may yet have to change some of their cherished beliefs about how galaxies form and evolve, and about the ultimate fate of the Universe itself. Whatever the outcome, the debate is heating up as experimenters around the world set up tests to check the original claims made by Reines's team and the Russians. Reines himself is running a new detector at Savannah River, one which can be set at different distances from the reactor core to see how the decay effect, if real, varies over different path lengths. We can be sure of only one thing at present—over the next year or two the neutrino puzzle will continue to make headlines, and one way or the other some cherished ideas are going to go out of the window. It is a long way from a detector buried in a gold mine in South Dakota to the heart of the Sun, and even farther to the outer limits of the visible Universe. Yet it looks at least possible that Ray Davis's tank of fluid may answer one of the deepest and most puzzling questions of science, that of the ultimate fate of the Universe and the overall curvature of spacetime. The incident of the dog in the night may have been curious, but to describe the ins and outs of this particular astronomical saga once again only the world of Lewis Carroll seems really appropriate—"Curiouser and curiouser!" as Alice cried, early on in her adventure down that other, even more famous, hole in the ground. And Carroll even had a turn of phrase to describe, more neatly than any particle physicist, the way some solar neutrinos may change into a different flavor of neutrino on the way to Earth. It's simple, of course—some Snarks are Boojums!

7

The Shrinking Sun

Whatever the truth about solar neutrinos, the Sun itself no longer looks so steady and reliable as we used to think. It shakes and shrinks, on a time scale of decades and centuries, and these changes could explain climatic cycles on Earth.

While the saga of neutrino mass was unfolding in the late 1970s and early 1980s, new insights into the nature of our Sun were being obtained by observers and theorists using a totally different approach. It is one of the frustrations of science that people working even in closely related fields of study seem, all too often, to be working in isolation, unaware of all the ramifications of the work going on next door in a related discipline. Of course, it is impossible to keep up to date with everything that is happening in astronomy, and the problem gets worse when astronomy turns out to overlap with particle physics and the study of climatic change. Everything is connected to everything else, and you have to draw the line somewhere. With hindsight—and having just run through the story of the solar neutrino puzzle—it does seem odd, however,

130

that most astronomers were startled in 1979 when Jack Eddy, of the High Altitude Observatory in Boulder, Colorado, claimed that the Sun was shrinking, at such a rate that, if the decline did not reverse, our local star would disappear within a hundred thousand years. The story of Eddy's claims, and subsequent developments in the study of the Sun and of climatic changes here on Earth, really has nothing directly to do with the story of spacewarps. But it is a fascinating story in its own right, and closely related to the story of solar neutrinos. So let's make a little detour to take in some of the most intriguing current work in astronomy, with profound implications for all of mankind.

Working with mathematician Aram Boornazian on a study of measurements of the Sun's diameter made at England's Royal Greenwich Observatory between 1836 and 1953, Eddy found evidence of a decline in solar angular diameter of 2 seconds of arc—equivalent to 0.1 percent—per century. Since we have very good evidence indeed that the Earth and the Sun have existed with essentially the same relationship to each other as at present for at least 4 billion years, such a discovery could only imply that the Sun is at present in a temporary phase of contraction, which must soon be halted and reversed.

Startling though these claims seemed to many people, to others they were almost welcome. A shrinking Sun could resolve the solar neutrino puzzle, because a shrinking Sun generates some of its heat by the release of gravitational potential energy, reducing the amount of energy generation required from nuclear reactions in its heart to explain the observed surface luminosity. With a reduced output from the central powerhouse, fewer neutrinos would be produced, perhaps in line with the numbers actually detected by Ray Davis. But alas for such hopes, Eddy's initial claims quickly turned out to be too much of a good thing. The observations at Greenwich on which the claims were based had been made by different observers at different times, using techniques which depended, to some degree, on the observer's skill and expertise in his chosen technique. And they proved to have been subject to persistent human errors which accounted for at least part of the apparent change in the size of the Sun.

How Big Is the Sun?

It is surprisingly difficult to measure the size of the Sun with the precision needed for this kind of study. To put the numbers in perspective, the angle subtended by the Sun on the sky—its angular diameter—is, in round terms, 32 minutes of arc, just over half a degree; its linear diameter, just over 108 times that of the Earth, is 1,392,000 km, and it looks so small only because it is at a distance of just under 150 million km from us. What astronomers actually measure is the angular diameter, which can be converted to a linear diameter, or radius, since the distance to the Sun is known; when they talk about the "angular radius" what they mean is half of the measured angular diameter. And, of course, changes measured as percentages are the same whether we are talking about angular measurements or linear ones, radii or diameters. One way to measure the angular diameter of the Sun is to time the passage of the Sun, from limb to limb, across a fixed suspended wire, called a meridian wire. Because we know how fast the Earth rotates, we know the angle covered by the movement of the meridian wire in that time and this tells us the angular diameter of the Sun. Another technique depends on measurements of the image of the solar disk using a micrometer screw at the eyepiece of a telescope. Both techniques were used by the nineteenth-century astronomers at the Royal Greenwich Observatory, whose records Eddy used in his first attempt to determine how the Sun's radius had changed during historic times. Although his first estimates of such solar variations proved wrong, they provided a debating point for astronomers, and triggered a flurry of new work.

Theorists were quick to point out that any such change in the size of the Sun ought to produce a detectable change in the measured energy output of the Sun—the solar constant, as it is usually called. Measurements of the solar constant over the period since 1850 show, however, that unless our understanding of how stars work is seriously at fault, the solar radius must have been constant to within 0.3 seconds of arc per century—less than half the variation in the Greenwich records. In mid-1980, the case against Eddy's interpretation of the old records seemed to be settled when Irwin Shapiro, of the Massachusetts Institute of Technology, published a study of solar diameter measurements based on yet another technique, the transits of the planet Mercury across the face of the Sun. This technique is rather like the meridian wire technique, except that a whole planet—Mercury—is used instead of a fixed wire. It depends on knowing the distances to Mercury and the Sun, the speed with which Mercury moves in its orbit, and the rate at which the Earth turns on its axis, but these are all now well established. In addition, the technique works only when the Earth, Mercury, and Sun are suitably aligned, so that transits of Mercury have been observed just twenty-three times since 1736. On the other hand, the very rarity of such an event has ensured that on every possible occasion for the past 250 years the transits of Mercury have been very carefully monitored by astronomers.

Taking all of the available measurements of the past twenty-three transits of Mercury (the most recent was in 1973), Shapiro concluded that any decrease in the angular diameter of the Sun, as viewed from the Earth, must be less than 0.3 seconds of arc per century, a result, as he put it, "incompatible" with the size of the decrease reported by Eddy on the basis of the observations made at the Greenwich Observatory. To most astronomers, "less than 0.3 seconds of arc per century" seemed close enough to zero to mean that the Sun is not shrinking and that its diameter has been constant over historic time. By late 1980, the issue seemed clear-cut. The old Royal Greenwich Observatory records contained errors, and Eddy had been wrong to take them at face value. But then the plot began to thicken, and now the story of the shrinking Sun really begins.

Conflicting Claims

In mid-December 1980, both of the two leading weekly science journals, *Nature* and *Science,* carried scientific papers reporting work stimulated by the claims of Eddy and Boornazian. As far as the numbers that came out of their calculations were concerned, the two papers reached exactly the same conclusions. Yet the interpretation of those numbers by the two teams involved led to diametrically opposed conclusions, as typified by the titles of the two papers. In *Science* (vol. 210, 12 December 1980, p. 1243), David Dunham, Sabatino Sofia, Alan Fiala, David Herald, and Paul Muller presented their analysis under the heading "Observation of a Probable Change in the Solar Radius Between 1715 and 1979," while at the same time in *Nature* (vol. 288, 11 December 1980, p. 548), John Parkinson, Leslie Morrison, and Richard Stephenson were proclaiming to the scientific world "The constancy of the solar diameter over the past 250 years." A close look at those two intriguing papers shows how even the most objective scientist can unwittingly color his conclusions to suit his expectations, but leaves the question of solar size variations still very much open.

The solar constancy argument is essentially the one I have already outlined. Parkinson and his colleagues pointed out that out of seven regular observers using the Royal Greenwich Observatory's meridian circle since 1851, five produced self-consistent observations of the Sun's diameter over each of their periods as observer, and the other two were full of "strong, erratic personal biases." In other words, five of the observers always made the same "mistakes," though not the same as each other, and the other two couldn't be trusted at all. Together with the Mercury transit data, this reinterpretation of the old records led to the conclusion that the maximum extent of any change in the Sun's radius since 1850 was no more than a decline of 0.08 seconds of arc per century, with a possible error range of plus or minus 0.07. Within the range of possible error, the Sun's diameter might be constant—the conclusion proclaimed in the *Nature* headline—or it might be shrinking, although at only one-tenth of the rate claimed by Eddy. It might not seem obvious which of the two conclusions to take on board, if it were not for the happy coincidence of the simultaneously published *Science* paper. For the conclusion reached by Dunham's team was that the Sun has indeed been shrinking, and that its radius— or, strictly speaking, half the measured angular diameter—has contracted by 0.34 seconds of arc over 264 years—in round terms, almost exactly in line with the decline of some 0.1 seconds of arc per century suggested by the reexamination of the Greenwich records!

The technique used by Dunham's team is disarmingly simple in concept, but it does depend upon the precise accuracy of some observations made in 1715 under the direction of Sir Edmund Halley, later Astronomer Royal and known to this day for the comet which bears his name. In that year, there was a total eclipse of the Sun visible from Britain on May 3. Halley organized observations of the eclipse from different parts of the country, and the duration of totality at each observing site provides an important clue to the size of the Moon's shadow on the Earth, and thereby to the size of the Sun at the time of the eclipse. An observer just half a mile inside the edge of the path of totality, for example, would see a total eclipse lasting for just fifteen seconds, and thanks to Halley's efforts valuable observations of this kind were made at both the northern and southern edges of the eclipse path in 1815.

In the north of England, Theophilus Shelton, Esquire, made observations from Darrington (a small town located just north of 53 degrees 40 minutes latitude, near the city of Leeds) and recorded that the Sun "was reduced almost to a Point, which both in Colour and Size resembled the Planet Mars," concluding that the northern limit of totality was just south of his location. In the south of England, the edge of totality was bracketed by observations just on either side of the line, south of the village of Cranbrook (which lies in the heart of the county of Kent, just south of latitude 51 degrees 10 minutes), giving a precise guide to the extent of the Moon's shadow.

Now, the path of the edge of totality depends on the precise geometrical alignment of the Sun, Moon, and Earth at the time, and this can be calculated very accurately from the standard equations of celestial mechanics. It also depends on the size of the Moon, but no one suggests that this has changed since 1715, and on the size of the Sun. Comparing Halley's data for the 1715 eclipse with similar observations of eclipses in 1976 (visible from Australia) and 1979 (watched by hundreds of amateur astronomers across North America, as well as by the professionals), Dunham and his colleagues concluded that there was no measurable change in solar radius between 1976 and 1979, but that between 1715 and the 1970s the diameter of the Sun had shrunk by 0.34 seconds of arc, with an uncertainty of plus or minus 0.02 seconds of arc. This disagrees with the earlier claim by Eddy and Boornazian, but falls within the limits previously set by theorists on the basis of measurements of the solar constant. It is also consistent with the Mercury transit data, used by Parkinson's group as evidence for the constancy of the solar radius, but which actually say only that any change is smaller than 0.15 seconds of arc per century.

But It Does Shrink

If those two papers had appeared out of the blue, with no preparation of the scientific ground, they would surely have made an enormous impact both among astronomers and in the wider world. For, of course, a shrinking of the Sun at a rate of merely 0.01 percent per century still implies its total disappearance in a million years, or that it was twice its present size a million years ago (both ludicrous suggestions on the basis of everything that has been learned over the past half century about how stars work), or that the present contraction is simply one phase of a long, slow pulsation which might have a cycle time of hundreds or thousands of years.

The snag was, all the headlines had already been written when

Eddy and Boornazian came up with the suggestion that the Sun was shrinking at a rate of 0.1 percent per century. Contraction at just one-tenth of this rate seemed small beer by comparison, and was presented by the popular media (when they took any notice at all) as just another example of a way-out scientific idea that had had the rug pulled from under it by more careful studies. Metaphorically, we can imagine theoretical astronomers breathing a sigh of relief and saying, "Oh, so the Sun is only shrinking by a tenth of a second of arc per century, not a full arc second after all. Nothing to worry about." It seems to have taken several months for the message to sink in that here was plenty to worry about, with deep implications for the inhabitants of planet Earth.

The immediate cause for concern is that changes in the Sun's diameter are indeed linked with changes in its heat output, and changes in the solar constant by even a fraction of 1 percent can have a pronounced influence on the climate of the Earth. Eddy's own interest in the old records from the Royal Greenwich Observatory had developed from his study of the changing level of solar activity as indicated by the numbers of dark spots—sunspots—on its surface. Sunspots come and go with a cycle which lasts for roughly eleven years, but is much "stronger" (that is, produces more spots) in some cycles than in others. The spots only became of interest to astronomers when Galileo discovered them in the early 1600s, although they had been known to the ancients. And the sunspot cycle was identified only in the late nineteenth century. The reason it took so long to make the identification of the cycle's repeating rhythm was that there had been very few sunspots observed in the seventeenth century, so it was only the Victorian astronomers who had enough good data to identify a cycle eleven years long.

Now, it happens that the dearth of sunspots in the seventeenth century—a succession of very "weak" cycles indeed—exactly coincided with the coldest period of a climatic fluctuation that is known today as the Little Ice Age. Twentieth-century astronomy and space-borne instruments have shown that the sunspot cycle is just the most visible manifestation of a fundamental rhythm affecting the whole of the Sun's activity. Could it be that when the Sun was quiet, in the seventeenth century, it was actually giving out less heat, and that is why the Earth cooled? Before that question could be tackled, someone had to prove that the old records were reliable—that the absence of records of sunspots in seventeenth-century documents really does mean that there were fewer sunspots, not just that astronomers hadn't bothered to take note of them. Eddy proved during a thorough reanalysis of old observations that the records are indeed reliable; when spots did occur, their presence was recorded in tones of wonder which left no doubt that the astronomers of the time were actively studying the Sun, and—as we might expect—were thoroughly intrigued by Galileo's discovery of sunspots.

So the coldest decades in recent history really did coincide (if that is the right word) with an interval when the Sun was remarkably free from these dark spots, although they have come and gone with a period of roughly eleven years ever since. Eddy's original interest in the old records of solar diameter measurements stemmed from this discovery. Might changes in the size of the Sun be linked both to the surface activity manifested by sunspots and to small-scale climatic changes on Earth? Curiously, in their paper suggesting the constancy of the solar diameter, Parkinson and his colleagues did mention that the Mercury transit data, in addition to showing an overall decline in solar radius of less than 0.15 seconds of arc per century, shows hints of a periodic variation in the Sun's size with a cycle time of about eighty years. The special significance of this number is that a similar long-term cyclic pattern shows up in the record of the changing number of sunspots, modulating the stronger eleven-year rhythm, and in climatic patterns, revealed by historical records of temperature, the width of the annual growth rings in trees, and so on. Some powerful hints of what was to come were there to be seen by the knowledgeable in December 1980. But it was not until the fall of 1981 that the bombshell finally exploded.

The Shaking Sun and Climate Cycles

Hardly surprisingly, the breakthrough came from one of Eddy's colleagues, Ronald Gilliland, who also works at the High Altitude Observatory. Perhaps a little more surprisingly, it was published not in the pages of *Nature* or *Science*, where hot news is usually aired for rapid communication among scientists and where, it has to be said, some of the publications prove on sober reflection to have been a little overhasty, but between the sober covers of the *Astrophysical Journal*, a pillar of respectability among the astronomical establishment, and not a journal prone to giving space to half-baked ideas. Gilliland based his study on no less than five sets of data, including the old Royal Greenwich Observatory records with the correction for systematic observing errors, similar meridian circle measurements from the U.S. Naval Observatory in Washington, D.C., two sets of Mercury transit observations, and the solar eclipse data. His first conclusion, from a battery of statistical tests, was that the overall decline in solar diameter of about 0.1 seconds of arc per century since the early 1700s is real. And when standard statistical tests aimed at revealing small, regular changes in the pattern of variability were turned on the meridian circle data, they showed an unambiguously clear trace of a periodic variation with a repeating rhythm seventy-six years long—almost exactly matching up with the periodic variation present in the Mercury transit data (*Astrophysical Journal*, vol. 248, 1981, p. 1144).

This regular pulsation is much smaller than the longer term decline in the Sun's size. It covers a range of only 0.02 percent of the Sun's radius, but it has been stable over the full 250-year span covered by the various sets of observations, and it shows a clear relationship with sunspot activity, with by and large fewer sunspots being present when the Sun is bigger. If the same anticorrelation can be applied to the longer term decline in the Sun's diameter, it may provide a clue to the dearth of sunspots during the height of the Little Ice Age, 300 years ago, when the Sun's angular diameter was about two-thirds of a second of arc greater than it is today. And as the icing on the cake, Gilliland also reported a smaller, but clearly present, fluctuation in solar size tying in with the eleven-year sunspot cycle. The periodic variations are unambiguous. As for the longer term decline in solar diameter, the discovery which started the whole ball rolling, Gilliland was cautious in his claims. "Given the many problems with the data sets," he said, "one is not inexorably led to the conclusion that a negative secular solar radius trend has existed since A.D. 1700, but the preponderance of current evidence indicates that such is likely to be the case."

With rhythmic variations eleven and seventy-six years long now identified in the measurements of solar diameter, however, it seems straightforward to interpret the longer trend as part of a similar but longer cycle, posing no real problems for astrophysicists' and geologists' faith in the long-term stability of our nearest star. Gilliland, however, had a parting shot to fire in his *Astrophysical Journal* paper—at present, if his analysis is correct, the Sun is ap-

proaching a maximum of the seventy-six-year cycle, and will start
to decline in size once again at about the end of the present decade. But the accepted textbook value of the solar radius, 959.63
seconds of arc, is based on nineteenth-century observations, which
became enshrined in the textbooks at a time when the Sun was
close to a minimum of the seventy-six-year cycle. If Gilliland is
correct, the true value of the mean solar radius is more like 959.8
seconds of arc. Best of all, though, his claims are testable—existing
techniques are accurate enough to measure such changes in the
Sun's size directly, and monitoring programs set up in the wake of
these various claims and counterclaims will resolve the issue, one
way or another, before the decade is out.

But while astronomers were still digesting the import of Gilliland's study, and observers were metaphorically girding their loins
to meet the challenge of testing these claims, an unobtrusive paper
from another theorist added a new twist to the shrinking Sun saga.
Carl Rouse, of the General Atomic Company in San Diego, California, revived the idea that a decline in the size of the Sun might
account for the lack of detectable solar neutrinos in a paper published in the journal *Astronomy and Astrophysics* just a few weeks
after Gilliland's paper appeared in the *Astrophysical Journal*. Apparently ignorant of all the fuss about Eddy's claims and the activity they had sparked off—he made no reference to any of the work
I have discussed here—Rouse put forward his proposal purely on
theoretical grounds. The solar neutrino puzzle can be resolved if
the heart of the Sun is 10 percent cooler than standard astrophysical models imply, and Rouse showed how a slightly different form
of mixing of material in some regions of the Sun could produce a
cooler core and a contracting outer layer (*Astronomy and Astrophysics*, vol. 102, 1981, p. 8).

So where do we go from here? One path, clearly, leads back to
the puzzle of just how the Sun works, and why it is producing so
few neutrinos just now. If a contracting Sun explains the solar neutrino puzzle, then maybe neutrinos do not have mass after all. The
two conclusions don't necessarily go hand in hand; the Sun might
be contracting and producing fewer neutrinos, whether or not those
neutrinos have mass. As I have explained, many—perhaps a majority—particle theorists now expect the neutrino to have mass
in order to fit in with their simple Grand Unified Theories. The
situation is intriguing, but the scientific jury's verdict is not yet in,
and this would not be the place to delve deeper into that particular
can of worms. But another path leads inexorably in a different di-

rection, into the detailed study of the workings of the Earth's atmosphere and climatic systems. In his search to determine more
about solar variability, Gilliland has now been forced to unravel
the complexities of recent climatic changes on Earth. It is difficult
to see how these changes in solar diameter, both the seventy-six-
year cycle and the longer term decline, could fail to have affected
the temperature of the globe, but so many other factors also affect
the climate that the only hope of detecting the solar "signal"—and
thereby, ultimately, learning more about what makes the Sun tick—
is to subtract out the other main influences from the historical record of changes in temperature in the Northern Hemisphere.

It might seem a daunting task. But in recent years climatologists
have begun an intensive study of temperature changes on Earth,
driven in large measure by a concern that the buildup of carbon
dioxide in the atmosphere—a by-product of our dependence on
energy from fossil fuels—could trap infrared radiation near the surface of the Earth and warm the planet through the so-called
"greenhouse effect." By and large, climatologists agree that two
"perturbations" have been affecting temperature trends during the
present century: the warming influence of this buildup of carbon
dioxide, and the variable cooling influence produced when great
volcanic eruptions spread dust high into the stratosphere, blocking
some of the heat from the Sun. Most of the changes in temperature over the past hundred years can be broadly explained by these
two processes at work. But Gilliland found that the real temperature record could be matched much more closely by adding a third
factor to the calculations—varying solar heat output tied to the
seventy-six-year cycle of solar size variations.

Gilliland is at pains to point out that this does not prove anything about the way external influences affect the workings of the
weather machine. His study certainly provides food for thought,
though. He has taken the well-established record of annual changes
in the average temperature of the Northern Hemisphere since 1881,
and obtained the best possible fit to this pattern by combining the
three external influences, each modified by a scale factor to adjust
the agreement between the model and the real world, and with an
adjustable time lag in the volcanic and solar influences to allow for
the time it takes the temperature of the atmosphere and oceans to
respond to outside influences. With so many variable factors, it
ought to be possible to provide a "fit" to almost any pattern of
temperature fluctuations; the interesting point of the study is
whether or not the scale factors you have to put into the equations

seem to be telling you anything meaningful about the real world.

The main features that any such model has to explain are a slight warming of the world (at least, of the Northern Hemisphere, for which good records are available) from the late nineteenth century up to the 1940s, and a subsequent cooling into the 1970s. Gilliland gets a reasonable fit between actual temperature records and his model if he leaves solar variations out altogether and works only with the buildup of carbon dioxide and the influence of volcanic products on the atmosphere. The early part of the present century was quiet in volcanic terms, and the warming might be explained as a result of dust clearing from the stratosphere, while the recent cooling trend coincides with increasing volcanic activity. But in such a variation on the theme, the carbon dioxide influence has to be set very small, only one-tenth of the strength most climate modelers currently accept, otherwise it would have overwhelmed the volcanic influence and caused the Earth to continue warming through the 1940s, 1950s, and 1960s.

The Best Explanation

The best fit of all between theory and reality comes, however, when Gilliland adds the third factor, solar variability. Now, the warming trend is explained as due to a combination of solar and volcanic influences, with a twenty-four-year lag between the maximum of the solar diameter in 1911 and the peak warmth of the 1930s—the dustbowl era in North America. From about 1940 to the 1970s, on this picture, both the solar and volcanic influences were acting to cool the Earth, more than compensating for the rapid buildup of carbon dioxide. Over the past few years, climatologists have developed a standard computer model of the way the carbon dioxide buildup may affect the Earth. As more fossil fuel is burned, and more tropical forests are destroyed, the experts see a real possibility that the amount of carbon dioxide in the atmosphere will double, compared with the level of the middle of the twentieth century, within about fifty years. The standard computer model tells us that such a doubling of the carbon dioxide concentration would warm the surface of the Earth by an average of 2 degrees C, with a bigger increase in the polar regions, and a lesser influence in the already warm tropics. One of the puzzles about this forecast is that if the computer models are correct we should already be able to detect the first stages of warming due to the carbon dioxide greenhouse effect, but in fact the world cooled from

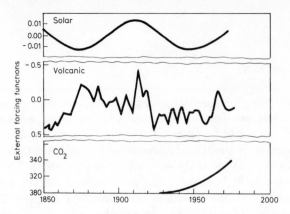

Figure 7.1 Three different external influences are used by Gilliland as "forcing functions" in his computer model of climatic change. The solar influence, as a percentage change in heat output the same as the percentage change in radius, is shown at the top. The volcanic influence, determined from studies of the acidity record of a core drilled from the Greenland ice cap, is shown in the same units as an equivalent change in solar "constant." The carbon dioxide buildup in the atmosphere is measured in parts per million by volume; standard climate models suggest that doubling the concentration of carbon dioxide in the atmosphere will warm the Earth by about 2 degrees centigrade.

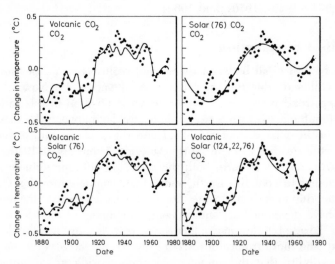

Figure 7.2 Adding either the volcanic influence or the solar influence to the carbon dioxide greenhouse effect (solid lines) gives a fair simulation of the actual temperature record of the past 100 years (dotted). But with only volcanic dust and carbon dioxide in the model, the best agreement comes (top left) when the carbon dioxide greenhouse effect is only one tenth as strong as the climatologists believe it to be. With the standard greenhouse effect numbers *and* the solar influence combined with the volcanic variations, the agreement with reality is even better (bottom left). And for the icing on the cake Gilliland gets an almost perfect agreement between climatic history and the computer model by adding in solar variations over 12.4 years and 22 years, corresponding to the two main sunspot cycles. While intriguing, this final curve should not yet be taken as definitive since so many variables are involved. (*Both figures supplied by Ronald Gilliland.*)

about 1940 into the 1970s. There are maverick theorists who argue that the standard model is wrong, and that the real greenhouse effect may indeed only be one-tenth as strong as the established theory predicts.* But Gilliland can now offer an alternative explanation, that the Sun's cooling over this critical recent period masked the first stirrings of the greenhouse effect.

All this is very intriguing. It resolves the puzzle of why the Earth cooled even while the concentration of carbon dioxide was continuing to grow exponentially, and all it requires is a peak change in solar luminosity of just 0.28 percent over the seventy-six-year cycle, producing a maximum influence on surface temperatures on Earth of just 0.28 degrees C. These figures are well within the range of possibilities set by observations of the solar constant from the Earth; as Gilliland says, on this picture "low temperatures of the last two decades result primarily from a minimum of the solar seventy-six-year cycle." But while resolving one puzzle about the greenhouse effect, his analysis raises new concern about its future influence on mankind.

If the standard greenhouse effect calculations are indeed correct, as they must be to produce the best possible agreement between Gilliland's model and the real world, then over the next thirty years temperatures are likely to rise by a full degree (Centigrade) as ever-increasing quantities of fossil fuel are burned. But now the solar influence is just turning around to contribute a further warming influence up to the year 2010, boosting the greenhouse effect where for the past thirty years it has been counterbalancing it. The result is a forecast of much more rapid and pronounced warming of the globe than has previously been thought likely, setting in by the end of the present decade. At first, this might seem beneficial as the 1990s see a return of the excellent conditions for world agriculture that prevailed in the 1950s. Beyond the turn of the century, however, the forecast implies a rapid warming into conditions unseen on Earth for a thousand years or more, heralding a super dustbowl era far worse than the 1930s across the Great Plains of North America.

So, in the space of just three years, the curious puzzle of the shrinking Sun has taken researchers from studies of dusty old records locked away in the files of the world's most famous observatory to speculations about the internal workings of the Sun and a

---

*For a discussion of the whole greenhouse effect debate, see my book *Future Weather*.

grim warning of the possible climatic future that will confront the next generation of human beings on an already overcrowded planet. Halley and his successors at the Royal Greenwich Observatory would surely have been fascinated to learn of the unexpected uses to which late-twentieth-century astronomers would put their solar observations. A century or two ago, though, who could have imagined any practical benefit to mankind from such erudite research as studies of the exact path of an eclipse, or painstaking measurements of the angular diameter of the Sun? And how can we imagine the uses which future generations—assuming they survive the coming climatic crisis—might make of the seemingly impractical observations of present-day astronomers—measurements of quasar red shifts, speculations about the black hole in Cygnus, studies of the atmosphere of Jupiter, and all the rest? Who would have thought, even half a decade ago, that there might be a connection between the mass of the neutrino and the climate on Earth?

For those who like to speculate about the interconnectedness of things, here is a grand speculation indeed. If the neutrino has mass, then the solar neutrino puzzle is solved and the Universe is probably closed by the resulting spacewarp. If the neutrino does not have mass, however, then the best way to solve the solar neutrino puzzle is to accept that the Sun is shrinking, and this would be very strong supporting evidence that all of Gilliland's work on solar size variations is correct. If the Sun's size does vary, then we are in for a climatic surprise in the next two decades, says Gilliland; and again, if the Sun's size does vary, then there may be no need to invoke neutrino mass (neutrinos could still have mass, or they might not), and that might imply that the Universe is open and will expand forever. Perhaps, throughout this chapter, you have been puzzling over why the story of climatic change gets into a book about spacewarps. Now you know—if the Universe is open, then we can expect a pronounced climatic shift within our lifetimes; if it is warped back on itself to make a closed segment of spacetime, then Gilliland may well be wrong and it may be much more like business as usual, in climatic terms!

I am writing, of course, with my tongue firmly in my cheek. But who knows? Ideas that seem esoteric to one generation often turn out to be of practical benefit in a later age. Surely, though, no one could imagine a possible practical benefit for the following extraordinary and exotic idea, although it does take us back firmly into the study of warped spacetime.

8

Timewarps Revisited

Since space and time are two sides of the same coin, the existence of spacewarps implies the existence of timewarps as well. Einstein's theory says that time travel is possible; one theorist has described mathematically how to build a time machine. But it may not be as useful as you hoped.

Is time travel possible? When I wrote *Timewarps* I answered that question with a qualified "yes." Time travel is possible, I concluded, but it all depends what you mean by time travel. Now, I'm not so sure that the qualification is needed. The reason for my change of heart, or mind, is the work of a remarkable American mathematician, Frank Tipler, Associate Professor of Mathematical Physics at Tulane University, New Orleans. Tipler seemingly delights in turning conventional ideas on their head, using detailed statistical and mathematical arguments to claim, among other things, that time travel really might be possible in our Universe, and, as we shall see in Chapter Nine, that we may be the only intelligent

145

beings in the Universe, or at least in our Galaxy. The work may
owe something to the "devil's advocate" school of thought, and
like Fred Hoyle before him Tipler prods his colleagues into con-
templating possibilities they might not otherwise consider, throw-
ing down the challenge to them to find the mistake, if any, in his
calculations. The role is an invaluable one in science, emphasizing
that nothing should be assumed to be "obvious" in this Universe
we inhabit, a lesson that the triumphs of relativity theory ought to
have brought home to all physicists and astronomers, but one
which, it seems, has to be relearned at least once in every generation. In the spirit of driving that lesson home, most of this chapter
will be devoted to a summary of Tipler's description of how to
build a time machine, a description drawn in part from a very
mathematical paper published as long ago as 1974 in the highly
respectable journal *Physical Review* (D, vol. 9, p. 2203), and in
part from discussions and correspondence I had with Tipler in 1980,
when I reported some of this work in *New Scientist*. Before getting
into the details, however, I ought to say something about our views
of the nature of time; a fuller background can be found, of course,
in the pages of *Timewarps*.

Does Time Flow?

We all have an instinctive feeling for the passage of time, and
the difference between the fixed, historical past and the unknowable future. More objectively, the Universe shows us a clear direction, or arrow, of time in the processes of change which have taken
it from a compact, hot fireball to a sea of dark space dotted with
stars, some of them orbited by planets, on one of which at least
intelligent life has evolved. The progress, if that is the right word,
from Big Bang to mankind is, however, a misleading image of the
arrow of time, suggesting the development of order out of chaos.
By contrast, physicists define the arrow of time in terms of processes which generate increasing disorder—drop an ice cube into
a glass of water and the ice melts, making an undifferentiated mass
of liquid. In the real world, we do not see a glass of water spontaneously creating ice cubes, although there is nothing in the laws
of physics at the Newtonian level to prevent this. It is when those
laws are applied to a mass of particles—atoms and molecules—that
statistical processes come into play, and have the effect of producing chaos out of order, destroying information and increasing the

measure of the thermodynamic quantity called entropy. On this picture, the development of the order represented by life on Earth has happened only at the cost of increased disorder—increased entropy—elsewhere. An industrial example makes the point. A house, say, is a fine example of order, and the appearance of a house out of the ground, as a result of random movements of molecules, would fly right in the face of our understanding of thermodynamics. But people can build a house. In the process, though, they burn fuel, cut down forests, dig rock and metal from the ground, and along the way use large quantities of energy and create a great deal of waste somewhere else. The local decrease in entropy represented by the house is more than offset by the greater increase in entropy involved in all these background activities.

There are problems here that the philosophers and thermodynamicists still debate. How can order arise out of chaos, even locally? Did the Universe contain, in some sense, a store of information at the beginning, which is the basis of the order we see around us but which must eventually be used up, with all the matter in the Universe disappearing into black holes, where order is smeared out of existence and chaos reigns supreme? If the Universe is like a clock running down—an analogy sometimes made to highlight the inevitability of the increase of entropy—who wound it up in the first place?

Leaving aside the philosophical puzzles, it is far from clear that our "commonsense" view of the inevitability of the flow of time "works" at a fundamental level. Nobel prizewinning physicist Richard Feynman developed the idea that in the world of particle physics the "antiparticle" counterpart to any particle—the positron partner to an electron, say—can be represented as its particle partner moving backward in time. This is not just a mathematical trick; Feynman's new insight into quantum mechanics greatly simplifies the equations used by physicists to describe the behavior of particles, and can be interpreted as literally meaning that a positron is an electron traveling backward in time. Feynman says that he got the idea from a throwaway remark of his former teacher, John Wheeler,* when Feynman was still a graduate student at Princeton. Wheeler commented that all electrons, everywhere in the Universe, could be regarded as the same electron which traveled forward and backward in time, to and fro across space, in a zigzag

---

*Incidentally, Wheeler is the man generally credited with first applying the name "black hole" in its now standard astrophysical context.

dance through spacetime that made it visible to us, here and now, as an array of particles across the Universe. What we see is a cross section through the knotted path of the electron, its world line, and our view changes as time passes and the cross section moves in the time direction through spacetime.

These are tricky concepts, suggesting that perhaps all of history, future as well as past, is fixed in spacetime and only our view changes as time "passes." Even the people who develop the ideas and the equations generally hasten to point out that this is just one way of looking at them; Feynman's insights, so valuable to quantum mechanics, can be interpreted in ways which do not involve particles traveling backward in time. Nobody "seriously" suggests that the entire material world is just our view of the tangled world lines of one or two particles zigzagging through spacetime along fixed paths. Nobody "seriously" accepts Tipler's calculations, either. But this may tell us more about the sort of people who make careers in science these days than about the way the Universe actually works.

The Theory of Time Travel

By a nice touch of irony, Tipler's thoughts on the possibility of time travel are probably known to a wider readership than most esoteric scientific ideas, but that readership may not appreciate that these ideas are "real science." The reason is that the ideas first emerged into the world beyond the readership of the *Physical Review* in one of the shortest stories by SF writer Larry Niven, a piece with the catchy title, "Rotating Cylinders and the Possibility of Global Causality Violation," a title which Niven acknowledges he stole from Tipler's 1974 paper. The story depends on the assumption that the work described by Tipler in that paper can be taken at face value, implying that it is possible to construct a working time machine based upon the rotation of a very long, massive, and suitably rigid cylinder constructed in space.*

That's all very well, but usually such exotic ideas are aired in the scientific literature hedged about with caveats to the effect that "this is not expected to apply in the real Universe," or some such qualification. So when I contacted Tipler to find out whether he really believed, as of 1980, that time travel was possible, I was

---

*Niven's story can be found in the collection *Convergent Series* (New York: Del Rey/Ballantine, 1979).

both surprised and pleased by the positive tone of his response that "my current view is that there is indeed a real theoretical possibility for causality violation in the context of classical general relativity," and his only caveat was the remark, "that is, I feel the question is still open." "Causality violation" is what you or I mean by "time travel." The point is that if time travel in the fullest sense is possible, then effects can be seen to precede their causes, instead of following. Causality is violated, for example, if you walk into a room and the light comes on, and then you flip the switch which allows the current to flow; or if the winner of the 3:15 at Hialeah is announced and then I pop back to 2:30 to place my bet on the winner.

There is a widespread and general assumption among mathematicians and physicists (and others!) that causality cannot be violated—but this is no more than an assumption, based on the commonsense view ingrained by everyday experience. So deeply is this view ingrained in us that any theory which allows, or predicts, causality violation is usually regarded on those grounds alone as a "bad" description of reality. But this is only a prejudice; Tipler and a few others argue that we should at least keep open minds at present. General relativity has stood every other test over the past half-century; now it is seen to predict causality violation, and there is as yet no proof that it is wrong on this count, either.

So to attempt to answer the question, "Is time travel possible?" Tipler has used the best mathematical description of spacetime that we have, and he has broken the problem down into three main parts.

First, do the equations allow in theory for the existence of journeys through spacetime in which the traveler returns to his starting point in both space and time, having traveled "backward in time" for part of the journey?

Second, if so, is it possible for the conditions under which such journeys are possible to arise naturally in the Universe?

And, third, is it possible, in principle at least, to create such conditions artificially, that is to build a working time machine?

It turns out that the answer to all three questions, within the framework of general relativity, is "yes." But first, let's take a quick look at that theoretical framework.

What we learn from special relativity is that time intervals experienced by people and measured by physical clocks depend on the particular path they follow through spacetime. If two spacetime paths coincide initially and intersect later, and one path is accelerated while the other is not, then the time length of the accelerated path will be shorter—less time will have passed for the traveler following this path. But he can never exceed the speed of light (at which time would stand still for our hypothetical observer), and can never travel backward in time. Our passage through the four-dimensional fabric of spacetime is confined within a region bounded by paths corresponding to light rays radiating from the here and now, a region called the "future light cone." And our knowledge of past events in the Universe is confined to information coming from a similar four-dimensional cone extending into the past, the "past light cone." In practice, relativists compress the three dimensions of space into one representational dimension, allowing them to plot two-dimensional diagrams on paper, with the flow of time represented as "up the page" and movement in space as "across the page." On such a spacetime diagram, a quarter of the page represents the future light cone, a quarter the past, and fully half of spacetime is inaccessible and unknowable, and called "elsewhere."

But special relativity takes no account of the effects of gravity, and one such effect, spelled out by general relativity, is that the presence of matter in a region of spacetime causes nearby light cones to "tip over" in the direction of the matter (light rays are "bent" by gravity). If the matter is rotating, it further distorts spacetime in its vicinity, creating a dragging effect which tips the light cones over in the direction of rotation. And if the mass involved is big enough, and the rotation is fast enough, then the light cones tip over so far that the coordinate used to measure space and the coordinate used to measure time become interchanged. In practical terms, the roles of space and time have been reversed, and by the entirely legitimate process of changing his local space coordinate—moving through space—a traveler would move through time, as viewed from the region of spacetime outside the influence of the rotating mass. In Tipler's words, "a traveler could begin his journey in weak field regions—perhaps near the Earth—go to the tipped-over light-cone region and there move in the direction of negative time, and then return to the weak field region, without ever leaving the region defined by his future light cone. If he traveled sufficiently far in the minus-t direction while in the strong field, he could return to Earth before he left—he can go as far as he wishes into the Earth's past. This is a case of true time travel." In other words, the first part of the puzzle has been

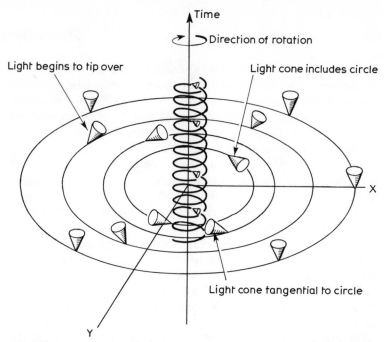

Figure 8.1 Near a massive rotating object, spacetime is distorted, so that the light cones in local regions (see Figure 1.4) tip over. A traveler, or message, can only move forward in time within a light cone, but if the light cone points backward, then time travel is possible. (Based on figure supplied by Frank Tipler.)

solved—general relativity does imply the theoretical possibility of causality violation. But is it practicable?

Building a Time Machine

There is no guarantee that because a region of spacetime like the one described by Tipler as "the strong field region" *can* exist, then such a region *will* exist. Crucially, how much mass must there be in the rotating object, and how fast must it be rotating, for causality violation to occur? A slightly more subtle point is that because the light cones are not tipped over until the massive rotating object comes into being, there is no way to travel back further in time than the instant of creation of the "time machine," whether it is natural or man-made. If we built such a time machine tomorrow, we could not use it to travel back in time and study the ancient Greeks; but if we found a natural time machine left over from the creation of the Universe, then we could.

The realization that rotation can scramble the orderly picture of

151

space and time is nothing new. Einstein himself tackled aspects of the problem, and Kurt Gödel developed a mathematical description, a model, of a rotating universe which came to some similar conclusions. Gödel's model was developed thirty years ago, and contains features that most theorists find disturbing. In particular, it allows journeys in which the traveler, by following a circuitous route through spacetime, returns to his starting point in both space and time, Tipler's eminently reasonable criterion of time travel. Such routes through spacetime are called "closed timelike lines," and the general reaction to Gödel's model is that the presence of closed timelike lines rule it out as a valid description of the Universe, because "of course" causality violation is impossible. A closed timelike line (CTL) is simply a path through spacetime that returns to its starting point, making a closed loop and therefore looping backward in time for part of its path. If a rotating universe contains CTLs, then in the eyes of most cosmologists that "proves" the Universe is not rotating.

The question is rather academic, however, because even if the Universe contains CTLs we would still have to find the right path through spacetime, and it is hardly likely that such a path passes within range of our rather limited spacefaring capacity. Even if we could find it, it might even involve traveling around the entire Universe to get back to the starting point. To find a natural time machine, it is more sensible to focus our attention on more local regions of spacetime, and lesser quantities of matter, than the Universe itself. Here, the mathematics gets too hairy for me, and like you I have to accept Tipler's credentials, and those of the journals in which his work has appeared, interpreting for you only the conclusions of his work, not the arguments themselves.* There is no doubt that general relativity permits the existence of CTLs, but the standard way to test the physical reality of mathematical solutions to Einstein's equations is to change the parameters being fed into the equations ("perturb the initial conditions") and see if the same solutions still come out. But it is hard to test whether CTLs are "stable" in this sense, because when dealing with a loop in time it is rather difficult to decide what you mean by the "initial"

---

*The *Physical Review* is not the only learned journal to have published the relevant work; other papers have appeared in *Annals of Physics,* vol. 108, p. 1; *Physical Review Letters,* vol. 37, p. 879; and in the book *General Relativity and Gravitation: One Hundred Years After the Birth of Albert Einstein,* vol. 2, p. 97, edited by A. Med and published by Plenum in 1980.

conditions. In terms of the practicality of time travel in our Universe, Tipler's results lead, even so, to one important and seemingly unambiguous conclusion. A time machine cannot be created from ordinary material under ordinary conditions; CTLs can arise only if at least some matter passes through such extreme conditions that a singularity is created.

A singularity is a region where the matter density becomes infinite, and there is no way in which matter with arbitrarily large density can be considered "ordinary." On the other hand, most relativists accept that singularities do occur in the ultimate collapse of matter within black holes. Such a singularity cannot be seen, because it is surrounded by an event horizon, and the snag for prospective time travelers is that while they might be able to cross the horizon on the way to the "time machine," they could never get back into our local weak field region of spacetime. You cannot, in other words, have a practical time machine without a naked singularity, one that is not surrounded by a black hole event horizon.

All is not lost, however. As Stephen Hawking has shown, black holes aren't black, and tend to evaporate over a long period of time, eventually exploding outward and exposing the singularity inside to outside view. If the singularity also had angular momentum—if it were rotating—it would be a working time machine with CTLs. Such a time machine could arise naturally from a small black hole left over from the Big Bang—and although in that case the high field region of distorted spacetime would be too small for even an electron to take advantage of the time traveling opportunities thus presented, that means that the second part of the time travel puzzle can also be answered in the affirmative. All that remains is to find a way to create such a time machine artificially. It might be done, in principle, by capturing a mini-black hole and cooling space around it to speed up its evaporation until a naked singularity appeared. We might even imagine means of manufacturing such a black hole in the first place, using powerful nuclear fusion devices. But the best prospect is the one picked up by Larry Niven—take a compact rotating body and speed up its rotation enough, while somehow ensuring that it doesn't collapse along its axis (which, says Tipler sadly, would be very difficult to arrange for a rotating cylinder with any finite length). When the rotation is fast enough, a naked singularity will form at the center of the rotating cylinder, and CTLs will come into existence.

The naked singularity need not remain in existence for any appreciable time, however, since once the CTLs are formed they are forever tied to the singularity, no matter how brief its existence, by their curved paths through spacetime. That does a great deal to make up for the obvious difficulties in constructing such a machine, since it only has to exist for a fleeting instant to open up all of the future of the Universe to exploration.

So Tipler concludes that not only are CTLs not ruled out by any fundamental physical principle, the construction of a working time machine is a theoretical possibility. The problems that remain, although impressively large, are essentially engineering problems. It would be possible, with the use of some sophisticated and expensive engineering, to set up a time machine.

How sophisticated and expensive would the engineering have to be? Some idea of the difficulties still to be overcome can be gleaned from some very "iffy" numbers Tipler quotes. If the approximations in his calculations which apply, strictly speaking, to infinitely long rotating cylinders still hold for finite cylinders, then the ratio of length of the cylinder to its radius would be about 10 to 1. If this finite cylinder has the same field effect in the CTL region as an infinite cylinder, and if stabilizing could be done without the need for extra mass (Tipler stresses that in his view this may be impossible even with extra mass), then a cylinder with a mass density of about 10^{14} grams per cubic centimeter (the density of the nucleus of an atom, or of a neutron star), a radius of 10 km, and a length of about 100 km, having a total mass roughly equal to that of the Sun, and rotating twice every millisecond so that the rim of the cylinder was moving at half the speed of light, would be a working time machine. In other words, a time machine would be like an elongated, rapidly rotating neutron star. Apart from the stability problem, the specification is remarkably like that of a young, recently formed pulsar, although no known pulsar rotates quite that fast—but the quickest, the "millisecond pulsar," actually spins once every 1½ milliseconds, and that is getting very close indeed to Tipler's requirement. None of the popular reports of this remarkable discovery seem, however, to have noticed how closely this fast-spinning pulsar fits the description of a working time machine.

It is a very surprising and dramatic discovery that a working time machine should bear such a close resemblance to objects that occur naturally in the Universe, and the suggestion doesn't seem to have caused anything like the stir in astronomical circles—and outside—that it should. Bearing in mind the advances in engineering we have made on Earth in the past millennium, the prospect of tweaking up a naturally existing pulsar to create, for the brief instant that is required, a working time machine looks entirely feasible for a civilization not much more advanced than our own. But before you get too excited, Tipler has a parting shot to impart. Would such a working time machine actually be of any practical use?

Operating Difficulties—and New Possibilities

"I would imagine," says Tipler, "that if such a device were created, it would be used only to send messages, not physical objects, back into time. It would take enormous energies to send a physical body back—energy at least as great as the rest mass of the body. You can see this by imagining a body of mass M sent back in time and returned close to the event at which it started; far away from the time machine, there would be two bodies with mass M, and the extra rest-mass energy has to come from somewhere. In effect, the machine acts as a matter duplicator."

Another operating difficulty would be posed by the enormous tidal forces associated with the strong gravitational field of a small time machine; but Tipler stresses that there is no theoretical barrier to the movement of particles of matter through the time machine, and for small masses even the energy cost of the matter duplication process would be less than the energy costs involved in building the time machine in the first place. A civilization rich enough, in energy terms, to build the machine would probably not be daunted by the cost of running it. And even the prospect of sending messages through time is enough to pull the rug from under the "causality is common sense" school of thought. When I pressed him to provide me with a definitive, quotable answer to the question, "Are CTLs possible?" Tipler would respond only with a "definite maybe," which he then explained as meaning that "we are a very long way from completely resolving the causality violation question." This is a very different point of view from the conventional argument that "of course" causality. violation is impossible. Dismissing any idea as "obviously" impossible is certainly bad science, and Tipler is encouraging good scientists to think more deeply about some cherished beliefs. It is in this spirit that he quotes with a slight paraphrase (italicized) the famous comment of American astronomer Simon Newcomb, published shortly before the Wright brothers took to the air: "The demonstration that no possible combination of known substances, known forms of machinery, and known forms of force can be united in a particular machine by which men *shall travel back in time*, seems to the writer as complete as it is possible for the demonstration of any physical feat to be."

If Tipler doesn't quite anticipate that developments in his lifetime will pull the rug from under this statement, at least he won't have as much egg on his face as most other astronomers if developments do overtake it in the way that Newcomb's statement was overtaken by events at Kitty Hawk.

Things haven't quite progressed to that stage yet. But by one of those occasional strokes of serendipity that make you wonder just who does set up the chains of causality that rule our lives, in the very week that I was drafting this chapter a young radio astronomer working at Jodrell Bank reported some seemingly esoteric interpretations of data from statistical studies of the properties of radio sources. Paul Birch was set one of those boring tasks that supervisors like to dump on research students, taking the raw data on the magnetic properties of radio sources studied with the big Jodrell Bank telescopes, and similar data gathered by other observatories around the world, and putting it all into some kind of order. The kind of order he found, however, was totally unexpected; the magnetic polarizations tend to "point" one way in half of the sky, and the other way in the opposite half of the sky. In one direction, double-lobed radio sources tend to be left-handed, and in the other right-handed—a curiosity best understood in everyday terms by imagining the radio galaxies to be roughly "S" shaped in one direction on the sky, and roughly "Z" shaped in the other. The pattern is far from being overwhelmingly obvious, and it could be just a statistical fluke. But one possible interpretation of such a pattern is that the whole Universe is rotating.*

The announcement of the discovery gave the headline writers in the "quality" newspapers an opportunity to trot out lines like "Universe in a spin" and for the writers of the stories beneath those headlines to succumb to the temptation to talk punningly about an "astronomical revolution." The real story is a bit less dramatic than that, and most astronomers remained cautious about the announcement, preferring to wait and see if more studies bear out

*Nature, vol. 298 (1982), p. 451.

the preliminary findings. Of course they were—and are—interested in the implications. If the whole Universe is indeed rotating in line with Birch's observations, then several of the standard cosmological models can be ruled out. The rate of rotation that comes out of these measurements is rather high, as cosmologists regard such things, at a cool 10^{-13} radians per year, implying one rotation every 6×10^{13} years (which is about 40,000 times the present age of the Universe), and John Barrow, of the University of Sussex, was quick to point out that this much rotation would rule out all of the simple "closed" models, and might mean, taken at face value, that the Universe is open. On the other hand, it could just be a "local" effect by the standards of the whole Universe. After all, our Milky Way Galaxy rotates, and nobody views that as a sign of universal rotation. It may just be that we have to redefine our ideas of what is "local" in the Universe to include a volume of spacetime covering a billion parsecs.

Writing in the summer of 1982, it is, tantalizingly, about a year too soon for me to be drawing any valid conclusions about the implications of Birch's study. But just suppose the data can be taken at face value, and the Universe is rotating. Its present leisurely rate of spin would, of course, have been more dramatic when the Universe was denser, closer to the Big Bang (remember the spinning ice skater drawing in her arms). And if those Big Bang cosmological models can be taken seriously, then it seems our Universe was born out of a singularity. As far as we are concerned, this is very much a naked singularity. If the Universe is open, then the singularity is open to an infinite stretch of spacetime; if our Universe is closed, a finite region of spacetime bounded by a surface akin to a black hole event horizon, the singularity is still naked as far as we are concerned, because we are inside the "black hole" along with it. The Universe, then, may have been born out of a rotating naked singularity. Gödel's equations may have been nearer to the truth than anyone has ever given him credit for, and it no longer looks as certain as people have assumed that causality is built into the fabric of spacetime. Closed timelike lines and causality violation may very well be inherent in our Universe, even if their effects are not obvious here on Earth.

Compared with such mind-blowing possibilities, the question of whether we are the only intelligent species to have emerged in our Galaxy, or in the entire Universe, seems almost mundane. But in recent years astronomers—and some biologists—have taken up the puzzle of the interrelationship between life and the Universe, in the belief that there must be some clue here to the nature of the chunk of spacetime that we observe with our telescopes. We are surrounded by the bizarre effects of spacewarps (and time-warps!) on the Universe; the Universe itself is a spacewarp, an expanding chunk of bent spacetime. Life on Earth, very clearly, is a product of the Universe we inhabit. But does that mean that "life as we know it" must be a common occurrence in our Universe? One of the many other strings to Frank Tipler's professional bow is the opposite argument, that the absence of any signs of visitors from space in our Solar System means that we are alone—an argument based, ironically, on the very ease of space colonization to a civilization scarcely more advanced than our own. And somewhere in the wings our old friends Hoyle and Wickramasinghe have recently espoused yet another idea, that life is so unlikely a phenomenon that it cannot have emerged in our Universe even in the time available since the Big Bang. Since we are indeed here, their argument is that the Universe is much older than the 15 billion years or so implied by a simple interpretation of its present expansion. The relationship between life and the Universe is clearly very complicated, and certainly merits a chapter of its own, even in a book primarily devoted to the physical effects of warped space-time.

9

Life and the Universe

We live in a Universe governed by the rules Einstein discovered. Life like us can only exist in a Universe like the one we see around us. Does that mean the Universe is tailor-made for humankind? Or does it imply that life is common in the Universe? Can other kinds of universe exist? Parallel worlds.

Life is so unlikely a phenomenon that we may well be the only intelligent beings in our Galaxy, perhaps in the whole Universe. Alternatively, the way the Universe is constructed, life like us is an inevitable product of a planet like the Earth, and the Universe is probably swarming with intelligent beings. Those two diametrically opposed views sum up our state of ignorance about life and the Universe. The arguments, on either side, are largely philosophical and the viewpoint you favor is largely a matter of faith rather than of solid scientific evidence. My own "gut feeling" is that the Earth is far from being a special place in the Universe, and I subscribe to what has been called the "principle of terrestrial mediocrity," which says that our home in space is an ordinary, unexceptional place and that if life, including intelligent life, can emerge here then it has surely emerged in other places as well. So, in order to give the opposing viewpoint a fair crack of the whip, I will start this chapter by putting forward, as best I can, the counterargument, that we are alone in our Galaxy.

That argument has been expressed most cogently, and most vociferously, by the same Frank Tipler who makes a convincing case that time travel is possible. He starts by defining an "intelligent being" as a member of a living species that is capable of developing a technology comparable to ours, and which, like our species, is interested in using this technology to communicate with other intelligent species, and is also interested in exploring and/or colonizing the Galaxy. As Tipler acknowledges, this is a restrictive definition. We can imagine a philosophically inclined intelligence that had no interest in rude mechanics or in exploring the Galaxy; some people might argue that the whales are every bit as "intelligent" as us, but do not come within this definition of intelligence. However, the definition is entirely reasonable when it comes to the search for extraterrestrial intelligence (SETI), because this is the only kind of intelligent life that we are likely to detect, and the only kind we could possibly detect using the radio telescopes which are the basis of current searches.

The philosophy underlying Tipler's approach to SETI is biological. Many biological experts claim that the evolution of an intelligent species from a single-celled organism is the result of a chain of evolutionary steps so improbable that we are likely to be the only intelligent species ever to have existed. This sounds like a piece of scientific evidence, but it is based on prejudice, and cannot be tested until we find another planet on which life exists. The only real measure of the probability of intelligence evolving is the fact that we exist—so we know the probability is bigger than zero, but without some basis for comparison we cannot specify how much bigger than zero. If, on some other planet as well as Earth, the "primitive" single-celled organisms have evolved into creatures as complex as whales, monkeys, or honey bees, then the argument falls down; alternatively, if we found such a planet covered with "simple" plants and animals, then the argument would look a little better. But it is impossible to generalize meaningfully from the single example of life on Earth, so I do not see this argument as a serious objection to the possible existence of extraterrestrial intelligence. On the other hand, as we shall see, there are those who not only accept this argument but take it several steps further.

Whatever the validity of this argument, however, it is only the introduction to Tipler's main idea on SETI. This is such a beautiful argument that it deserves to be true. What he says is that space travel is so easy for any species that meets his definition of intelligence that, if one existed, it would already have colonized the Galaxy and would be here on Earth. Since we do not see evidence of such extraterrestrial visitors in our own cosmic backyard, the Solar System, that is proof that no extraterrestrial intelligence exists.

Are We Alone?

This is certainly an idea worthy of a full description. The first point is that the human species has already sent out four space probes at velocities so great that they will leave the Solar System altogether—Pioneers 10 and 11, and Voyagers 1 and 2. So we know for sure that it is possible to send a probe to another star system, and any of these four probes could have been so targeted, although it would take thousands of years for such a probe to reach the nearest star. If we assume only modest advances in rocket technology, complex payloads could be sent to other star systems with ease, and at low cost. But what sort of payload? The mathematician John von Neumann proved that it is possible in principle to construct a machine (a computer) which is capable of making copies of itself. It is only a small step from this to envisaging a machine with near-human intelligence, capable of building anything for which it has the raw materials and a blueprint. In honor of von Neumann, Tipler calls such a device a "von Neumann machine."

It may sound farfetched, but anyone reading this book is likely to have some idea of how rapidly computer technology has progressed in the past twenty years, or even in the past ten years. When I began my writing career, it was unimaginable that in 1982 I would be writing a book not using a typewriter but my own personal computer, yet today my computer is regarded by some of my colleagues as almost laughably old-fashioned, being based on technology from as long ago as 1978. (Jerry Pournelle puts the computer explosion in perspective in one of the essays in his thought-provoking collection *A Step Farther Out*. An engineer who worked on NASA's space program, he is also among the writers who have described the potential of self-replicating robots.) Computer scientists believe that a von Neumann machine could be built within a hundred years, and once one is built it could produce others virtually for nothing, so that such machines would become cheap and commonplace. By then, we would also have the technology to send such a machine to another star system, as a von Neumann probe.

What might it find there? The one thing we can be sure of is that any star will be surrounded by debris, asteroids and comets, which the probe could use to make copies of itself. These could be launched to other star systems, while the original probe sets about exploring its new home and, perhaps, sending data back to Earth. Eventually, for the cost of just one von Neumann probe, the entire Galaxy would be colonized. And since the von Neumann machines come free, the cost of the probe is simply the cost of the rocket vehicle, which Tipler estimates at around $3 to 4 billion at today's prices. That is well within the budgets of many private concerns, and almost small change for the government of a major industrial power.

So Tipler argues that there must be, among any intelligent species, some group of individuals that will send such a probe on its way. They may be motivated by idealism, or militaristic visions of expansion. It doesn't matter—as long as just one such probe gets a start on the job, before too long the Galaxy will be crawling with them. And they could do a pretty good job of transforming the Galaxy. Each probe would be capable of building anything it wanted, including a habitable space station. It could very well be capable of synthesizing a living replica of the species that launched it, copying the genetic code carried in our DNA, for example, into an artificially manufactured "fertilized egg." It could seed a planet it found with synthetic single-celled life forms, or produce two or more copies of the species that made the probe, and set them loose on the surface of a suitable planet. The possibilities are endless, but the most relevant one, in Tipler's view, is the ease with which such a probe could contact any intelligent beings it found.

This is where the present searches for extraterrestrial intelligence fall down. With radio searches, we can only contact civilizations that also use radio. Perhaps other civilizations use totally different techniques for communication—beams of neutrinos, or gravity waves, or something we have yet to discover. But, as Tipler says, if a probe had arrived in our asteroid belt in the seventeenth century, built a landing craft, and set it down in front of

Buckingham Palace, the event would have been noticed even though our ancestors at the time had no knowledge of radio!

Using technology barely in advance of ours, Tipler calculates that the entire Galaxy could be explored or colonized in this way within 300 million years. Since the Galaxy is 10 billion years old, there has been ample opportunity for any intelligent species to have done the job, so their absence implies they do not exist.

It is, indeed, a lovely argument. But I can poke holes in it almost without trying. Perhaps the Galaxy has been colonized, and we are part of a cosmic "zoo" or reservation. Perhaps the Earth *was* seeded from space by a von Neumann probe, 4 billion years ago, and we are the end product. The "Adam and Eve" scenario won't work, of course, since our DNA is almost identical to that of the other apes, and similar to that of all life on Earth, so such a seeding would have to have been right at the beginning of the story of life on Earth. But, perhaps again, the probe is sitting in the asteroid belt waiting for us to find it, the test by which we might prove our own intelligence to the others out there. Tipler's counter to these arguments would probably be that by now the Galaxy ought to be teeming with probes and some species or other would be inclined to make contact with us, whatever our state of development. But the fact that the arguments can be made shows that the simple argument "they aren't here, so they don't exist" cannot be taken as the last word on the subject.

One of the Crowd?

"We are alone in the Universe," says Tipler. But G.F.R. Ellis and G. B. Brundrit, of the University of Cape Town, claimed in the pages of the *Quarterly Journal of the Royal Astronomical Society* in 1979 (vol. 20, p. 37) that if the Universe is open then, so far from being alone, we are actually multiplied like photocopies of ourselves across the infinite stretches of space and time. Their point is that an open universe is indeed infinite. The infinite Universe, on this picture, is expanding and getting less dense, but it is still infinite, and always was, even just after the Big Bang. Using the usual mathematical description of the Universe, there must, therefore, be an infinite number of world lines through spacetime, each representing a galaxy, say. So there must be an infinite number of galaxies, and as long as there is any probability of life evolving, there must be an infinite number of planets carrying life, since any fraction of infinity is still infinite itself.

7. Two intertwined spiral galaxies, NGC 5432 and NGC 5435. (Lick Observatory Photograph)

But that isn't the end of the story. How similar to us could some of that life be? In a genuinely infinite universe, say Ellis and Brundrit, there must be an infinite number of planets like Earth—not just similar to Earth, although there must be an infinity of those too, but *indistinguishable* from our planet. Assuming there is life in the Universe, and the Universe is open, the Cape Town team concludes that an infinite number of "copies" of you exist out there, reading an infinite number of copies of this book. I don't believe it for a minute, but the idea could be compatible with Tipler's calculations provided none of the infinity of other life-bearing planets lies within range of our telescopes—that is, within the expanding bubble of spacetime, now 15 billion light-years across, within our light cone. The idea echoes the concept of multiple universes, which I discussed in *Timewarps* and which is much more appealing. But that is another story.

If you reject the idea on "philosophical" grounds, though, you are left, on the face of it, with no alternative but to accept that the Universe is finite, and therefore that it is closed and must one day collapse into a cosmic fireball. The mathematicians point out a complication in this argument. Because of the peculiarity of transfinite numbers, infinity multiplied by zero can still give you a finite number. So in a truly infinite universe, even if the probability of life evolving is zero, there might still be life on Earth. But if you think this is beginning to get too confusing, hold on to your seat.

So far, using seemingly reasonable arguments, we have "proved" that there is no other intelligent life in the Universe, and that in an infinite universe there must be an infinity of life. Tipler has picked up the latter point in a refinement of his own ideas to "prove" that the Universe cannot exist in a steady state. Although steady state cosmologies are unfashionable, it is in fact very difficult to rule them out as explanations of the Universe we live in. Almost any evidence in favor of the Big Bang can be interpreted in the context of an eternal steady state universe, unchanging over truly long stretches of space and time, within which our light cone encompasses only insignificant and local fluctuations. Sometimes the steady state arguments seem contrived. If we live in a bubble of spacetime that is indistinguishable from a Big Bang universe, but is "really" part of a bigger infinity, does it make sense to describe it in any other way than in Big Bang terms? Still, the steady state arguments can be made. But in a steady state universe, says Tipler, the Ellis and Brundrit argument applies with double force, since there is infinite time, as well as infinite space, to play with. In a steady state universe, an infinite variety of intelligent spacefaring life would have evolved an infinite time ago, on an infinite number of planets, and by now the entire universe would be colonized by the von Neumann probe technique, or some other method.

This looks very interesting. Using nothing more than common sense, it seems that we have established that the Universe is neither open nor steady state, which only leaves the finite, closed models. But just to save us from any complacency, Sir Fred Hoyle and his colleague Chandra Wickramasinghe at University College, Cardiff, have another idea. Hoyle believes that the probability of intelligent life arising in the Universe is not just small, but so tiny that it is quite unreasonable to expect life like us to have evolved in the time available since the Big Bang. So he says the Universe *must* be in a steady state, to provide the infinite time necessary for intelligence to evolve at all. And he believes that it is quite possible that the Universe *has* been colonized, seeded with living organisms scattered through space, and that we are the products of that seeding and colonization process. From the fact that we exist, Hoyle deduces that the Universe must be in a steady state, whereas from the "fact" that nobody else has visited us, others argue that we live in a closed, finite universe. I doubt if the debate will be resolved in my lifetime, if ever. But the biological background to the seemingly outrageous ideas put forward by Hoyle and Wickramasinghe in a series of pamphlets* deserves to make both biologists and cosmologists think again about some of their cherished beliefs.

Seeds of Life

Chandra Wickramasinghe has spent more than twenty years studying the nature of the dust grains that are found in space. These grains lie between the stars, part of the immense clouds of gas and dust that together may contain as much matter, or more, as we see in the bright stars of the Milky Way. The study of their nature is clearly important—in the first place, there is too much dust to ignore if we want to have any understanding of the Galaxy, and other galaxies; and secondly, such clouds are the birthplaces of stars. Our own Sun and Solar System were born out of the collapse of just such a cloud of gas and dust in space, so understanding the clouds ought to help us to understand how stars form. It is

*The Origin of Life, by Hoyle and Wickramasinghe, University College Cardiff Press, 1980; The Relation of Biology to Astronomy, by Fred Hoyle, UCC Press, 1980; Steady-State Cosmology Re-visited, by Fred Hoyle, UCC Press, 1980.

now known that the clouds are well laced with complex molecules, which are revealed by the way they absorb or emit electromagnetic radiation at radio frequencies. The largest molecule so far identified in this way has no less than eleven atoms of carbon strung together and joined to atoms of hydrogen and nitrogen to make cyano-deca-penta-yne, a chemical relative of acetylene. About a hundred molecules have been identified in interstellar clouds, many of them, like this giant, based on carbon atoms. They include molecules which can be regarded as the building blocks of the even more complex molecules, amino acids, which are themselves the basis of our form of carbon-based life.

This was a revolutionary discovery. Before it was made, biologists tried to explain how life could have arisen on Earth from the chemistry of simple molecules such as carbon dioxide, methane, ammonia, and water. Such mixtures can react to produce complex molecules such as amino acids, but all the evidence suggests that it would be a long, slow process. Yet the fossil evidence tells us that living cells existed on Earth only a billion years after the Earth formed. It makes the job of the biologists seeking to explain the emergence of life much easier if they envisage the Earth's early atmosphere, and oceans, laced with a brew of molecules such as formaldehyde and the rest, perhaps as a result of the impact of a comet with our planet. But Hoyle and Wickramasinghe go far further with their speculations.

First, Hoyle suggests that almost all of the Earth's atmosphere and water is the inheritance of a cometary impact, or series of cometary impacts. This is a controversial suggestion, and most astronomers and geophysicists accept that the Earth's atmosphere could have been produced entirely from the "outgassing" of water vapor and other gases by volcanoes, a process that is happening today and has presumably happened throughout antiquity. Why invoke unknown phenomena to explain what can be explained very well by known phenomena? Then, Hoyle interprets the statistics of living molecules as implying that the Earth is too small, the time scale available too short, and life itself too complex for molecules such as amino acids and DNA to have evolved on Earth, even starting from a chemical brew including the carbon compounds identified in interstellar clouds. Four and a half billion years ago, he says, the Earth was too hot for any organic molecules to persist; 3.8 billion years ago, life had arrived. "A hitherto sterile Earth might be said to have become infected with life." Where did

it come from? The answer, according to the two Cardiff researchers, is that it came from outside—that not just precursors to life
but living cells, bacteria, exist in interstellar space.

Hoyle and Wickramasinghe had been trying for twenty years to
explain the observed spectral properties of dust grains in space,
without success. They do not tell us just why they decided to compare this interstellar extinction curve, as it is called, with the spectrum of a mass of bacteria—a decision which Hoyle himself describes as an "outlandish idea," no doubt with intentional pun—
but try they did, convincing themselves, if few other people, that
a mass of dormant, dehydrated bacteria forming a cloud in space
would have exactly the observed properties of interstellar dust
clouds. The implied mass of bacterial cells in our own Galaxy alone
is about 10 million times the mass of our Sun.

From this jumping-off point, they have proceeded to a series of
striking conclusions. One, rather outside the scope of the present
book, is that many terrestrial diseases such as influenza, which strike
suddenly and infect many people before dying away, are actually
brought from the skies, trails of bacteria or viruses following cometary orbits around the Sun and infecting the Earth at more or less
regular intervals. This has no direct relevance to cosmology. But
working in the other direction, Hoyle has returned to the more
conventional astrophysical scene with views transformed by his
thoughts about life. Life is so subtle and complex, in his new view,
that its origins transcend not just our Solar System but even our
Galaxy, and the Big Bang Universe. He speculates that biology
may actually be in control of astronomical processes—"if the min-
uscule Earth can produce a creature with our own measure of intelligence, the whole galaxy should be able to manage an intelligence to which the manipulation of astronomical processes would
be reasonably straightforward"—and that the explosion of a galaxy
like M82, with its vast outpouring of matter, could be life's way of
seeding the Universe.

This has direct bearing on the classic philosophical counter to
Tipler's argument. Perhaps we do not recognize evidence of intelligent life because we are too stupid to know it when we see it.
Can we recognize signs of intelligence at work in our Solar System
any more than a flea sees signs of intelligence in the behavior of a
man? Like the debate about the number of angels that can dance
on a pinhead, that point can be discussed forever without reaching
a conclusion. But Hoyle goes further. "Life is even too complex

for it to be confined within our galaxy alone. The resources of the whole universe were almost surely needed for its development." Now, indeed, we are back to cosmology. But not the standard Big Bang cosmology of a white hole universe exploding outward from a singularity.

Hoyle accepts that the observed expansion provides a key insight into the nature of the Universe. But he sees the "age" of the Universe derived from studies of its expansion not as the true age since some unique beginning, but as a characteristic time scale, a repeating rhythm, or cycle time. Times and distances greatly beyond our observable bubble of spacetime provide the imaginative theorist with room to reinvent the steady state theory, or a variation on it. And the motivation for such ideas comes, in Hoyle's view, from the need for more time to explain how life could have evolved at all—"opening the cosmic time-axis into the past" as he puts it. Life represents a lot of information, which needed an enormously longer timespan than 15 billion years to build up, according to Hoyle. So now we have arrived at the opposite conclusion from Tipler. He says that if the Universe were in a steady state then it would be overrun with intelligent life, and that since we do not see it then the Universe must have a finite age. Not at all, we can imagine Hoyle replying. Life could never evolve at all in a universe like the standard Big Bang model, so the Universe must be in a steady state or we wouldn't be here. And besides, the place does seem to be swarming with intelligent life, if we could only recognize its activity represented by phenomena such as quasars and exploding galaxies.

I do not intend to take sides in this argument. If anything, I think that both are wrong. But having pointed to some obvious flaws in Tipler's ideas, it is only fair to poke a couple of holes in Hoyle's. First, if space is full of bacteria and the Earth has been seeded with life from space, why are our neighboring planets, Venus and Mars, so barren? Without going into details, we have the technology to seed Venus with bacteria ourselves, and in a few hundred million years they would transform its present superdense atmosphere into something much more Earthlike. It is a great surprise, if we take Hoyle and Wickramasinghe's published arguments at face value, that any planet in the Galaxy should not be rich in life. The second argument tackles Hoyle and Wickramasinghe, and by implication others who argue along the same lines, on statistical grounds.

The Odds in Favor

How probable is it that life evolved on Earth, in strictly mathematical terms? The Hoyle-Wickramasinghe argument is that the
basic constituent of life is a chain of amino acid molecules, containing perhaps twenty different kinds in a typical cell. There is a choice
from as many as thirty amino acids which have to be in the "right"
places in the chain for it to do its job, and the chance of such a
chain being put together at random is 20^{-30}, or 10^{-40}. Since a cell
needs a thousand such chains, or enzymes, the chance of a living
cell appearing spontaneously is $10^{40,000}$ to 1 against. But no evolutionary biologist seriously suggests that the first cell appeared as a
result of the random sticking together of thousands of molecules in
this way! The enzyme system of a cell is thought to have evolved
from simpler systems, and H.N.V. Temperley, writing in *New
Scientist* (19 August 1982) explained how such a "simpler system"
might be built up from one or two enzymes. One enzyme is needed
to act as a "jig" for the manufacture of other enzymes, and one
might be needed to act as a "cutter" to separate pieces of chain.
All that life needs for evolution to do its work is a large number of
such chains, which are protein molecules; and the one or two simple enzymes needed to churn out the chains could indeed arise
from ordinary chemical processes in the oceans of the cooling Earth.
Professor Temperley, who recently retired from the Department
of Applied Mathematics at University College, Swansea, calculates
that with a volume of 10^{15} cubic cm of coastal water in which to
work, and 10^{20} amino acid molecules in each cubic centimeter,
chemical reactions proceed at such a rate that 10^{60} configurations
would have been "tried out" during the history of the Earth. The
"spare" factor of 10^{20} in the calculation, compared with Hoyle's
erroneous estimate, tells us that not only is this process virtually
certain to have happened when the Earth was young, but that there
is a very fair chance of something much more complex than Temperley's simple system evolving from chemistry.

Of course, it is all just number juggling. The point is not that
Temperley's numbers are necessarily the best, but that Hoyle's
numbers are certainly not the best. However, there is another reason for taking note of what Temperley says. He is the author of a
book called *A Scientist Who Believes in God,* * and says, "My conclusion, which, for religious reasons I do not particularly like, is

---

*London: Hodder and Stoughton, 1961.

that what must surely have been the first step in the evolution of the primitive soup could have occurred by accident and that it is therefore unnecessary to invoke either divine creation or the appearance of proto-life from interstellar space to 'explain' the initial step." Here is a man whose own religious feelings are strong enough for him to have stood up to be counted among the scientific community, but whose faith in science is such that he is equally ready to be counted on the side of evolutionary theory, and who can accept the evidence that life could have evolved here on Earth.

Wherever life did begin, though, the chemical reactions which produced the first amino acid chains themselves depended on the nature of atoms and molecules, and the forces acting between them. The religious scientist can still keep faith with both God and science by seeing the rules by which the Universe works as God's design. Many scientists, indeed, see it as more than a coincidence that life like us should inhabit a planet like the Earth, circling a star like our Sun, at this particular moment in the evolution of the Universe. They do not usually talk about the hand of God, or God's design, but rather of the "anthropic principle," the puzzle that the Universe seems to be tailor-made for man.

The Anthropic Principle

In its modern form, the anthropic principle stems from an investigation by Princeton's Robert Dicke, in the 1960s, of some strange numerical coincidences noticed by Paul Dirac thirty years earlier. When physicists make measurements in the real world, they find that while many measurements, or equations, involve the quantities of length, time, and mass in various combinations (like $E = mc^2$), some numbers without any of these dimensions can be constructed by suitable juggling of the equations so that the dimensions cancel out. These "dimensionless constants" must reveal something fundamental about the nature of the Universe, runs the argument,* and the curiosity Dirac noticed is that several of these numbers come out to have the same, rather large, value—10^{40}.

One of these numbers is a measure, in dimensionless terms, of the strength of the gravitational force (10^{-40}); another represents a dimensionless measure of the age of the Universe (10^{40}); and a third is an estimate of the number of particles, protons and neutrons, in the Universe (10^{80}, which is the square of 10^{40}). Taking just the

*This is discussed in more detail in the next chapter.

first two of these, it seems strange at first sight that if we multiply the age of the Universe by the strength of gravity we get the "answer" 1. After all, the Universe is getting older all the time, so why should we just happen to be living at the special time when this relationship holds? Dicke answered the question by pointing out that people like us can only be around to ask questions like this at a certain stage in the life of the Universe. In order for people to be here at all, the original hydrogen and helium mixture of universal material must have been processed inside stars, in thermonuclear reactions, to make the heavier elements, notably carbon, on which life as we know it depends. The rate at which this process goes on depends on the strength of gravity. If gravity were stronger, stars would have to burn their nuclear fuel more rapidly to hold themselves up against gravity.

Our kind of life only exists in a Big Bang universe at a time after stars have formed, and before the universe has aged so much that most stars have died. So we must be here at a time in the evolution of the Universe which is closely linked to the strength of gravity, because that is what decides how quickly stars burn out.

These ideas can be extended to other properties of the Universe. The cosmologists calculate that there is an almost infinite variety of universes which could have emerged out of the Big Bang, and ponder over the reasons why our Universe should have come out with just the kind of properties it has—why, for instance, it sits so very close to the dividing line between being "open" or "closed." The conditions which lead to a universe like the one we live in are very restrictive. It has to be almost uniform, so that it expands nicely, but with just enough irregularity to produce galaxies and stars; it can't expand too slowly, or it will recollapse before stars ever form, and it can't expand too fast, or it will spread matter too thin for stars to form; and so on. The point is that all of these restrictions are requirements for the presence of life—specifically, for terrestrial, or human, life.

Brandon Carter, of the University of Cambridge, has expressed the implications most cogently in recent years. Copernicus revolutionized astronomy by demonstrating that we must not assume that we occupy a special place in the Universe, in particular that we are not at the center of the Universe. Modern cosmology depends on the assumption that the Universe is much the same everywhere, and looks the same in all directions, so that our view is a typical view. But Carter argues that the kind of coincidences I have just outlined show that we do live at a special *time* in the evolution of the Universe. What we observe in the Universe, says Carter, "must be restricted by the conditions necessary for our presence as observers," so that our position, while not being central, is inevitably "privileged" to some extent. This is the anthropic principle—not that the Universe is tailor-made for man, but that man can only exist to observe the Universe when certain conditions have been met.

Dennis Sciama, of the University of Oxford, is among the theorists who have pointed out some startling implications of this principle. All parts of the Universe are related to one another, and stem from the original Big Bang. If we understood thoroughly just how the pieces were put together, and how the interactions worked, it ought to be possible, in principle, to deduce all of the properties of the Universe by studying our local region. It seems quite likely, for instance, that there must be large numbers of distant galaxies, or there would be no life on Earth. More extravagantly, it might be possible in principle to deduce how fast the Universe is expanding, and whether it is open or closed, from such everyday observations as the temperature at which water boils. This is something for debate among the philosopher cosmologists rather than an issue of practical importance to astronomy today. But it is not the most extreme version of the anthropic principle, and it leads us into interesting territory, familiar to readers of *Timewarps* but worth touching on again.

If there is nothing in the laws of physics which says that the Universe had to turn out the way it is, but on the other hand it turns out to be one of the few variations on the cosmological theme in which we could have evolved, what has happened to all the "lost" versions of the Universe? Isn't it still odd that, just by chance, the Big Bang gave birth to a universe in which our sort of life is possible at all? There are two types of answer to this puzzle. The first stems from work by Hugh Everett, of Princeton University, and is based on the idea of uncertainty in the theoretical description of particle physics, called quantum mechanics.

The underlying principle of this work is that at a fundamental level it is impossible to decide whether fundamental entities, such as electrons or quarks, are particles or waves. An electron "in orbit" around an atomic nucleus, for example, is better thought of as smeared around the atom, with a finite probability of being anywhere in this shell at any time. When we make a measurement of such an object using the techniques of particle physics, however, we locate it at a definite position—we don't find half an electron here, a quarter over there, and the rest somewhere else. The wave function, which is such a useful description of the general behavior of the particle, seems to have collapsed into one point in space-time. Was the particle "really" there all the time? This is a puzzle which has caused intense debate among the experts for decades. Everett's answer is that the electron, or whatever, is "really" at all of the places the wave function says it can be, and that there is a separate world (a separate universe) corresponding to each possibility. For obvious reasons, this is called the "many worlds" interpretation of quantum mechanics. What happens when we make a measurement is that we select one possibility from an infinite range of probabilities, collapsing the wave function as far as we are concerned, but leaving the other worlds, real but unknowable, somewhere off to one side in spacetime.

Parallel Worlds

It is important to stress that this strange idea is entirely consistent with every experiment and every observation ever made. Yet, coming up from the level of particles to everyday life, it implies that there are real worlds, or universes, corresponding to every imaginable, and unimaginable, variation on the historical or cosmological theme. There really are universes where gravity is stronger, or weaker; there is a world where the United States never gained independence from Britain, and one where Europe was colonized by travelers from the Americas; and so on. But this is still not the end of the story. John Wheeler, of the University of Texas at Austin, takes the quantum mechanical argument a step further by pointing out that the "wave function" would never collapse at all unless someone was around to make an observation. This doesn't just mean poking around inside the atom with a particle accelerator; the term "observation" also applies in its more everyday sense of looking at things. The infinite array of possible quantum mechanical worlds only loses its ghostly aspect when life appears to take note of its surroundings. "Quantum mechanics has led us," says Wheeler, "to take seriously [the view] that the observer is as essential to the creation of the universe as the universe is to the creation of the observer."

Because all of the universe is interconnected, this applies with equal strength to the reality of the Universe now and in the past. A universe can still exist before observers appear to notice it; like Tipler's time machine which exists forever once it has appeared for an instant, one quick look at the entire universe is enough to collapse all of the wave functions describing it and ensure its physical reality throughout its life.

This really is the ultimate version of the anthropic principle. But there is still the other variation on the theme. So far, I have described alternative universes existing in some sense parallel to our own, displaced sideways in time. But suppose they follow our own Universe in some sort of chronological sequence? Some theorists, Wheeler again prominent among them, have suggested that if our Universe is indeed closed and will ultimately collapse back into a cosmic fireball, then it may represent just one link in a chain of such universes. Each collapse into the fireball is followed by rebirth, phoenixlike, from the fire, but each "new" universe will have its own properties, its own constants of nature (like the strength of gravity), and perhaps even its own laws of physics. Out of the infinite chain of such cycles, conditions which allow life to evolve occur very rarely. From here on, the argument is the same. We see such an unusual Universe around us because life like us can only evolve in such a universe. We are here because we are here, because we are here.

There is a counterargument to all of this, however. Some theorists argue that the state of the Universe is not so unusual at all, and that even if it started out nonhomogeneous and anisotropic early in the Big Bang, various interactions involving gravity, neutrinos, and so on would soon smear it into a uniform, homogeneous, and isotropic state. And there are even speculations about the nature of the Big Bang itself in the context of quantum mechanics. We have already encountered the physics underlying the speculation in the context of evaporating black holes. "Empty" spacetime can produce a pair of particles out of nothing. It can also produce a whole universe out of nothing, if you wait long enough. At the beginning there is a singularity, before which the universe does not exist, and there must also be a corresponding singularity at the end, after which the universe does not exist. The whole thing is simply a quantum fluctuation of the vacuum.

Such an occurrence is extremely unlikely, but has a nonzero probability. If the universe is "really" nothing but infinite empty spacetime, then at some places in that empty spacetime there will be fluctuations like our Universe—yet another variation on the many worlds theme, but with the interesting implication, established by Ya. B. Zel'dovich of the USSR Academy of Sciences, that all of the variations on the theme must be closed. An open universe can never be created by this process, because that would violate the conservation of energy and matter; matter and energy can be conserved in a closed universe, because everything eventually disappears back into the singularity.

This is as far as we can push such speculations today. There is a recurring theme here, though, which is perhaps the most important insight provided by this seeming confusion of ideas. All of the ideas incorporate, in one way or another, the idea that there is much more to spacetime than our little bubble. Hoyle says that the Universe may be infinite in time and space; Everett implies that there is an infinite variety of worlds across time; Wheeler suggests that an infinite number of universes follow one another in time; Zel'dovich speculates that a truly infinite array of empty spacetime may be pockmarked with temporary bubbles, quantum fluctuations, in one of which we live. And all of these exotic ideas are within the framework of physics as we know it—general relativity and quantum mechanics. It is astonishing that the theories developed on Earth can be pushed so far. But a few theorists go further. It is one thing to speculate that gravity may be different in another universe, or another cycle of our Universe. It is something rather different, and much closer to home, to speculate that gravity may vary as time passes in our own little bubble of spacetime, over the interval since the Big Bang. Everything in this book so far has been, in a sense, a tribute to the power of Einstein's theory. It is fitting, perhaps, to close with a look at the work of theorists probing beyond Einstein's vision of the Universe.

10

Beyond Einstein?

Einstein's theory is not the last word. Should it be scrapped in favor of a better description of the Universe? Or can a new theory be constructed that incorporates Einstein's ideas within it? Does gravity change as the Universe ages? "Supergravity" and the grand unification of physics.

The idea that gravity may vary with time occasionally generates "gee whiz" headlines. But behind those headlines lies a search for a deeper understanding of the Universe, unifying gravity with the other forces of nature. The Holy Grail of modern theoretical physics is the development of a unified theory in which gravity can be related to the other three fundamental forces—the strong and weak forces within the nucleus of the atom, and electromagnetism. One way to develop such a theory is to look at what happens to the laws of physics at very high energies, equivalent, in a cosmological context, to the early phases of the Big Bang in which, most cosmologists believe, the Universe was born. The basic idea behind a

unified theory is that all of the four fundamental forces—the strong
and weak nuclear forces, electromagnetism, and gravity—are facets of the same fundamental interaction which become independent of one another as the energy density of the Universe de-
creases and they decouple, breaking the original symmetries.

Gravity is so much weaker than the other forces that it is no
surprise that it is the last to be included in this new understanding
of physics, or, from the other point of view, that it was the first to
go its own way early in the history of the Universe. For the same
reason, the study of gravitational interactions in the large—the study
of the evolution of the whole Universe since the Big Bang—has
seemed for half a century to be a very different area of study from
the study of particle physics. But many cosmologists have been
concerned about the nature of gravity in much the same way that
particle physicists have been concerned about the nature of the
other fundamental forces. In particular, just as particle physicists
seek for symmetries and invariant properties of the forces that fall
within their domain, so cosmologists have worried over the asymmetries that are part and parcel of the theory of gravity. There are
many kinds of symmetry inherent in the physical laws which seem
to describe the Universe so well. The laws of motion, for example,
are time-symmetric, which means that the behavior of a collection
of bouncing snooker balls, say, follows Newton's laws both in the
real world and if we film their motion and then run the film backward (the same would be true of the motion of the planets in their
orbits around the Sun). Magnetism is symmetric in another sense,
having two equal and opposite polarities which may attract or repel
with equal strength; and electricity comes in two varieties, negative or positive. But there is only one kind of gravity; it always
attracts. Some of these concepts, and their deeper implications,
are discussed by Paul Davies in his book *The Forces of Nature.* *

The problem is that theorists would like to be able to describe
gravity mathematically using a theory—a set of equations—which
is scale invariant. Our understanding of the physical world is unchanged whether we measure in centimeters or meters, even
though the numbers that come out of our measurements differ by
a scale factor of 100. The way the Universe works "ought" to be
similarly independent of the scale of our measuring system. The
truth of the equations should not depend on the units by which

*Cambridge University Press, 1979.

we measure the parameters in the equations—but general relativity, the theory which is widely regarded as providing our best theoretical description of gravity and the Universe, is not scale invariant. Cosmologists describe the Universe in terms of coordinates, such as R and t to describe distances and times, and a good theory of the Universe should not depend on the coordinates we use. General relativity is, indeed, coordinate invariant. Replacing R and t by some function of R and t does not change the physical description of the Universe. But it also seems reasonable that the laws of physics should be independent of the scale of the coordinate system used, and at this point general relativity diverges from common sense.

Many cosmologists, therefore, have tried to find a theory of gravity that is scale invariant, the important point being that general relativity is not naturally a scale invariant theory, although scale invariance can be built into it. General relativity is a geometrical theory that describes the behavior of the Universe in terms of the geometry of curved spacetime. So the most fundamental quantity in the equations of relativity is the variable that corresponds to a measure of length. This is known as the line element, and is usually written d*s*. But d*s* has the dimensions of length, and if we change scales, even by such a simple step as swapping our measuring rods marked in meters for ones marked in centimeters, its size alters. Many theorists see this as undesirable.

Variable Gravity

One way in which scale invariance can be built into a theory of the Universe is to allow gravity to vary with time. This is the approach described by Vittorio Canuto, of the NASA Goddard Institute for Space Studies in New York.* The importance of this work is not actually that gravity varies with time, but that by choosing the right kind of variability for gravity, scale invariance can be built in to the system of equations developed by Einstein to describe the Universe. The goal of a scale invariant theory is the rationale behind most of the work on variable gravity cosmologies, cosmologies which might otherwise seem like exotic theoretical blooms with little root in reality. In fact, such studies are a fully respect-

*One article has recently appeared in the guide *Cosmology Today*, which I edited for *New Scientist*. See Bibliography.

able branch of cosmology, even though the occasional bursts of
publicity for the idea that gravity may be getting weaker, say, tend
to give the impression that they form part of the lunatic fringe.
One such speculation can be taken here to provide an example of
the way in which a different approach to an old problem can provide new insights.

In 1981, Paul Wesson, of the University of Alberta, Edmonton,
and Ron Goodson, of the Canadian Armed Forces, reported in the
journal *The Observatory* a bibliographical survey that listed 1,300
papers on variable-G cosmology published up to the beginning of
1979, and noted wearily that after that date Wesson "gave up in
despair his attempts to keep tabs on the subject" (*The Observatory*, vol. 101, p. 105).

Variable-G cosmologies have received most attention recently in
the form proposed by Vittorio Canuto and his coworkers. Recently, however, Ajit Kembhavi and Martin Pollock at the Institute of Astronomy in Cambridge have argued that Canuto's theory
does not stand up to detailed inspection—the Canuto model contains, they say, a scale invariant part and a scale breaking part, and
depending on how you choose to boil the equations down you either
end up with the equivalent of Einstein's equations and no variable-
G, or you end up with variable-G at the expense of including terms
which break the scale invariance (*Monthly Notices of the Royal
Astronomical Society*, vol. 197, p. 1087). This is a matter for esoteric debate among the specialists. But it does highlight the important point that the real name of the game is not variable-G, but
scale invariance. Recently Paul Wesson has been looking in detail
at the whole business of constructing scale invariant cosmologies
without invoking variable-G. His results show how, by applying
the same philosophical approach to the problem that particle physicists apply to the problems they tackle, it is possible to discern a
glimmer of a relationship between the very large (the Universe
itself) and the very small (the world of elementary particles).

The first serious attempt to construct a scale invariant cosmology
was made, as I hinted in the previous chapter, by Paul Dirac in
1938, who built on strange numerical coincidences originally noticed by Sir Arthur Eddington. Now let's look at those coincidences in a little more detail. The size of the electrical force between the proton and electron in a hydrogen atom is given by e^2/r^2
(neglecting a dimensionless constant), and the gravitational force
between the same two particles is $Gm_p m_e/r^2$. The ratio of these two

forces is a large dimensionless number, of the order of 10^{40}. Nothing remarkable in that, but if we define an atomic unit of time in terms of the charge on the electron, its mass, and the speed of light we have a unit e^2/mc^3. This is a very small unit, on the order of 10^{-23} seconds, and measured in such units the age of the Universe, about 10^{10} years, becomes 10^{40} atomic units of time. In other words, the ratio of the electrical and gravitational forces operating in an atom is strikingly similar to the ratio of the time scale appropriate for the Universe and the time scale appropriate for an atom. The age of the Universe appears in the calculation, so if all of the other numbers are true constants then this result is a very remarkable coincidence, true only at the present epoch of the Universe.

Like Eddington before him, Dirac found this too much of a coincidence to swallow, and argued that the two large numbers are in fact exactly equal, now and at every epoch. For this to be so, at least one of the "constants" in the equations must vary with time, and the simplest way to achieve the desired effect is to allow gravity to decrease as the Universe ages. Dirac developed a complete cosmology along these lines, with gravity declining at a fractional rate of 10^{-10} parts per year—well within the limits that can be set by observations of astronomical objects such as the Sun and Moon, and their orbits around one another. In the 1970s, Dirac returned to this field of study and developed his ideas further, to include matter creation within the framework of a variable-G scale invariant cosmology. Meanwhile, very similar ideas had been developed by Fred Hoyle and Jayant Narlikar, starting from a very different philosophical base. Their interest started from the steady state model of the Universe and concern about the possibility that the red shifts in distant galaxies and quasars may not be entirely due to the Doppler effect of recession in the expanding Universe.

The equations with which any theory describes the behavior of the Universe are the equations of motion of the Universe at large, and in the context of the curvature of spacetime discovered by Einstein the key feature is that they describe the motion of particles, or light, along the equivalent of straight lines through curved spacetime. These "straight lines" are known as geodesics, and P. Bouvier and A. Maeder, of the Geneva Observatory in Switzerland, have shown that the geodesic equations of all of these variable-G cosmologies are in fact identical. Dirac, Hoyle and Narlikar and others in recent years have all been tackling the same problem, albeit from different directions. They developed the same theory, derived from different starting points (*Astrophysics and Space Science*, vol. 54, p. 497; *Astronomy and Astrophysics*, vol. 79, p. 158).

Although variable-G cosmologies do not predict any change in G too great to be consistent with the known dynamical behavior of the Solar System, studies of the binary pulsar (PSR 1913+16) have closed in the limits on any possible variation of gravity with time, and it now looks as if a variation as large as 10^{-10} per year may not be happening in the real Universe in which we live. This, however, does not spell the end for scale invariant cosmologies, as there are other approaches which do not require G to be noticeably variable after all.

The numerical coincidences noticed by Eddington and Dirac depend on the construction of dimensionless numbers out of the equations of physics—ratios of forces, or of times, so that the dimensions themselves cancel out. Such dimensionless constants clearly tell us something important about the physical systems they describe, as a simple example makes clear. For an object with mass M and radius R, there is a unique dimensionless number GM/Rc^2 which decides whether or not the object is a black hole. Compress the object (that is, decrease R) until the dimensionless number reaches the value ½, and it can no longer hold itself up against the pull of its own gravity. This is true whatever units we measure in—change from the metric system to good old British units and all the numbers G, M, c, and R change, but the value of GM/Rc^2, which is the physically significant thing, does not. This is just a change of units, but the dimensionless constants are also invariant under scale changes. Gravity does not change alone, but a combination of changes "conspires," as Wesson puts it, to keep GM/Rc^2 the same. G and M may change, for example, so that their product doubles in size; as long as R and c vary at the same time in such a way that the denominator also doubles, we do not change the numerical value of the fraction itself, the number that determines whether or not an object is a black hole.

A New Theory

The concept of such dimensionless numbers provides the philosophical basis for Wesson's latest approach to scale invariant cosmology. Although it has so far failed to set the world on fire or make headline news, it is certainly of some interest to both astronomers and particle physicists. He starts from the fact that all of physics can be described in terms of quantities having dimensions composed of the three fundamental parameters: mass (M), length (L), and time (T). Particle physics involves three fundamental constants: e, $\hbar$, and c, which have the dimensions (denoted by square brackets) $[e] = M^{1/2}L^{3/2}T^{-1}$, $[h] = ML^2T^{-1}$, and $[c] = LT^{-1}$. These form a complete set of parameters, in the sense that only one dimensionless number can be formed from them. Gravitational theory—cosmology—on the other hand contains only two constants, c, which also enters into particle physics, and G, which has the dimensions $[G] = M^{-1}L^3T^{-2}$. No dimensionless constant can be formed from two numbers which themselves have different dimensionality, and so there is no gravitational counterpart to the dimensionless number of particle physics. Theorists such as Wesson argue that this implies that, in some fundamental sense, gravitational theory is incomplete.

Wesson has attempted to complete gravitational theory, in this sense, by looking at the way the four fundamental constants relevant to particle physics and cosmology (e, $\hbar$, c, and G) can be reconstructed to reveal fundamental physical properties of nature (*Physical Review* D, vol. 23, p. 1730). There are, for example, two constant masses $(e^2/G)^{1/2}$ and $(\hbar c/G)^{1/2}$ which emerge from the manipulations, and these combine to give a dimensionless ratio $e^2/\hbar c$. This is the fine structure constant, one of the most fundamental constants of atomic physics. "In other words," says Wesson, "if one is to find a way to a grand unified theory, it is expected to involve combinations of dimensional physical constants that do not yield other dimensional constants but rather dimensionless constants." The approach owes more to particle physics than cosmology, and it leads to a simple prediction of the constant required to plug the gap in gravitational theory. We need a third constant to complete the theory, says Wesson, so we will choose one and dub it p. Because we already have G and c, and we require the presence of one dimensionless constant formed from a combination of G, c, and p, we know that the dimensions of the new constant must be $[p] = M^{-1}L^2T^{-1}$. In the physical world, this is equivalent to saying that p must be a constant that relates angular momentum (J) and mass (M) in such a way that $J = pM^2$. Starting from an obvious asymmetry in the equations of physics, Wesson has produced a new equation, a prediction that the angular momentum of a rotating system dominated by gravity is proportional to the square of its mass.

There is no theory, as yet, that incorporates G, p, and c explicitly, although of course general relativity should turn out to be a special case of such a theory, with p going to zero. But it is very easy to test the prediction $J = p\mathrm{M}^2$. The equation only holds in a system where gravity is the only force present, so it can hardly be tested in the laboratory, where the objects we might whirl around to study are held together by electrical forces and affected by viscosity, solid state effects, and so on. The smallest object for which gravity really dominates is a planet, and the dominance of gravity over the other forces of physics increases as we go to larger scales. So Wesson has compared the angular momentum/mass relations of planets, double stars, star clusters, galaxies, and clusters of galaxies. In fact, the job had already been done for him. Peter Brosche, of the University of Bonn, has made just such a study, derived from a great deal of observational data. Using a logarithmic plot, he ends up with a straight line relationship with a slope of two, exactly as the $J = p\mathrm{M}^2$ relation requires.

Figure 10.1 Angular momentum is proportional to mass squared. Why?

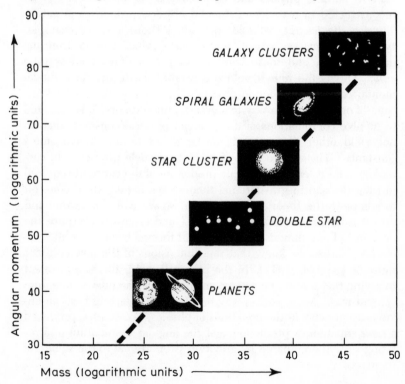

The data indicate a value for p of about 8×10^{-16} $g^{-1}cm^2sec^{-1}$, although this is less important than the hint that such a constant may have a place in the real world. But it is certainly reassuring that the constant is small enough to leave general relativity as a good approximation to reality. When Einstein developed a theory of gravity that went beyond Newton's theory, he found that Newton's equations are part and parcel of the equations of relativity, a special case that applies when we are dealing with weak gravitational fields. Like Newton's theory before it, general relativity has been very successful, and it would be astonishing to find a new theory of gravity which required us to abandon relativity theory altogether. It is much more in line with the steady progress of physics that a new theory should give us the same answers as relativity in many cases, but differ from relativity under extreme circumstances.

The story doesn't stop here. The characteristic constant of particle physics is the fine structure constant, $e^2/\hbar c$, which has the numerical value $1/137$, about 7×10^{-3}. The equivalent dimensionless constant in the new gravitation is G/pc, which has a rather uncertain numerical value of 3×10^{-3}, based on estimates of mass and angular momentum of real objects such as galaxies and clusters of galaxies. It is even possible that the two constants have exactly the same numerical value—"there appears to be only one dimensionless coupling constant . . . which just happens to turn up in two different (physical) guises," says Wesson, and this suggests that particle physics and gravitation may indeed be unified.

In mathematical terminology, the two subjects may be different representations of the same group, and their apparent differences may be a result of the very large differences in the mathematical languages that have been used to describe them. "The language mismatch," says Wesson, "is considerable, but there are signs that a link might be made."

So scale invariant cosmology is not an exotic bloom of no serious worth, but an attempt to get at the very heart of the nature of the physical world, a path toward the unification of gravity with the other fundamental forces in one self-consistent theory. The particular approach of Paul Wesson's that I have used as an example may not be the correct approach—although the angular momentum information derived by Peter Brosche must be telling us something about the nature of the Universe—but the search for symmetries

and completeness in the equations governing gravitational interactions is clearly a lot more than idle numerology.

Spacetime Bubbles

Scale invariant cosmologies can also provide a new perspective
on the Big Bang. I mentioned in Chapter Five that an alternative
way of looking at the Universe sees the Hubble red shift not as the
product of universal expansion away from a spacetime singularity,
but as due to the increase of mass of every particle in the Universe
as time passes. This is a scale invariant model of the Universe, one
which has been developed in detail by Fred Hoyle, Jayant Narlikar, and their colleagues. Within the framework of this model, there
are no spacetime singularities, but there are epochs—"places" in
spacetime—when particle masses vanish. This not only removes the
Big Bang singularity, but other singularities in spacetime, such as
the ones associated, in conventional relativistic cosmology, with
black holes.

Narlikar says that it helps to visualize the resulting model universe by imagining spacetime divided into different regions by what
he calls "zero mass surfaces." Inside one such bubble of spacetime,
mass may be positive or it may be negative, but it is the same
throughout the bubble; across the zero mass surface, mass has the
opposite sign, and so on. Just as in the spacetime diagrams of standard relativity theory, we can imagine the world lines of particles
extending across spacetime, and always keeping within their own
light cones. But what happens to a test particle when its world line
crosses a zero mass surface, passes through the bubble of spacetime inside it, and out the other side? To an observer whose world
line passes outside the enclosed bubble, this is equivalent, in terms
of general relativity, to the test particle first falling into a black
hole and then emerging from the singularity, bursting outward from
a white hole. The emergence from a singularity is exactly equivalent to the emergence of the Universe from the Big Bang singularity. But in the framework of scale invariant cosmology, although
mass does peculiar things there is no singularity and the test particle can proceed serenely through the spacetime bubble, crossing
the zero mass surface twice.

This alternative view of the Universe has provided Narlikar and
his colleagues with the incentive to investigate the properties of
white holes. Their main conclusion is that such objects can exist,
providing large bursts of energy into our Universe, but that an

amount of matter equivalent to a hundred thousand Suns is needed to give a high energy burst lasting just one second. This doesn't look too promising for anyone trying to explain quasar outbursts in such terms, but it does suggest that there may be something in the observable Universe that is beyond explanation in terms of standard relativity theory. It is certainly worth looking for these white holes, since their discovery would profoundly influence how cosmologists view the Universe. And, as Narlikar says, "whatever their conceptual shortcomings within relativity, the white holes hold one advantage over black holes. They are readily and directly observable." *

Revolutionary Thoughts

Other maverick theorists are less cautious in their assessment of the inadequacies of relativity theory. Victor Clube, of the Royal Observatory in Edinburgh, is one who has argued that we stand on the brink of a revolution in astronomy. After looking at all the evidence of bizarre phenomena in our Universe, including exploding galaxies, quasars with jets, and the anomalous red shifts, he concludes that something much more radically different even than Narlikar's ideas is needed to explain what is going on, and he believes that evidence of this radically different activity can be seen even in the behavior of the stars of our own Milky Way Galaxy. The key to this argument is the fact that although general relativity has stood every test so far, all of those tests involve what are really rather weak gravitational fields. The only exception (until somebody actually finds a black hole, brings it home, and measures its properties) might be the Big Bang itself, but even there what we see is outward explosion, not inward collapse. Clube's scenario, developed in collaboration with M. E. Bailey,** goes something like this.

We don't know what happens in the final stages of gravitational collapse, and our theory of gravity, good though it has proved in the case of weak fields, is not so securely established that we can trust it in the ultimate limit of such a collapse. We see explosions and outbursts at the centers of many galaxies—the quasar phenomenon being the most extreme example—and it looks as if all gal-

---

*Violent Phenomena in the Universe, p. 176. See also Narlikar's article in New Scientist, vol. 97, 24 February 1983, p. 516.
** See Clube's contribution to Cosmology Today.

axies go through such phases from time to time, perhaps at more or less regular intervals. Suppose that a massive object lies at the heart of the Milky Way, and that a similar object lies at the nucleus of each galaxy. When this object collapses due to the inward tug of gravity, it reaches a point where its behavior can no longer be described by the equations of general relativity. It first becomes highly supermassive, and then "bounces" outward again from the superdense, supermassive state, restoring what we think of as normality.

This looks like a very peculiar pattern of behavior, but it could explain many observations. First, it is one (rather contrived) way of locating the "missing mass"—on this picture, all galaxies are supermassive for part of the time, and that explains the dynamics of clusters and other associations of galaxies. Second, and much more intriguingly, this kind of behavior repeated every hundred million years or so, and lasting for a few million years each time, could explain some oddities about the movements of stars in our Galaxy.

If events have followed the pattern sketched by Clube and Bailey, our Galaxy has been repeatedly squeezed and relaxed. When the supermass switches on, every star is tugged inward by gravity and the whole Galaxy becomes more compact; when the supermass switches off, it expands outward again. It happens that Seyfert and N-type galaxies seem to be more compact than our own, and that high red shift objects are in general compact. But this is no more than circumstantial evidence. In our Galaxy, there is some evidence of outward expansion, which can be neatly explained if the center of the Milky Way emerged from a supermass state about 50 million years ago. The Solar System, for example, is moving, together with our local group of stars, outward from the heart of the Galaxy at a rate of 40 km per second, which is unexpected if the Galaxy is in a state of equilibrium and has been for billions of years. That is not to say that all of Clube's ideas are right, but it does point to interesting areas of research for theorists trying to probe beyond Einstein. If there is a better description of gravity than general relativity, then that better theory must tell us more about very strong gravitational fields and very high densities of matter than relativity does, while at the same time it must be exactly equivalent to general relativity in the weak field case.

But there is another way to probe beyond the reach of Einstein's theory. If we accept that general relativity is the best description of gravity, there is still the puzzle of how gravity and the other forces of nature can be combined into one great theory, which will contain within itself the explanations of both the very large (cosmology, gravity) and the very small (particle physics). We saw in Chapter Three how Grand Unified Theories (GUTs), incorporating all of the fundamental forces except gravity, have already proved their worth in the latest explanations of how the Universe emerged from the Big Bang, and how they provide at least a clue as to why the Universe contains matter without an equivalent amount of antimatter, and why it contains the amount of matter it does, compared with the amount of energy in the form of photons. But this is far from being the end of the story.

One of the underlying principles of this kind of study is symmetry. If the GUT interpretation of how the early Universe cooled from a superdense state into the state we see today is correct, we owe our existence to the breaking of some symmetries. At very high energy densities, the argument runs, all the fundamental forces were equally powerful and important; as the Universe cooled and thinned out, each force in turn fell by the wayside and went its own way as symmetry was broken. On a more modest scale, there is a lack of symmetry in the Universe in that it contains matter rather than antimatter, but this asymmetry is now seen as a consequence of the way the greater symmetries broke down. Can other visible asymmetries in the world about us be explained in similar fashion?

The Mainstream of Progress

According to the best unified theories, for example, electricity and magnetism ought to be completely symmetrical with respect to each other, and yet while single electric charges exist, until recently there has been no evidence that single magnetic poles—monopoles—exist. Magnets always seem to come in pairs, a north pole with a south pole, even though the GUTs predict that free monopoles should exist. This does not completely confound the theorists, since the GUTs may not be the last word. The previous step on the road to unified physics was a theory that combined electromagnetism and the weak nuclear force in one package, and that unified theory in itself does not predict magnetic monopoles, even though the GUTs, which add the strong nuclear interaction to the package, do. Nevertheless, the GUT prediction has led to some sophisticated experiments designed to catch any free monopole that may pass by, and in the early 1980s a couple of claims were made that one or more monopoles had been found. If those claims are borne out, they have far-reaching implications, since the GUTs tell us that the solo poles would have been made when the Universe was at least 10^{27} K hot, the point at which the energy density was low enough for the symmetry between the three interactions that are facets of the GUTs breakdown. Discovering just one monopole would imply that the Universe did indeed originate in a hot Big Bang. This story has echoes of the early days of the search for solar neutrinos, and in ten years' time there should be a story worth telling in detail. Meanwhile, there are other tests for the accuracy of GUTs. They predict that the proton itself should be an unstable particle, decaying with a lifetime of 10^{31} years. It isn't feasible to watch one proton and wait for it to decay, but in a mass of material a very few protons should decay by chance while they are being "watched." A joint Indian-Japanese team, monitoring a mass of 140 metric tons of iron buried in the Kolar Gold Fields, claims to have observed six events which might be explained by proton decay in the space of two years, a rate exactly right for this mass of material according to GUT theory.

So GUTs and the ideas of symmetry and symmetry breaking involving the fundamental interactions of physics are taken very seriously today. Some of the cosmological implications can be sketched in general terms, even though the ideas are so new, and are developing so rapidly, that it would be pointless to go into detail yet. One idea relates the expansion of the Universe itself to symmetry breaking. Just as changes in the phase of a substance from solid to liquid, or liquid to gas, are associated with changes in energy and temperature, so there are analogous "phase changes" early in the history of the Universe, associated with the breakdown of symmetry between interactions that started out with the same strength. According to some calculations, such phase changes can provide both the heat for the Big Bang and the origin of the outward expansion which is the most prominent feature of our Universe. In a tongue-in-cheek moment, theorists dubbed this model the "inflationary universe." Variations on the theme see our visible Universe as perhaps just one bubble of expanding, phase-changed material in a greater infinity of spacetime, or alternatively that in a "bouncing" universe it could be the phase changes associated with restoration of symmetry in the big crunch that halt the collapse and restore the universe to an expanding state.

It is all heady stuff. But even these speculations at the frontier of cosmological theorizing in the 1980s are still at least one step away from the big prize, the inclusion of gravity with the other forces of nature in one super-GUT, a supersymmetric theory. It is too early yet to be able to spell out the details of such a theory, but we may now just be able to see which kind of theory is most likely to emerge triumphant, perhaps before the end of this century. So, having begun this book with an instant guide to the best theory of gravity of the twentieth century, it seems appropriate to end with a similar guide, no matter how sketchy, to what might be the best theory of gravity of the twenty-first century.

Any such theory, unlike its predecessor general relativity, must include the interactions of particle physics. The first step toward such a theory is to look at the Universe in terms of matter ("particles") and forces between particles ("interactions"). The interactions themselves can be thought of as being carried by a different kind of particle from the matter particles, with electromagnetic forces, for example, operating by the exchange of photons between electrically charged matter particles, like a group of football players tied together by the rapid passing and repassing of the ball, or a set of balls. One essential difference between matter particles and interactions, however, is in the fundamental property which is called spin. Matter particles always have half-integer values of spin (½, 1½, 2½, and so on), but interactions have integer spin (1, 2, 3 . . .). This property is related to a phenomenon known as the Pauli Exclusion Principle, which holds that no two particles with half-integer spin can be in the same place at the same time. This is entirely in line with our everyday experience of matter particles, but it does not hold for interactions. For the record, we should also note that the matter particles can be subdivided into hadrons, which are composed of quarks, and leptons, which are not.

Interactions have integer spin and do not obey the Pauli Exclusion Principle. I have already mentioned the four basic interactions. In order of strength, they are the strong nuclear force, which interacts only with hadrons; electromagnetism, which interacts with all charged matter particles, hadrons or leptons; the weak nuclear force, which interacts with all hadrons and leptons; and gravity, by far the weakest, which interacts with everything. Two of the four interactions, gravity and electromagnetism, are long range; the other two operate only over a short range. The important consequence of this is that the fields associated with a collection of particles add up for gravity and electromagnetism to produce overall fields that can be detected at the macroscopic level. This, of course, is why they were the first two forces to be identified and investigated. General relativity, in a sense, combines the earlier theories of gravity (Newton's) and electromagnetism (Maxwell's), but it is deficient in the sense that it deals with quantities that are continuously variable and can be subdivided, in principle, to any accuracy. Such a theory is now called a "classical" theory. Study of the behavior of atoms and subatomic particles in the twentieth century has shown that quantum mechanics provides a better description of the workings of the Universe, at least at this level.

The underlying principle of quantum mechanics is that particles—such as an electron "in orbit" around an atomic nucleus—can only exist in certain places, separated by discrete intervals, or quanta. Similarly, energy cannot be emitted or absorbed by such a particle any old way, but only in quantities that are multiples of certain basic quantum units. This is fine when we are dealing with atoms. But it is much harder to apply to interactions, or particles isolated in space. The simplest version of quantum theory "predicts" that when an electron, for example, is not tied to an atom both its mass and its charge become infinite. There is a way to overcome this, called renormalization. The trick involves subtracting out infinite quantities from the equations in such a way that the amount left is the "correct" charge or mass. But the trick only works because we know the "answer," the mass and charge of the electron, that we are looking for. Renormalization could, in fact, give any value of mass and charge (or other quantities) that we chose, and we come back to the anthropic principle if pressed to provide a reason why such quantities should have the values they do have in our Universe. Renormalization smacks of "fiddling" the equations, but it is a fiddle which seems to work, and has now been extended to the unified theory of electromagnetism and the weak nuclear interaction, and to include the strong nuclear interaction in a theory of quarks called quantum chromodynamics.

From this approach, theorists have come up with the GUTs that suggest that at energies above 10^{15} GeV all the interactions except gravity combine into one field, that magnetic monopoles exist, and that protons decay. The fly in the ointment, however, is that gravity does not seem to be renormalizable. In order to get sensible, finite answers out of the equations involving gravity, it would be necessary to make an infinite number of infinite subtractions, which would leave an infinite number of unknown remainders. Yet there is a need for a unified theory including gravity, because even the classical theory—general relativity—predicts the existence of spacetime singularities, points in spacetime where, among other things, the strength of gravity becomes infinite. Before such extreme conditions are reached, the classical theory must become inadequate and quantum effects must become important. A quantum theory of gravity is essential if we are to develop an understanding of the earliest phase of the Big Bang universe, or of such exotic objects as black holes, white holes, and quasars. It would also help, perhaps, in explaining why the Universe possesses the detailed properties it has, without resorting to the anthropic principle. And it may be that such a theory will show that singularities cannot in fact occur, because of the importance of quantum effects in highly curved regions of spacetime, extreme spacewarps.

Supergravity

Most of the great theorists of the present day, such as Stephen Hawking of the University of Cambridge, see the best hope for a theory of gravity including quantum effects in an extension of general relativity called Supergravity. It is assumed, from analogy with other fields, that gravity is carried by an interaction, a particle called the graviton, which has spin 2. Supergravity relates fields with different spin to one another, and in the process blurs the distinction between matter (spin ½ particles) and interactions (integer spin particles). The intriguing thing about Supergravity is that many of the worrying infinities of quantum theory cancel out of their own accord. It has been proved mathematically that theories involving gravity must contain either an infinite number of such infinities, or none at all—they are either not renormalizable or finite. But it has not yet been established which category Supergravity fits—even with some infinities canceled out there could be an infinite number left, or it might be that, when the calculations are carried through in the right manner, all of them disappear.

If that proves to be the case, the theorists will be left with a theory which unifies all of the interactions and all of the matter particles in one framework, as well as bringing gravity into the fold, and which has no need of renormalization at all. It could be that the disturbing necessity for renormalization in the lesser theories is simply because they are incomplete descriptions of the Universe, and that the need for renormalization is, in a sense, the sign of their incompleteness. So even though Supergravity has not yet been fully worked out, the theorists are eagerly investigating any of its properties they can come to grips with. A key feature is that it predicts an end to the way particles seem to be made of subparticles, and subparticles of subsubparticles, like nesting Russian dolls. An atomic nucleus, for example, is made of protons and neutrons, held together by interactions involving energies of around 10^6 eV; the neutrons and protons are themselves made of quarks, held together by interactions at higher energies, about 10^9 eV. Many particle physicists suspect that deeper layers may lie within the quarks. But Supergravity says that there must be a limit to this nesting, down at a length scale of 10^{-33} cm, with energies around 10^{28} eV involved in the interactions.

That is still a very long way from the present, partly understood quark level. According to Supergravity, it is at these extremes that quantum effects break up the smooth structure of spacetime into a kind of foam. You might think that between this ultimate frontier and the quark level there is room for plenty more mysterious particles. But Supergravity seems not to permit this. There are only a few variations on the Supergravity theme, and the most comprehensive, called the "$N = 8$ extended Supergravity," sets strict limits on the number of types of fundamental particles that can exist. The $N = 8$ theory involves one graviton, 8 particles each with spin ½ (hence its name) called gravitinos, 28 particles with integer spin, 56 particles with half-integer spin, and 70 particles with no spin at all. These are large numbers, but not large enough to account for all of the "fundamental" particles that we already know about. The particles that carry the strong interaction are called "gluons," because they stick atomic nuclei together, and the 28 integer spin particles are insufficient to account for all of the gluons and their counterparts of the weak interaction. The implication is that interactions like gluons, and particles like quarks, are not really fundamental at all, but are composed of combinations of the really basic particles allowed for by the $N = 8$ Supergravity. The only way to test this is to predict, using the $N = 8$ theory, how particles such as quarks will behave when the particle physicists are able to probe them at energies higher than any yet reached—or to check out such possibilities as the existence of monopoles, produced at very high energies in the Big Bang but still roaming through the Universe. Such particles would, like massive neutrinos, help to explain the "missing mass" in the Universe, perhaps providing enough mass to make the Universe gravitationally closed. Indeed, gravitinos might fill an even more useful role. Late in 1982, a team headed by George Blumenthal, of the Lick Observatory, came up with the idea that massive gravitinos could account for the existence of galaxies in the Universe.

The calculations depend on the exact mass assigned to these particles, and no theory yet sets precise limits on this. But the important point is that whereas neutrinos, if they do have mass, check in at around 50 eV, or less, gravitinos could mass up to about 1 keV, one five-hundredth the mass of the electron. As the Universe emerged from the Big Bang, each kind of particle would tend to produce characteristic irregularities in the Universe, on a scale related to the particle masses. Neutrinos with masses of 50 eV would tend to cause the expanding universal cloud to break up into clumps on the scale of superclusters of galaxies; but 1 keV gravitinos would be associated with lumps massing around 10^{12} (a thousand billion, or a trillion) times the mass of our Sun, just right to produce a typical galaxy like our own, including its dark halo, which might be rich in gravitinos. The calculations are suggestive rather than compelling, but provide further evidence, if only circumstantial, in support of recent claims that less than one-tenth of the gravitational mass of the Universe is in the form of baryons, and that the Universe is most probably closed.*

The crucial calculations may be made within the present decade. Testing the predictions may take a little longer, but it is not foolhardy to foresee the ultimate test of Supergravity, one way or another, coming in our lifetime, perhaps within a hundred years of the development of special relativity. The theory may yet fall, but at present it has a great deal going for it as the prime contender in the probe beyond Einstein's theory. It is the only theory which includes gravity, which is four-dimensional, and which (we hope) is finite without any infinite subtractions. Since we live in a Universe which is clearly dominated by gravity, which occupies four dimensions, and which seems intelligible in finite terms, those are powerful credentials for the $N = 8$ Supergravity. The story of spacewarps is the story of gravity; the story of Supergravity is the story of the Universe and everything in it. I hope to be able to report that story, in all its glory, before I quit writing.

*George Blumenthal, Heinz Pagels, and Joel Primack, *Nature*, vol. 299, 1982, p. 37.

Bibliography

All of the works cited here should be accessible to the interested reader who has no specialist knowledge of physics. I have included a few articles from scientific journals, but only those written as "review" articles, which are intended for a wider audience than the place of publication might indicate. These provide detailed references to the original scientific papers on which progress in the study of the nature of spacetime is based, and some of those papers are specifically referred to in the text of the present book. If you *are* frightened by equations, however, it would be best to avoid the items marked with an asterisk.

Bath, Geoffrey, ed. *The State of the Universe.* London: Oxford University Press, 1980.

Bleecker, Sam. "John Eddy: Sunspots . . . and then there were none." *Star & Sky* (June 1979), p. 12.

*Burke, William L. *Spacetime, Geometry, Cosmology.* Mill Valley, California: University Science Books, 1980.

Carroll, Lewis. *The Annotated Alice.* Ed. by Martin Gardner. London: Penguin, 1965.

Clube, Victor, and Bill Napier. *The Cosmic Serpent.* London: Faber & Faber, 1982.

Coleman, James. *Relativity for the Layman,* rev. ed. London: Pelican, 1969 (reprinted 1979).

Davies, Paul. *Other Worlds.* London: J. M. Dent, 1980.

*———. *The Accidental Universe.* Cambridge: Cambridge University Press, 1982.

Doyle, Arthur Conan. "Silver Blaze," in *The Penguin Complete Sherlock Holmes*, pp. 335–350. London: Penguin, 1981.

*Eddington, Arthur. *The Internal Constitution of the Stars*. Cambridge University Press, 1926.

*Gilliland, Ronald. "Solar, Volcanic, and CO_2 Forcing of Recent Climatic Changes." *Climatic Change*, vol. 4 (1982), p. 111.

Gribbin, John. *White Holes*. New York: Delacorte; London: Granada, 1977.

———. *The Death of the Sun*. New York: Delacorte, 1980.

———, ed. *Cosmology Today*. London: IPC, 1982.

Harrison, Edward R. *Cosmology*. Cambridge University Press, 1981.

Hawking, S. W. "The Quantum Mechanics of Black Holes." *Scientific American* (January 1977), p. 34.

Hewish, Antony. "Pulsars." *Scientific American* (October 1968), p. 25.

Hoffman, Banesh. *Albert Einstein*. London: Paladin/Granada, 1975/77.

*Hoyle, Fred. *Steady-State Cosmology Re-visited*. University College Cardiff Press, 1980.

*———. *The Quasar Controversy Resolved*. University College Cardiff Press, 1981.

———, and Chandra Wickramasinghe. *Space Travellers*. University College Cardiff Press, 1981.

Kaufmann, William J., III. *Black Holes and Warped Spacetime*. San Francisco: W. H. Freeman, 1979.

Lindley, David. "In the beginning." *New Scientist* (12 March 1981), p. 685.

Narlikar, Jayant V. *Violent Phenomena in the Universe*. London: Oxford University Press, 1982.

———. *The Lighter Side of Gravity*. San Francisco: W. H. Freeman, 1982.

Ostriker, Jeremiah P. "The Nature of Pulsars." *Scientific American* (January 1971), p. 48.

Penrose, Roger. "Black Holes." *Scientific American* (May 1972), p. 38.

Pournelle, Jerry. *A Step Farther Out*. New York: Ace Books, 1980.

———. "The Insurmountable Opportunity," in *Destinies*, vol. 2, no. 4, p. 27. New York: Ace Books, 1980.

Shipman, Harry L. *Black Holes, Quasars, and the Universe*, sec. ed. Boston: Houghton Mifflin, 1980.

Silk, Joseph. *The Big Bang*. San Francisco: W. H. Freeman, 1980.

*Smith, F. G. *Pulsars*. Cambridge University Press, 1977.

*Tayler, R. J. "Neutrinos in the Universe," *Quarterly Journal of the Royal Astronomical Society*, vol. 22 (1981), p. 93.

Thorne, Kip S. "Gravitational Collapse." *Scientific American* (November 1967), p. 88.

———. "The Search for Black Holes." *Scientific American* (December 1974), p. 32.

Weinberg, Steven. *The First Three Minutes*. London: Andre Deutsch, 1977.

In addition, anyone with a serious interest in the nature of space-time and gravity can do no better than study *Gravitation*, by Charles Misner, Kip Thorne, and John Wheeler (San Francisco: W. H. Freeman, 1973). Be warned that this text runs to 1,279 pages and is intended to give competence in gravitation physics at the Ph.D. level; but if you can find it in a library, and you have enough math to cope, even dipping into it will provide the detailed background to many of the concepts of curved spacetime discussed in the present book.

Index

Page numbers in italics indicate illustrations.